FROM DESPAIR TO DELIRIUM

Two Seasons that Transformed a Football Club

Howard Falshaw

Grosvenor House
Publishing Limited

This book is published by
Grosvenor House Publishing Ltd
Link House
140 The Broadway, Tolworth, Surrey, KT6 7HT.
www.grosvenorhousepublishing.co.uk

A CIP record for this book
is available from the British Library

ISBN 978-1-80381-643-2

Dedication

In Memory of John Falshaw

Contents

Acknowledgements

Thank you to Ben Holmes for permission to use the cover photograph; to The News and Star, Carlisle United matchday programmes and the Carlisle United website for quotations; to Dean Zaltsman and Becky Banning at Grosvenor House Publishing Ltd. for their help, advice and support in getting this book published; to the Facebook friends who provided valuable feedback when this book was in its original blog form; to John Clarke for kindly writing the foreword to this book; and to the players and staff of Carlisle United who took us on a fantastic ride!

Foreword

Your team is your team and you stick with it. This is an attitude embedded in all true football fans, an attitude which prohibits the possibility of changing allegiances for a more successful, fashionable team, or a bigger club. Glory seeking is reprehensible, your team is your team and you stick with it.

Sticking with it involves accepting that there is often rough to follow smooth, troughs to accompany peaks, and an equal acceptance that these qualities are often not mixed equally. Most football fans are well-acquainted with the pain of losing and the despair engendered by constant under-achievement, recognising that triumphs shine brighter against a backdrop of mediocrity. Those that don't, those whose expectations are of wall-to-wall uninterrupted success are generally deluded and widely regarded as obnoxious. They are not true followers; they don't realise that when you pledge to support a team you sign up for the full thick and thin package. For every trip to watch your team walk out on the sunlit turf of Wembley there are the countless number of trips like the one to Grimsby where the game is abandoned due to a rain storm before the first half has even been completed. Trips where the voices sing in your head that this is all folly. But you are committed, your team is your team and you stick with it.

My team became my team sometime in the late sixties when my dad took my brother and I along to be lifted over the turnstiles to be let into the ground and to take our places at the front of the terracing next to the half-way line. We kicked loose cinders over our shoes and leant against a metal bar which was held in place by a series of concrete posts which ran the length of the pitch. One of the early games we witnessed from this viewpoint was an F.A. Cup game where a 3-1 deficit was overcome by means of a glorious second half hat-trick. It was the afternoon where things were set immovably in place: Carlisle United became my team and Hugh McIlmoyle became my hero.

And that is how it has remained. But all of these years on and living 120 miles from Carlisle has made supporting the Blues in any practical sense quite difficult. My support has been of the occasional away match but largely listening to the radio on a Saturday afternoon and hoping for the best variety. It has been highly frustrating and far from satisfactory. But I use the past tense because last season things changed dramatically like floodlights being turned on for the second half of an afternoon match in October. I found out that there was a fellow Blue living not five miles from my house in West Yorkshire. Much more assiduous in his support than I was, a season ticket holder who kindly offered me a lift to away matches which were deemed feasible, and also indeed for the long trek to Scotch Corner and over the A66 to Brunton Park as appropriate. I accepted his offer and what a season for this to take place.

I first met Howard Falshaw through our mutual interest in the written word. We soon found out that we also shared a revered memory of Chris Balderstone, the player and the person. In addition, I was highly engaged by Howard's optimism and his continual assertion that whenever Paul Simpson starts a season as manager, Carlisle get promoted. I'm sure he didn't need reminding that only too recently the gaping jaws of the National League had been ready to snap around the club. It turns out that Howard was writing weekly match reports in the form of a blog: lively, erudite and fair-minded reports which were a joy to read. He told me that he was going to have the collected reports published in book form and I was delighted at the prospect of a great addition to the worthy canon of Carlisle United-related literature.

I was equally delighted when he asked me to write a foreword for the book. Delighted and honoured because after all, his team is my team and we stick with it.

John Irving Clarke
August 2023

INTRODUCTION

My introduction to Carlisle United came on Saturday 26 August 1967, as an impressionable nine-year-old. And what an impression that afternoon made! It was the beginning of an obsession that remains equally strong, probably stronger, more than fifty-five years later.

The game in question was an entertaining 2-2 draw against Middlesbrough, watched from the terraces of the long defunct Scratching Shed. If my memory serves me right, the team that day included Chris Balderstone, Allan Ross and George McVitie, all subsequently to become club legends. I soon became a regular in the kids' enclosure before graduating to The Paddock which has become my spiritual home. I've occasionally indulged in seats in the Main Stand or East Stand, but sitting down at Brunton Park has never really seemed quite right. I even watched one game from the Waterworks (or Petteril) End, a late-season friendly against Dutch team MVV Maastricht.

Those were good times to be a Carlisle United supporter. The club was well established in the old Division 2 and reached the semi-final of The League Cup in the 1969-70 season. Four years later the club achieved the seemingly impossible by winning promotion to Division

One. No less a person than Bill Shankly (a former Carlisle manager himself) described the event at the time as "the greatest achievement in the history of football". I was at Brunton Park on 24 August 1974 when a twice-taken Balderstone penalty secured a 1-0 win over Spurs, and took the club, all too briefly, to the pinnacle of English football. I still have that league table in a scrapbook somewhere on the loft!

Other significant moments include celebrating promotions at Chester City, Stoke City (play-off final) and Mansfield Town, as well as attending all of the Football League Trophy final appearances except the 4-1 defeat to Southampton. Most memorably I was at Brunton Park to see Jimmy Glass score his iconic goal to save Carlisle United from probable oblivion. I cannot imagine that anything in my time as a Carlisle supporter, past, present and future, will top that moment. It was a very special moment to meet the man in person before last season's home game against Sutton United.

But this book is about the club in the present, not the past. So, I'd like to provide a little bit of context about how this book came to be.

Ironically, having taught children how to write well for over forty years in my job as an English Teacher, I'd done relatively little writing myself. That changed during the first Covid lockdown in the spring of 2020. A Facebook friend nominated me to list my Top Ten albums. I duly obliged, writing an explanation or justification of each of my choices, and posting my choices on Facebook on a daily basis. I'd enjoyed the writing so much I decided to write and post some further Top Ten lists. They tended to reflect my own interests, comprising subjects such as sport, literature, music, TV, film and politics. You can read all of these, should the fancy take you, on my website "Too Many Thoughts Left Over".

At the start of the 2021-2022 football season, I decided to add a second string to my writing bow, by posting a review after every game of Carlisle's season. The 2020-2021 season had proved ultimately be one of disappointment and frustration for Carlisle fans. An effective and successful brand of "Beech Ball" had seen Carlisle hit the top of League Two on New Year's Day of 2021. Over the next five or six weeks, a combination of Covid outbreaks at clubs, frozen pitches, waterlogged pitches and even a power failure on one occasion meant that Carlisle didn't play a game for well over a month. When they finally resumed, the momentum had gone, and while the players no longer had Covid, it was evident that they were not at the levels of stamina and fitness they had displayed in the first half of the season. In the end the team didn't even make the play-offs.

However, hope springs eternal, and there was a hope that, with good recruitment over the summer, Chris Beech could recover the formula that had seen the team show such promise in the first half of the previous season. Furthermore, the purchase of my first half-decent car for many years meant that the 270-mile round trip from Wakefield to Carlisle appeared less daunting, and that our range for travelling to away games was extended. Nonetheless, I was still teaching full-time, which meant that there was a limit to how many games I could attend. Paul Simpson's first home game back in charge in February 2022 was the first midweek game at Brunton Park during a working week that I'd attended since a League Cup tie against Spurs back in the 1990s.

A year later, following The Great Escape engineered by Simmo, and with the first season of this journal complete, there came another significant development. I'd already decided to retire from teaching in the summer of 2022, when Lisa, my wife, made a dramatic and unexpected suggestion. Perhaps fearful of me having too much time on my hands, or perhaps ignorant of just what it would involve, she proposed that I bought Carlisle United season tickets for Adam (our sixteen-year-old son) and myself. I didn't need asking twice! It might have taken over half a century in coming but it's been worth the wait. I missed just two home league games in the 2022-2023 season, both for family reasons.

If we were going to make a 270-mile round trip for home games, that set the bar for away games. Any ground that was a similar distance or less from Wakefield was on the agenda. That meant we attended about two-thirds of the away fixtures as well.

At this point I should introduce a few of the key characters who feature in the narrative that follows. As a former English Teacher, I should probably list them as the dramatis personae!

Lisa – my lovely, long-suffering and remarkably tolerant wife. Lisa organised a great night out in Leeds for me on the day I retired last year, but the suggestion of a season ticket for Brunton Park was possibly the best retirement present I could have imagined. Lisa was a Saturday cricket widow in the early years of our marriage, and to subject herself to a similar fate, albeit for a different sport, almost three decades later was an act of impressive selflessness. She's only ever been to one Carlisle game with me, when we were 'courting'. It was an away game at Doncaster Rovers' ramshackle former Belle Vue ground, before the then owner tried to burn it down in an insurance scam. Despite a packed away end and plenty of goalmouth incident, the result was a 0-0 draw. She's never been to a game since! She may be only mentioned rarely in the pages that follow, but without her this book would never have happened.

Adam – my sixteen-year-old son. Adam has been my constant companion at every Carlisle game I've attended over the last two seasons. For better or worse, he's inherited my obsession with Carlisle United, but had yet to experience the euphoria of promotion or winning a trophy. In his early years he professed to being an Arsenal fan, strongly enough for me to take him to St James Park to see Arsene Wenger's Gunners take on Newcastle United. Coincidentally the assistant to Steve McClaren, the Newcastle manager at the time, was one Paul Simpson! We also attended a memorable game at The Emirates Stadium when Arsenal legends took on Milan legends in front of nearly 60,000 fans.

His conversion came on a cold evening at Grimsby Town's Blundell Park. As we drove home after the match, he told me he'd got a confession to make. He wasn't an Arsenal supporter after all, he really supported Carlisle. He only professed to supporting Arsenal to avoid mickey-taking at school. I can pinpoint the moment at which the penny dropped. At the end of the game, we went down to stand behind the advertising hoardings and acknowledge the Carlisle players. As the players came over to salute the fans, Charlie Wyke caught his eye and gave him a thumbs up. That was the moment that Adam realised that this was real, a genuine connection between players and supporters. It was a far cry from seeing overpaid Premier League "superstars" as distant figures on the pitch from the upper reaches of a vast and soulless stadium.

That connection was re-enforced a few weeks ago, as we travelled home from a game at Carlisle. We made our usual stop at Scotch Corner Services, and as Adam queued to collect his order at Burger King, who should he bump into but Alfie McCalmont, on loan at Carlisle from Leeds United at the time, and now a fully-fledged Carlisle player. Alfie was happy to engage with him, discussing the afternoon's game.

Ben Smith – Ben is Adam's best mate and also leading scorer for Durkar Devils U17s, the team that Adam plays for and captains. I'm not quite sure how he managed it, but a couple of years ago Adam somehow convinced Ben that he too should support Carlisle United, and he's with us for the majority of matches, when he's not sprinting for Yorkshire. Many's the time on a Sunday morning that Ben has been given offside because the referee can't believe he was quick enough to reach a pass without having an unfair advantage!

John Clarke – John needed no persuasion to become a Carlisle United supporter. He was born and brought up in the city and his sister still lives within walking distance of Brunton Park. Interestingly, during the 2022–23 season, his visits to his sister seemed to increasingly coincide with Carlisle home games, when we'd meet up in The Paddock! He's also become one of the Wakefield branch of the Blue Army on our trips to some of the more local (to Wakefield) away fixtures.

Like me John devoted his working life to teaching English, which gives us a further connection. Since my dad died three years ago, he's the only person with whom I can reminisce about the First Division days, and even players who predate that era! I came to meet John entirely by coincidence. Lisa entered a poetry competition for which John was the organiser. When Lisa won one of the prizes, I accompanied her to the awards event, which was when she introduced me to John. It soon transpired that we had a bond that was much stronger than that of poetry. Ever since Lisa has accused me, whenever John is mentioned, of "stealing" her friend.

To conclude this introduction, a brief author's note.

All the entries in this journal were originally composed and posted within, at most, three days of the match they describe. They are very much an account of how things felt at the time. I have resisted the temptation to edit any of my comments and opinions with the benefit of hindsight. I hope that this book will be enjoyed by those who were also part of the journey, and that it might also be appreciated by those who weren't but may enjoy an insight into the week-to-week reality of supporting a League Two football club.

Journal of a Cumbrian football season 2021–2022

AUGUST 2021

Saturday 7 August 2021. Carlisle United v Colchester United. Brunton Park. EFL League 2.

The start of a new football season is always a bit special. It's that magical time when any outcome is possible, and unavoidable optimism briefly triumphs over the realism of decades of crushing disappointment! It has added resonance this year, because it's the first time in almost twenty years that I've actually attended the first match of the season, and also because it's the first time in a year and a half that there have been no restrictions on fans attending. Add to that the fact that Adam's best mate Ben, who has somehow been persuaded by Adam to join us as a Carlisle supporter, would be attending his first match at Brunton Park, then anticipation was high.

Further to that, in my first digression into non-football matters, I'd bought a new car (new to me, not brand new!) and this trip was the first extended opportunity to explore and enjoy all its impressive bells and whistles.

We set off in good time, the intention being to visit the club shop and then enjoy an extended build-up to kick-off once inside the stadium. We flew up the A1M to Scotch Corner where we took a brief comfort and food break. Alas, within five minutes of resuming our journey along the A66, we hit the back of a long queue of traffic. As we crawled forward at a snail's pace for most of the next hour, it became evident that not only would we miss kick-off, but we were also likely to miss a substantial part of the first half. I was very conscious of the fact that days of anticipation and excitement for the two fifteen-year-olds in the back of the car were rapidly evaporating, not to mention my own feelings!

When we finally reached the front of the queue, the cause of the delay was revealed – a traditional traveller horse-drawn caravan. Although much of the journey from Scotch Corner to Appleby is along dual-carriageway, stretches of single-carriageway meant that the progress of cars was limited by the speed of the horse and caravan.

I grew up just ten miles from Appleby and quickly realised that the delay was a consequence of the Appleby Horse Fair, an annual traveller event that dates back almost 250 years. Romanies and travellers from across Europe converge on Appleby for this event, one of the major features in their annual calendar. Suffice to say, my notions of political correctness were a little strained by the time we finally overtook the admittedly impressive horse-drawn caravan!

Fortunately, the new car now came into its own, and I was able to make up enough lost time to mean that we were only likely to miss the first 10-15 minutes of the game. Finally, as we were about to exit the M6, just a mile from the ground, came evidence that the gods had decided to smile on us. Adam announced that the kick-off had been delayed by fifteen minutes.

A hastily found parking spot, a brisk walk down Warwick Road, and we were just in time to witness a rather touching minute's applause for people associated with the club who have been lost during the pandemic, whose names and pictures were displayed on the electronic scoreboard.

Now here's a thing. Due to the pandemic, I had never seen a single player who started the game for Carlisle play in the flesh before. What exactly is it that makes me retain my loyalty to an institution that is so far removed from the club and team that I first engaged with in the late Sixties and early Seventies? Answers on a postcard please!

As for the game itself, it was an anti-climactic 0-0 draw. We dominated the game, and I'm not sure how we failed to score, but at least it dampened any premature euphoria about what lies ahead!

Tuesday 10 August 2021. Sheffield United v Carlisle United. Bramall Lane. Carabao Cup Round 1.

Having drawn the highest ranked team in the first round of the competition, we still travelled with high hopes. This naïve optimism was based on the fact that two years ago we played Barnsley at the same stage of the competition. Like Sheffield United they were new to the Championship, though they arrived there through promotion rather than relegation! We proceeded to smash Barnsley 3-0 on their own patch, in one of our best performances of recent seasons (notice how I've already slipped into the collective 'we'?!) hence the high hopes on Tuesday evening.

Tuesday's experience contrasted to last Saturday's experience in several ways: we had a much shorter distance to travel to the game; there were no horse-drawn traveller caravans on the M1; it was an away game. Let me expand on the latter point.

In many ways away matches are a better experience than home ones. Typically, we are part of a travelling contingent of 500-600 fans. These are the hardcore supporters, who follow the team almost everywhere, and are very vocal in their support. There were relatively few periods on Tuesday night when the supporters were silent. And when those moments occurred, there was usually an individual who would come out with a piece of abuse aimed at Sheffield United striker Billy Sharp.

I have no idea what kind of a person Billy Sharp is. Most of the comments on Tuesday night centred around his ability as a footballer and his weight. Some were amusing, and some were just bigoted. A rather mean part of me was hoping that he'd respond and provoke further abuse, and another part of me was embarrassed that I was thinking like that! I like to think of myself as reasonably broad-minded and liberal, and yet there's something about the primal and tribal nature of being a football supporter that I find irresistible.

There was to be no repeat of the triumph at Barnsley, though a 1-0 defeat was a creditable performance.

Saturday 14 August. Swindon Town v Carlisle United. The County Ground. EFL League 2.

A strange one this. A seven hour plus round trip was always out of the question. Not only that, the return of fans to grounds meant that the game was not streamed live through the online platform I-Follow, so I was reduced to regularly checking my phone for score updates. That became particularly fraught when I checked at about ten to five, fully expecting to see the final score, only to discover we were in the fifth minute of additional time, with another nail-biting four minutes to follow. Suffice to say that the added time allowed for a Swindon player to be sent off, rather than them grabbing a late equaliser. So, we achieved our first win of the season by 2-1 and occupy sixth place in the largely meaningless early-season league table.

On reading the latest blog from my mate Ian Cusack, I realised that while Adam and I were at Bramall Lane on Tuesday night, Ian was just down the road at Rotherham's New York Stadium. If I'd known you were looking for a midweek game Ian, I'd have invited you to join us at Bramall Lane.

Despite its proximity to where I live, I've yet to visit Rotherham's relatively new ground. However, I did visit their previous home at Millmoor on a couple of occasions, which is the cue for an anecdote which, if it does nothing else, will at least pad out this post!

Back in the day, there was a tendency for opposition fans to abuse Carlisle supporters as 'sheep shaggers'.

This insult has its origins in the very rare occasions on which Carlisle appeared on 'Match of the Day' in the Seventies. The programme director, who obviously could not resist the most obvious of visual cliches, would invariably start the coverage with a distant shot of the Lakeland fells, before focusing on a field of grazing sheep not far from the stadium. The camera would then pan over the Waterworks End of the ground onto the pitch itself.

It was on a Saturday afternoon at Millmoor in the late eighties, that the Carlisle fans took their revenge. At about quarter to three we got our retaliation in early, with the immortal chant of 'We've come to shag your sheep'!

Tuesday 17 August. Port Vale v Carlisle United. Vale Park. EFL League Two.

The basic details of the evening are as follows. The game itself was a 0-0 draw, and not the most entertaining of evenings, with limited goal-scoring opportunities for either side. A couple of players made their first appearances for Carlisle as substitutes and made reasonably positive impressions. The referee managed the impressive feat of alienating both sets of supporters. When are Carlisle actually going to wear their away kit? And we must stop taking Ben with us to matches. Whenever we do the result is invariably a 0-0 draw, and we experience significant travel problems on the way to or from the match!

Tuesday's trip was the first game for some time where I've visited a ground that I've never been to before. Initial impressions were very positive. There was designated parking for away fans, and once we'd found a parking space, we had to walk all of fifteen yards to the turnstiles! Not so good for a quick post-match getaway though. Very friendly and helpful stewards too, with generous comments about a good and safe journey home. The ground itself is a very neat all-seater stadium, deserving of better crowds than Port Vale are currently able to provide.

And away grounds are the focus of the rest of this post. I'm going to be unashamedly blokeish and Nick Hornbyesqe in providing you with statistics about away grounds I've visited. A quick look at the League tables suggests that I've visited 23 of the 92 grounds in the Football League. However, this number increases significantly when I add in clubs whose old ground I've visited before they moved to a new stadium. These include Sunderland (Roker Park), Middlesbrough (Ayresome Park), Arsenal (Highbury), West Ham (Upton Park), Rotherham (Millmoor), Doncaster (Bell Vue) and Reading (Elm Park). The number increases further when I include grounds which no longer feature in the Football League. These include Bootham Crescent (York City), Blundell Park (Grimsby Town) and Feethams (Darlington).

I'm actually quite disappointed with the overall count, which I expected to be higher. At least I'll be adding another ground to the list when we head to Hartlepool a week on Saturday.

Saturday 21 August. Carlisle United v Leyton Orient. Brunton Park. EFL League 2.

This is unbelievable! Match 5 of the season proper, and we've been to four of them in person! This is unprecedented in over fifty years of supporting Carlisle United!

Live attendance at this match was never on the agenda until seven days ago. That was when I received a letter, which I quote in full and with Adam's full permission.

"Dear Dad

Yes, I have written you a letter, and instead of being an annoying nagger I will instead talk to you through this letter, firstly to practise for my GCSEs and also to show you that I am even willing to write a letter to try and get to Carlisle games. I'm writing this to convince you for us to go to the Leyton Orient game on Saturday, and I understand how you have already driven a lot and you will be even more throughout the holidays, but I will give my perspective on things and why I believe we should go.

The first reason I think we should go is that despite it taking up a lot of the day, personally whenever we go to Carlisle games, I always enjoy myself so much, from the journey to the game itself and even the greasy Gregg's sausage rolls. Even if we lose, I always thoroughly enjoy myself. And I think after missing out on so much recently due to Covid it would be great to go. Also, if you are worried about time, you don't have to go to the Salford game on the 4th and me and Ben can take the train. Back to my point, I don't think I can explain how much I enjoy going, it gives me something to look forwards to beforehand, something to enjoy while I am there and something to look back on once it is over. Going to Carlisle games is always when I'm at my happiest, apart from when I'm in History class of course! And I have a statistic for you, going to football matches means it is 80% more likely a fifteen-year-old called Adam Falshaw will be a very happy person and will be unbelievably thankful of his Dad for going with him, just saying...

Another reason I think we should go is because of how well the team is doing, I mean seriously, who doesn't want to watch Clough, Riley and Mellish (a.k.a. the beast) live in the flesh? Beech Ball is at its best and Chris Beech's league winning blues will beat Orient, and hopefully we'll be there to see it. It may also be Clough's competitive debut, and even you said he's the player you're most excited to see. Just imagine – 92nd minute, Abrahams wins a free kick on the edge of the box, Clough takes, and smashes it in at the Warwick Road End, the Paddock erupts, you know deep down you don't want to miss out on that. Oh, and a quick bonus, Ben can't make it so you don't have to get a booster seat for him (Ben is not very tall!).

Now this isn't a reason as to why I think we should go, but more that I am willing to do jobs around the house to make up for lost time if you go to the game on Saturday. Whether it's making my own meals, helping buy the shopping or even something as simple as loading the dishwasher.

Back to reasons as to why I think we should go, I know you wouldn't want to go because of journey time and how it takes up a lot of the day, but instead of that perspective I'll put my more positive view on this. Firstly, it is more time to spend in your very nice new car, you clearly enjoy driving it and who wouldn't want to spend more time in the luxury of heated seats, six gears and electric windows that always work! And if we ever get bored, we can always bring back the old game of counting Eddie Stobart trucks like we used to.

Thanks for reading this and I hope you consider everything I've mentioned, I think it'll be a really good day out where we will watch Carlisle (hopefully) hammer Orient at Brunton Park with a Clough hat-trick."

What father could resist persuasion like that?! And although he's my lad, I think it's a lovely example of just how much supporting a team can mean to a football-obsessed teenager.

So it was that yesterday found Adam and me heading up the A1, A66 and M6 to Brunton Park again.

Unfortunately, the reality of the game didn't quite match the dramatic end exciting scenario Adam painted in his letter. We did see a live goal for the first time this season, from an early penalty. Carlisle dominated the first half and should really have had the game won by half-time. Unfortunately, the score remained just 1-0, and to his credit Kenny Jackett, the Orient manager, made two half-time substitutions which changed the balance of the game. Carlisle failed to sustain the levels of the first half, and we ended up with a 1-1 draw.

Memo to self. Don't take Adam to any more games with me. He's been to a fair few now and has only ever seen them win two or three times. This season is a case in point. We go to four of the first five games and witness three draws and an honourable 1-0 defeat against Sheffield United, newly relegated from the Premier League. The one game we've missed was a 2-1 win away to Swindon Town.

Saturday 28 August. Hartlepool United v Carlisle United. The Victoria Ground. EFL League 2.

Another in-person attendance, and another new ground. I'm not sure this momentum can be sustained! Once again Ben, Adam and I headed north, though north-east this time rather than north-west, just two days before the family headed in the same direction for our short break in Northumberland.

This was a game which summed up what League One and Two football is all about – raw and visceral. Hartlepool are newly promoted from the National League. Carlisle have not enjoyed a promotion season since 2006, but still brought a travelling support of 1,000 to this game. In a ground that has a capacity of around 8,000, and with a home support of 5,000 plus, it made for an atmosphere that was febrile to say the least. The sense of confrontation was increased by the fact that the packed away end confronted the vocal home support, who were positioned at our end of the side of the ground. I have to admit that Hartlepool's home support was among the most noisy and impressive I've seen in a long time.

Well before kick-off, Hartlepool supporters laid into us with a chant of "You're just a small town in Scotland." Never lost for words, the Carlisle fans responded instantly with "You're just a town full of smackheads." Some vague remnants of political correctness made me hesitate about joining in. Then I remembered that the citizens of Hartlepool voted in a Tory MP at a recent by-election and gave it full voice! Coincidentally, I'm sure, police seized a £6 million haul of cocaine from a yacht on Hartlepool Marina just three days after our visit.

Unfortunately, the game itself failed to match the build-up. In what was Carlisle's worst performance of the season to date, they were lucky to escape with a 2-1 defeat. A change of formation was a dismal failure, giving the impression that this was a team without any clear plan or direction. With the transfer deadline looming, and significant interest from other clubs in some of our players, this was not a day to remember.

Adam and Ben are now on a warning that I will no longer continue to take them to games if they continue to jinx the results. The only game none of us have seen is the one game we won, and between us we've now seen five games without a win.

Tuesday 31 August. Carlisle United v Hartlepool United. Brunton Park. Papa John's Trophy group stage.

No, we weren't actually at this game. By Tuesday evening we were firmly ensconced in the depths of Kielder Forest, just south of the Scottish border. I did point out that the journey from Kielder to Carlisle would be the shortest journey we'd made to a game, other than our trip to Bramall Lane, but for some reason that didn't wash with anyone. And rightly so. The Papa John's Trophy is a third-rate competition, supported by a third-rate sponsor. In previous incarnations it has offered lower division clubs the chance of Wembley glory, and Carlisle have experienced that winning feeling twice, at both old and new Wembley, as well as four unsuccessful final appearances (also including the Millenium Stadium in Cardiff) giving us the record for final appearances.

However, the competition was devalued from the moment it was decided to admit U21 teams from Premier League and Championship clubs.

As it happens, we probably should have gone! The game was a 3-3 draw, meaning we missed more goals than we've seen in the five games we've attended. That was followed by a 4-3 penalty shoot-out victory to avenge our defeat at Hartlepool's hands three days earlier.

I've noticed that all the crowd shots from the game feature an apparently well-populated paddock and main stand. That's because they were the only parts of the ground that were actually open to spectators!

SEPTEMBER 2021

Saturday 4 September. Carlisle United v Salford City. Brunton Park. EFL League 2.

This may prove to be our last football road trip for some time, with a new school year imminent, and distant destinations such as Crawley starting to appear on the fixture list. Mind you, the 270-mile round trip to Carlisle isn't exactly a short hop! Yet again Adam, Ben and I hit the A1M for the journey North, and this time we were unimpeded by traveller caravans, or festivalgoers leaving Leeds Festival at Bramham Park, which had caused us a horrendous two-hour delay between Wakefield and Wetherby just five days earlier, as the family headed for Northumberland. On this occasion we were able to have a decent break at Scotch Corner and still arrive in time to secure an excellent viewing position in the Paddock, close to the half-way line.

The day's opponents were Salford City, the nouveau riche club of League 2. For some they are tainted by their association with the Manchester United 'Class of '92', others are less than impressed by their efforts to buy their way out of League 2 by offering ridiculous (by League 2 standards) salaries to attract players. However, while cash may attract talent, it doesn't always bring commitment with it, and before this game they were languishing below halfway in the League table. The sense of them being a manufactured club is enhanced by their poor fan-base. Despite the journey from Salford to Carlisle being twenty miles shorter than our own journey from Wakefield, they brought with them just over a hundred travelling fans.

And so to the game. Despite an early goal, the first-half performance was less than impressive, culminating in a Salford equalizer just before half-time. At that stage, following our poor showing at Hartlepool a week earlier, I'd pretty much decided I wasn't that keen on travelling again to see mediocre performances, irrespective of a new school term. Fortunately, things improved significantly in the second half, with two debutants, signed on transfer deadline day, to the fore. New right back Kelvin Mellor nearly stole the show with an outrageous bicycle kick that just cleared the Salford crossbar, but the day, and the man of the match award, rightly belonged to last season's talismanic midfielder and top scorer Jon Mellish. He gave a barnstorming performance from box to box, crowning it with the winning goal, lashed home with venom from all of two yards!

After five previous live attempts, it was lovely to get that winning feeling again. For Ben it was just nice to get the winning feeling at all, as he'd never seen Carlisle win before.

Crawley Town v Carlisle United. Saturday 11 September. The People's Pension Stadium. EFL League 2.

There's not a lot to say about the game itself. Firstly, we weren't there. The trek to Crawley is officially

Carlisle's longest trip of this season, so in-person attendance was never on the agenda, particularly on a term-time weekend. Secondly, we lost, in what was a very discouraging result! However, the game did prompt thoughts on a number of football-related topics.

Seven games into the league programme, it could be argued that the season is beginning to take shape. Carlisle have won two games, lost two and drawn three. Our goal difference is zero, having conceded exactly as many goals as we have scored. We are in twelfth place in a division of twenty-four teams. You couldn't get much more average than that! The early season excitement of new signings has largely evaporated as said signings, while not disastrous, have yet to set the world on fire. Furthermore, a couple of important players left before the transfer deadline. So, as the league table begins to assume some sort of recognisable form, I'm left to contemplate whether I'm going to be confronted with yet another season of underachievement and mediocrity: not bad enough to be in danger of relegation, not good enough to challenge for automatic promotion, or even the play-offs. And that in turn prompts me to wonder why I put myself through this torture year after year, for over five decades now. It's over fifteen years since we last experienced the euphoria of promotion for god's sake. And after a spirited victory over Salford a week ago, we really should have been capable of beating Crawley, who languish near the foot of the table. Whatever happens, I know my addiction is fated to continue, and I just hope my pessimism about the rest of the season is unjustified.

After the disappointment of Saturday afternoon, the evening brought a brief diversion from football and a reversal of fortune. In 1974 the legendary Bill Shankly described Carlisle United's promotion to Division 1 as "the greatest feat in the history of the game." Well, Emma Raducanu's achievement in winning the U.S. Women's Tennis Open, without losing a set, and having had to play three qualifying rounds before even entering the competition, must rank as possibly the greatest achievement in any sport and in any era.

The name of Crawley's ground, The People's Pension Stadium, set me thinking about the ridiculous monikers some clubs will accept in exchange for a few thousand pounds extra in corporate sponsorship. Among others, Carlisle will play this season at the VBS Community Stadium, the Mazuma Stadium, the One Call Stadium, the Lamex Stadium, the Peninsula Stadium, the Sands Venue Stadium, the Crown Oil Arena, the Jobserve Community Stadium, the Breyer Group Stadium, the Dunes Hotel Stadium, the Envirovent Stadium, the Utilita Energy Stadium, and best of all The Fully Charged New Lawn (Forest Green Rovers). I challenge you to recognise any of the above clubs by the name of their ground. A lot of the grounds have a capacity of under 10,000 and yet they have the temerity to describe their pokey little ground as a stadium! I don't think any ground that has a capacity of less than at least 15,000 should be allowed to describe itself as a stadium or arena! All credit to those clubs who stick with traditional names for grounds, the names that long-time fans recognise.

Carlisle United v Scunthorpe United. Saturday 18 September. Brunton Park. EFL League 2.

This is the first home league game we've not attended, and given the outcome, I can't say I'm sorry we missed it. Following last week's demoralising defeat at lowly Crawley, this was another opportunity to pick up three points against another basement team. But no, we managed to concede a goal after three minutes, and managed to ship another just minutes before half-time. All my pessimism of the previous week seemed fully justified. Admittedly we fought back in the second half, finally clinching a point with an equaliser in the fifth minute of added time. But the momentary euphoria of such a late strike shouldn't obscure the fact that this was another game we clearly should have won if we're to achieve anything this season.

That's about it really! Nothing to get excited about and nothing to digress about!

Match Day Number 11. Sutton United v Carlisle United. Saturday 25 September. VBS Community Stadium. EFL League 2.

After my last Carlisle post I remarked to Lisa that my football posts seemed to be mirroring Carlisle's performances – heading all too rapidly into mid-season mediocrity. Little did I realise how quickly things would get worse. Yesterday's 4-0 defeat by newly promoted Sutton would be flattered to be described as mid-season mediocrity. Yet again we conceded a very early goal and another shortly before half-time, but this week there was no added-time equaliser to salvage an undeserved point. Just two more goals, probably three if the referee hadn't blown the full-time whistle as Sutton were about to score a fifth. Oh, and one of our substitutes was sent off after only twenty minutes on the pitch. The News and Star, Carlisle's daily newspaper, summed it up nicely – "The performance was abject, the football dire, the punishment only appropriate to a degree. This we know. Now it's a case of asking what happens next."

Thankfully I engaged with the game on a very limited level. I spent most of the afternoon with Lisa in the garden, constructing a large trampoline, with periodic score updates from an increasingly miserable Adam. It was probably the best way to spend the afternoon, though my back and arthritic knee are currently sending me a rather different message,

In an attempt to ensure this post rises above Carlisle's dreadful performance yesterday, I'm prompted to reflect on why I continue to engage with an institution that provides me with so much disappointment. Apart from the fact that it's now a habit of some fifty-three years, and therefore not all that easy to break, it's hard to find any rational justification! There have been some great moments – sitting at the top of the English football pyramid (however briefly), the unforgettable Jimmy Glass goal, visits to Wembley (new and old) with the occasional trophy, and a few promotions. But it's well over a decade since the last of those moments occurred, shortly before I turned fifty. I've been trying to drink at an empty well ever since.

I wouldn't keep buying the mediocre music of a formerly loved band for that length of time, in the forlorn hope that they'd rediscover a modicum of the magic that made me like them in the first place. I wouldn't keep buying crap novels by a writer who'd clearly lost their muse. Maybe it's time I applied the same logic to my sporting interests!

Carlisle United v Everton U21s. Tuesday 28 September. Brunton Park. Papa John's Trophy group stage.

An advance warning – not much of this post is going to be about football!

I've had a distinct feeling of déjà vu today. We're back to wearing face masks at school in all settings. I emerged from a pre-school briefing, in which we'd all dutifully worn our masks, into a main hall that was absolutely rammed with pupils. I couldn't help but wonder what the hell was the point of wearing face masks when there's no pretence at social distancing, and when schools have no control over pupils' social interactions and covid-cautious behaviour outside the school setting.

Secondly, I called at the supermarket (Asda) on the way home from work, to find the familiar sight of significant gaps on shelves. It might not be toilet rolls and pasta that are in short supply at this particular moment, but it was sadly reminiscent of the panic buying of last spring.

Talking of panic buying, another factor that is not part of my feeling of déjà vu, but adds to my sense of despair, is the current crisis over fuel supply. The issues here are far too complex for this post but suffice to say that sensationalism in certain sections of the media, individual selfishness, and inevitable government incompetence over management of the supply chain, make this current crisis all too predictable. The sense of déjà vu does actually intrude here. I've been mildly encouraged by Facebook memes today showing pictures of queues of cars outside petrol stations, along with the slogan 'Brexit isn't working'. For those who are not of a certain vintage, this is a reference to a Saatchi and Saatchi advertising campaign on behalf of the Tories from the late seventies, showing a fabricated image of a dole queue alongside the slogan 'Labour isn't working'.

In yet another bit of déjà vu, Adam and I watched tonight's Carlisle game on iFollow. For the uninitiated, iFollow is an EFL (English Football League) streaming platform, which allows certain games to be streamed live for a one-off payment of £10. The main criterion for allowing games to be shown is that live streaming won't impact significantly on in-person attendance. With largely empty grounds last season, due to Covid, that meant that virtually every Carlisle game was streamed live, so I probably saw more games live in the season than I've ever seen in my fifty-plus years as a supporter, albeit not in person. So, tonight was yet another case of reverting to the habits of dark Covid days.

Anyway, finally onto tonight's game. What was largely a Carlisle reserve side beat Everton U21s 2-0 in a meaningless competition, to more or less guarantee progress to the knock-out stage, thanks to two goals from an eighteen-year-old Aston Villa loanee who has yet to start a league game. Cynical as I might be about the tournament, a cup run might be just what we need as an antidote to the mediocrity of our league campaign. After all, we have won the competition twice, and hold the record for the most final appearances - two at the old Wembley, two at the National Stadium in Cardiff, and two at the new Wembley.

OCTOBER 2021

Carlisle United v Forest Green Rovers. Saturday 2 October. Brunton Park. EFL League 2.

Sadly, the start of a new month brought no change to Carlisle's fortunes. Forest Green came to Brunton Park as League 2 leaders, on a good run of form. Chris Beech, the Carlisle coach, spoke of it being a positive and encouraging performance against a strong team, but the bottom line is that it was yet another defeat, and yet more goals conceded from set-pieces. Our slide towards the relegation zone gathers pace!

The real interest in this game was off the pitch. The owner of Forest Green Rovers is 'eco-entrepreneur' Dale Vince, and FIFA has hailed the club as the world's first carbon neutral club. At the weekend, Vince took exception to the dress-code for the Carlisle director's box, which required him to wear a tie, and announced very publicly that he would slum it with the travelling fans (if he could find them – there wouldn't be much competition for seats in the away section, with just 114 Forest Green supporters).

This is just the latest instalment in an ongoing petty feud between the two boardrooms. A couple of seasons ago, when Carlisle travelled to Forest Green, the pre- and post-match catering for the Carlisle dignitaries was strictly vegan, with no meat alternatives. Carlisle director Andrew Jenkins, who just happens to own Pioneer Foods in Carlisle, renowned for its meat pies and sponsorship of the East Stand at Brunton Park, took exception to this, suggesting that there would be an almighty fuss if Carlisle adopted the same approach and only provided a meat-based menu when Forest Green next came to Carlisle. Needless to say, they didn't. The ball would currently appear to back in Carlisle's court. Such is the minutiae of life in League 2!

Bristol Rovers v Carlisle United. Saturday 9 October. The Memorial Stadium. EFL League 2.

Before I deal with this game, I need to provide an update on the Carlisle and Forest Green boardroom feud. The first picture in the Forest Green match gallery on the Carlisle website was of the away section. Behind the Forest Green supporters was a large and prominently placed advert for Pioneer Foods meat pies – no coincidence I suspect!

This was the weekend the roof fell in. The enthusiasm of travelling to numerous early season games now seems a distant, and barely believable memory. A term-time trip to Bristol was never on the cards, but the international break meant that the game was streamed live on iFollow, which meant that I forked out a tenner for Adam to watch the dismal events unfold in real time. Me? I must have managed to find something else to do – urgent hoovering, much needed ironing, that kind of thing.

In brief, we lost 3-0, a result that plunged us to 22nd in League 2, just one place above the relegation zone. Disappointment I can cope with, but a second relegation from the Football League would test my loyalty to the hilt. It was little surprise that by Sunday lunchtime Carlisle United had issued a statement that head coach Chris Beech had left the club with immediate effect. It was a sad end to his two years in charge. Last season had us really believing in him as the club soared to the top of the division with a convincing style of play, before Covid and winter weather totally derailed our season.

Since then, there has been much speculation about who will be the new manager/coach, most of it centring around ex-Carlisle players who are now in management or coaching, and even a couple who aren't. On a sentimental level the idea of a returning hero quite appeals, particularly when I look at the names being touted who don't have any history with the club! However, history has tended to prove that players returning to their former club as manager rarely enjoy significant success.

Carlisle United v Tranmere Rovers. Saturday 16 October. Brunton Park. EFL League 2.

I recall I referred to last week's events as the weekend the roof fell in. I'm struggling to find a metaphor to describe this weekend's fiasco. Perhaps it should be described as the weekend the wheels fell off (no cliché is too predictable for this journal!).

With previous assistant coach Gavin Skelton (brother of BBC presenter Helen Skelton) and youth coach Eric

Kinder in temporary charge of first team affairs, we took on Tranmere Rovers at home, a team without an away win, or even an away goal so far this season. Well, one of those unenviable records remains intact. They may have notched their first away win by beating us 1-0, but we did the hard work by scoring their goal for them. We then tried to consolidate their lead by giving away a penalty, but newly signed goalkeeper Mark Howard obviously hadn't read the script as he proceeded to save it.

The result means that we're now next to bottom of League 2, occupying one of the relegation places. Yet Director of Football David Holdsworth, the man who really should have been sacked last weekend instead of coach Chris Beech, maintains that the club are not in a relegation battle! I think it's obvious where the problem lies. We've won one point out of eighteen in the last six games.

Off the pitch, things got even worse. A certain Michael Knighton was spotted sitting in the directors' box at the game. For those of you who are unfamiliar with this arsehole, he is the charlatan who launched a bid to take over Manchester United in 1989, shortly before they began their dominance of English football. Having failed in that attempt (the Manchester United board must have had a good bullshit detector) he switched his attention to the other end of the Football League (no Premier League then) and became the owner of Carlisle United in 1992, when they sat at the bottom of the Football League.

A couple of promotions and Wembley appearances ensued, in each case followed by rapid relegation as Knighton failed to strengthen the playing squad, and sacked popular managers who he felt were getting the praise and limelight that was due to him. It even reached the point when he decided to manage the team himself. His record speaks for itself – Played 68, Won 19, Drawn 12, Lost 37, win % 27.9.

After the club were put into voluntary administration, ownership of the club was finally prised from his grasp in 2002. So relieved were the Carlisle faithful that over 10,000 of us turned up to watch the first game of the new era, which was a 3-0 home defeat to Hartlepool, but it was a day on which the result really did not matter. We'd got our club back. Michael Knighton brought Carlisle United to its knees, and very nearly destroyed the club. The current board of directors claim that Knighton arrived at yesterday's game unannounced. Knighton claims he was invited. The man is a pathological liar, but on this occasion, I'm inclined to believe him. For the board to invite him into the directors' box, at a time when the club is probably facing its biggest crisis since Knighton's tenure, shows utter contempt for the club's supporters. Michael Knighton should not be allowed within ten miles of the club he came so close to destroying. As a supporter of 53 years' vintage, who was present when we topped Division 1 in 1974, who was present when Jimmy Glass saved us from relegation to the Conference in 1999, I am giving serious consideration as to whether I can continue my support for the club.

Newport County v Carlisle United. Tuesday 19 October. Rodney Parade. EFL League 2.

This game in some respects marked a return to the good old days of lockdown, in that this was one of this season's rare games to be streamed live on iFollow. Not that I was sitting glued to the laptop screen. No, given our recent run of results I had much more enticing attractions, delights like marking and planning lessons. My indifference was immediately tested when Adam started shouting and screaming within the first minute. Joe Riley had scored after 38 seconds, one of, if not the fastest, goal in Carlisle's history.

Of course, it couldn't last. Two goals in quick succession meant that we went into half-time trailing to Newport. Things improved slightly in the second half when a Newport defender conceded a penalty, earning himself a red card in the process. Zack Clough duly equalised, and when a second Newport player was sent off, it appeared the win was there for the taking.

It wasn't to be. Numerical advantage counted for nothing, and on a rain-sodden night in Newport we clocked up our seventh game without a win. Still, I suppose 2 points from a possible 21, is a better ratio than the 1 from 18 before the game.

Lots of speculation, but no signs of progress in the process of appointing a new manager/coach. These are desperate times indeed.

Carlisle United v Oldham Athletic. Saturday 23 October. Brunton Park. EFL League 2.

Still no movement on the managerial front, but this game saw the return to Brunton Park of one of our previous managers, Keith Curle, who for all his egotistical faults, at least managed to get us into the League Two play-offs and was responsible for signing probably one of the best Carlisle players of recent seasons, Nicky Adams. He's now in charge of Oldham, one of the two teams in the Football League who are statistically worse than Carlisle at this moment in time.

Predictably, given the current circumstances of each club, the result was a dire 0-0 draw.

I appreciate this post is very short – a reflection of my current disengagement with Carlisle United.

Northampton Town v Carlisle United. Saturday 30 October. Sixfields Stadium. EFL League 2.

At least we went into this game with a manager. Earlier in the week the Board announced the appointment of Keith Millen as the club's new manager. Who? – that was exactly my reaction! He's spent most of his career since retiring from playing as an assistant manager to various others, and an occasional caretaker when the man in charge got sacked. None of that makes him a bad choice, but we've just sacked Chris Beech, who arrived at Brunton Park with a very similar managerial CV. I desperately hope he's successful, but I worry that the Board have failed to learn any lessons from their previous appointment.

Perhaps most importantly, Millen is a former team-mate of David Holdsworth, Carlisle's 'Director of Football', which suggests that the real problems at the club exist at a higher level than the manager. At least four managers – Keith Curle, John Sheridan, Steven Pressley and Chris Beech – have tried and failed at Brunton Park, while Holdsworth has remained in post. Can the board not see after so long that the key issue might be at a higher level?

Any hopes that there might be a new manager 'bounce' were quickly dashed as the team fell to a depressing 3-0 defeat. From the brief highlights I've watched, and the snatches of radio commentary I caught, they currently appear to be a team without direction, without motivation, without skill and without talent. Two points from the last available twenty-four tells its own tale.

NOVEMBER 2021

Carlisle United v Horsham FC. Saturday 6 November. Brunton Park. F.A Cup Round One.

You may infer from the fact that I'm posting this on Sunday evening that this has been a better weekend from a footballing point of view, and you'd be absolutely right!

However, one shouldn't get too carried away with Carlisle's first victory in ten games. It came against Horsham, a team over sixty rungs below us on the football ladder and would appear to be a rather laboured victory. These games are always a no-win situation for the bigger club. Lose, and you suffer abject humiliation. Win by anything other than a convincing margin, and you're damned with faint praise. So here goes with the faint praise! In our 2-0 win, it took seventy minutes to break down a non-league defence, and the second goal came in the 90th minute. It hardly fills me with confidence for the next League Two encounter.

It looks like Adam, Ben and I will be at that next game. We'll be heading North for the Cumbrian 'derby' between Carlisle and Barrow next Saturday. The Barrow squad has a significant number of ex-Carlisle players, all of whom will be keen to put one over their favourite team. Add to that the fact that Barrow have sold 1500 tickets for the game, and that all their fans will be in one section of the ground, unlike the home fans, and will therefore appear to make much more noise than us, and I'm not exactly filled with optimism, particularly as yesterday's attendance was a paltry 2,581.

Morecambe FC v Carlisle United. Tuesday 9 November. The Mazuma Stadium. Papa John's Trophy group stage.

Not a lot at stake here. We'd already qualified from the group by winning our first two games, so all that remained to be decided was whether we would get a home or away draw in the first knock-out round. There was a little bit of local pride at stake, as Morecambe are our nearest neighbours, but not enough to take the attendance into four figures!

The bare facts are that we won 2-0, against a team from a division higher than us, and with a significantly changed team from Saturday. That makes it two wins on the bounce, albeit against a non-league team, and then in a meaningless midweek competition. Adam watched the game on iFollow and said the performance was quite good. Maybe things are starting to look up?

Actually, it's a bit unfair of me to dismiss the Papa John's Trophy as meaningless. The Football League Trophy has almost always suffered from pretty naff sponsors who have been granted naming rights to the trophy, but it's provided me with some great days out at finals at both Wembleys and the (formerly) Millenium

Stadium. The last time we won it, we defeated Brentford in the 2011 final. They're now in the Premier League, while we occupy one of the League Two relegation places.

Foolishly, I've agreed to take Adam and Ben to Saturday's Cumbrian derby against Barrow. I fear the slight improvement of the last few days may come crashing back to earth against a team with lots of ex-Carlisle players who will no doubt want to prove a point, and who will be bringing over a thousand supporters. And yes, I know Carlisle and Barrow are not as close as Goodison Park and Anfield, but when you're as remote as Carlisle, anywhere within a hundred miles counts as a derby!

Carlisle United v Barrow FC. Saturday 13 November. Brunton Park. EFL League 2.

Since my last post there have been two cup draws, which mean we'll be playing Shrewsbury at home in Round 2 of the F.A. Cup, and Lincoln City at home in the Round of 32 in the EFL Trophy (or the Papa John's Trophy, to give the competition its branded name). Two fixtures to really set the pulse racing, eh?!

As mentioned in the previous post, this weekend's Cumbrian 'derby' marked the first League fixture in front of fans for fifty-six years, most of which time has seen Barrow languishing in various non-League divisions. They brought 1500 fans to this game, which meant a decent home crowd of almost 7,500, well above recent attendances. That, the resumption of a local rivalry, an early 1.00 o'clock kick-off and a surprisingly warm and sunny afternoon for November, meant that expectations were slightly above mediocre, given our current League position. Furthermore, Adam, Ben and I were in relatively good heart after another trouble-free journey north.

We should have known better. We witnessed a tedious 0-0 draw between two very mediocre teams. Carlisle's best chance came in the first minute and although we did hit the woodwork late-on, other goal-scoring opportunities were few and far between. We did keep a third clean sheet in a row, but I couldn't help thinking that any team better than Barrow would have punished us more harshly for some woeful defensive lapses.

A couple of by-lines. New manager Keith Millen's comment on some of Barrow's foul play was "I didn't realise we were swapping shirts <u>during</u> the game.' And talking of shirts, Barrow's away shirt has to be one of the worst I've seen in some years – an insipid pink with white trim, clashing perfectly with a bright green and red shirt sponsor's logo.

Exeter City v Carlisle United. Saturday 20 November. St James' Park. EFL League 2.

The journey to Exeter is a 700-mile round trip for Carlisle supporters, which for at least one fan required a 4.30 a.m. start yesterday morning. God knows what time he got home! For 155 supporters to make the journey when their team has not won a League game since 4 September (77 days) is a testament to their dedication (or should that be blind stupidity in the face of overwhelming evidence?!).

Put Carlisle's woeful run together with the fact that Exeter went into the game unbeaten in nineteen games in all competitions and you'll understand why expectations were low. Add to that the fact that our talismanic midfielder Jon Mellish was sent off just before half-time, and that our captain Callum Guy was serving a one-match suspension, and a 2-1 defeat doesn't look too bad. However, the reality is that we're back in the relegation zone, there's no tangible bounce from the appointment of a new manager, and I fear for the viability and future of the club if we lose our League status.

I was sorry to read today of the death of Joe Laidlaw, a former Carlisle player. 'Smoking' Joe, as he was known to fans, was a mainstay of the Seventies team that won promotion to, and, all too briefly, competed in Division 1. As well as reminding me of my own mortality (he was only seven years older than me) his death means that over a third of that iconic team have now passed away. Alan Ross (goalkeeper and record appearances for Carlisle), Bill Green (centre-half and captain) and Chris Balderstone (midfielder and England cricketer as well) are also no longer with us. Even my precious memories are on the way out!

Match Day Number 22. Carlisle United v Harrogate Town. Tuesday 23 November. Brunton Park. EFL League 2.

It was against Harrogate that the wheels started to come off for Carlisle last season. Having just topped the

League Two Table, we travelled to their Wetherby Road ground with high expectations, only for the game to be abandoned after eight minutes because the referee had misjudged the iciness of the pitch. A second attempt to play the game failed when, after the team had travelled again, a local power cut meant that there were no floodlights. Postponements for waterlogged and frozen pitches followed, along with a Covid outbreak at the club, meaning that we went over a month without a game, while others were playing regularly. When we finally resumed playing the momentum had gone, and the Covid outbreak meant that a number of players, while available, were far from fully fit. We didn't even make the play-offs.

This season the wheels have already come off by the time we face Harrogate! We have sacked our head coach, replaced him with someone whose only previous experience of managing a team has been in a caretaker capacity, and we sit in the relegation zone. Last night's defeat was particularly depressing, because Harrogate really didn't play very well, but had little difficulty beating us 2-0. That means we've now gone twelve League games without a win, the longest such run in League Two, and have failed to score a single goal in our last five home League games. Jon Colman, who reports on Carlisle for the local newspaper 'The News and Star' offered a damning verdict. "Show me a more toothless team in the history of Carlisle United. Sorry - there isn't one. This, sad to say, is getting serious."

I'll conclude by returning to a topic raised in a previous post, namely the role of Carlisle's Director of Football,

David Holdsworth, in the current debacle. A series of bungled contract offers and negotiations by Holdsworth in the summer meant that a number of key players from last season's team left, in one case finding playing in the National League more attractive (and lucrative!). Chris Beech was left trying to plug gaps as the season started. When will the board stop making managers the fall guys for Holdsworth's shortcomings, and get rid of the incompetent fool? There's a Holdsworth meme currently doing the rounds which quite reasonably and accurately labels him 'Director of Failure'.

Perhaps most depressing is the fact that the crowd was just over 3,100, barely 40% of the attendance at the previous home game against Barrow.

We lost 2-0 by the way.

Carlisle United v Walsall. Saturday 27 November. Brunton Park. EFL League 2.

Perhaps there is light at the end of the long, dark tunnel we've been travelling through! It was after a convincing win at Walsall that Carlisle went to the top of League 2 back at the beginning of this January (my word, does that seem a long time ago, in so many respects!) before everything went horribly pear-shaped. And who knows, yesterday's win against the same club might just herald the beginning of a revival and better things ahead. Ironically, having gone top of the table against Walsall, at one point during yesterday's game we were bottom of the table as the scores stood.

Yesterday's 1-0 win means that I can reflect on a League victory for Carlisle for the first time since 4 September (yes, it really is almost three months!). Little did Adam, Ben and I realise, as we celebrated that win on the Brunton Park terraces, what barren weeks lay ahead. The goal yesterday was also Carlisle's first league goal in front of the home fans in well over 500 minutes.

I've not read any match reports yet, but it appears to have been a pretty laboured win, with not many chances, and the winning goal only coming in the 88th minute. But at the moment, any kind of win will do just fine!

The next two games are also both at home and represent two opportunities to take a step closer to Wembley, against Lincoln City in the first knock-out round of the Papa John's Trophy, and then against Shrewsbury Town in Round 2 of the F.A. Cup. I can always dream! Indeed, if I didn't, I wouldn't still be following this damn team and writing about it!

Carlisle United v Lincoln City. Tuesday 30 November. Brunton Park. Papa John's EFL Trophy: 2nd Round, Northern Section.

OK – it was only a miserably wet late November night in Carlisle; it was played in front of just 884 fans, the fourth lowest crowd for a senior game in Carlisle's history; it was a game in a third-rate competition with a third-rate sponsor; and we only went through on penalties. But it was a win, and against higher-level opposition as well. It's also a win that leaves us just three games away from a potential Wembley appearance.

Adam streamed the game (at my expense and on my laptop!) on i-Follow, and although I only dropped in to watch the odd moments, I was reasonably impressed with what I saw. Carlisle faced a team with a good passing game and clearly superior technique and managed to largely contain them and keep them away from danger areas. Fortunately, I managed to catch key moments, particularly Carlisle's equaliser. Manny Mampala executed a beautiful turn, drove forward, and laid on a beautiful pass for left-back Jack Armer to run onto and calmly slot just inside the far post.

And so to penalties. Things didn't start well when John Mellish hit the first penalty with ferocious power, only to see it ricochet off the crossbar. Fortunately, Lincoln's first penalty taker outdid Mellish by blazing about five yards over the bar. The remaining penalties were all dispatched efficiently until Lincoln's final taker also missed the target.

I was hoping to find a video clip of Brad Young's outrageous fourth penalty. Young is a nineteen-year-old striker on a season-long loan from Aston Villa. After a short run up, he took the most outrageous hop before side-footing the ball past a bemused goalkeeper. He'd have looked a complete dick if he'd missed, but all credit to someone so young and inexperienced for having the brass neck to try it and pull it off.

DECEMBER 2021

Carlisle United v Shrewsbury Town. Saturday 4 December. Brunton Park. F.A. Cup 2nd Round.

This represented Carlisle's second opportunity in four days to take a step along the road to Wembley, though obviously the F.A. Cup offers a much less likely route! Perhaps that's why I felt slightly disengaged from this game, despite the return of two Former Carlisle strikers in Shrewsbury's squad. Having beaten League One opposition on Tuesday evening I was hopeful (rather than optimistic!) we might do the same again, and also hoped for the anticipation of drawing a Premier League team if we made it into the Third-Round draw.

Despite those vague hopes I wasn't particularly surprised or disappointed when it didn't happen. A 2-1 defeat might sound like a reasonable performance, but the one goal for Carlisle came in the 91st minute, a bit late to spark a late comeback. The game was watched by a miserable 2,794 fans, and 350 of those were from Shrewsbury. Those who did bother to attend showed their dissatisfaction by throwing tennis balls onto the pitch in an effort to disrupt the game, also unfurling a banner that urged the board to "Get out of our club'. At least it gives me the opportunity to trot out one of the oldest, hoariest and worst football clichés, "Well, we can concentrate on the League now." – My god, we certainly need to.

As for our other potential route to Wembley, we've been drawn away to Tranmere Rovers or Harrogate Town in the last sixteen of the Papa John's Trophy. Adam is fervently hoping Harrogate make it through, as Harrogate represents one of our shortest away trips. I'm certainly not up for a trip to The Wirral on a school night in January!

By the way, Carlisle would have played Liverpool if they'd beaten Shrewsbury!

Mansfield Town v Carlisle United. Tuesday 7 December. Field Mill. EFL League Two.

We lost 1-0 after conceding an early goal in the 6th minute. Apparently, we created plenty of chances but failed to convert any of them. We're still in the shit.

The fixture did remind me of happier days at Mansfield for Carlisle, including a promotion celebration that I was present to witness in 2006, featuring one Michael Bridges. With about ten minutes remaining, the stadium announcer mistakenly announced that Bridges had been substituted. Moments later he went on a mazy run before shooting narrowly wide, prompting the memorable chant "There's only two Michael Bridges."!

Stevenage F.C. v Carlisle United. Saturday 11 December. Lamex Stadium. EFL League Two.

This was a bit more like it. We had the rare experience of going into the half-time break actually in the lead. The goal was scored by Jon Mellish who was signed as a defender and was converted into a midfielder by previous manager Chris Beech, going on to be our leading goal scorer last season. Current manager Keith Millen played him as a striker today – he'll probably be in goal next week!

The win was secured by a second-half penalty from Jordan Gibson and was all the more valuable for coming against another struggling team. Supporters needed some good news in a week when it was announced that long-running negotiations over a possible takeover of the club had fallen through.

Carlisle United v Bradford City. Saturday 18 December. Brunton Park. EFL League Two.

Didn't happen! This was all set to be the beginning of our mini-Carlisle binge over the festive period, with tickets already purchased for three games. Our trip up the A1M, A66 and M6 never happened. By Friday afternoon the rampant spread of the Omicron variant of Covid 19, aided and abetted by our shitshow of a government, meant that infections at Bradford City led to the game being postponed.

This is eerily reminiscent of a year ago, when Covid infections had a massive (and entirely negative) effect on our season. The one difference is that then we were at the top of the table, rather than hovering precariously above the relegation zone, as we are at present.

I self-tested for Covid this evening for the umpteenth time, using the inevitable (and probably highly unreliable) lateral flow test. I can't help falling prey to suspicion and conspiracy theories when I recall that Covid 19 originated in Wuhan Province in China, and every single lateral flow test kit I've used in the last year has been manufactured in the People's Republic of China. In amongst all the billions that were squandered on Covid related contracts for Tory chums and donors, was there not even one of our wonderful British entrepreneurs who could develop a British produced testing kit? Think of all the benefits to the environment of not having to transport so many millions of those tests halfway round the world. Or are we all just fall guys in a vast conspiracy of international capital?!

The 2021 part of this journal is ending with an emphatic whimper rather than a bang. What was going to be a little Christmas binge of Carlisle games is gradually unravelling as Omicron continues its spread, while the Government continues its inaction. First the pre-Christmas game against Bradford was postponed (Bradford Covid), to be followed by the Boxing Day game against Rochdale (Carlisle Covid). Now the Wednesday game against Salford has also gone (Carlisle Covid), with upcoming games at Scunthorpe and Harrogate also in doubt, all of which we've got tickets for. Things would appear to be so bad that my good friend Paul Fisher was today reduced to watching Belper Town in the Northern Premier League Division One Midlands. I put this down to the fact that he must be visiting family in the Belper locality or is just desperate for some live football!

JANUARY 2022

Scunthorpe United v Carlisle United. Saturday 1 January 2022. Glanford Park (or to give it its sexy sponsor's name. The Sands Venue Stadium). EFL League Two.

The first attempt to play this game was postponed, setting the tone for the rest of the holiday period. That might explain why I was unreasonably excited this morning about a trip to Scunthorpe, of all places. Not only was a Carlisle game actually taking place, but it was a game we could go to.

Glanford Park is a neat but unprepossessing stadium, with a capacity of just over 9,000, all-seated apart from the home end, and none of the stands receding that far back from the playing area. However, the match day experience is quite good. Most of the hour-long journey from Wakefield is by motorway, and the ground itself is barely a quarter of a mile from the motorway exit. Not only that, but there is also ample car-parking right next to the 'stadium', meaning that it's only a couple of minutes from your car to your seat in the ground. And when the gate is as low as today's crowd of just over 3,000, it doesn't take long to get out of the car park post-match either!

A bit of context for today's game. On New Year's Day 2021, Carlisle won convincingly 2-0 away to Walsall to go the top of League 2. If we lost today and other results went against us, there was a very real possibility that we would start 2022 at the bottom of League 2. The times they are a changing.

After recent Covid cancellations, Carlisle were at least able to raise a match-day squad today, though they were a player short on the substitutes bench. And if anyone had told me on the opening day of the season that our New Year's Day strike force would consist of Jon Mellish (signed by Steven Pressley as a defender, converted by Chris Beech last season into a goalscoring midfielder) and Sam Fishburn (a novice teenager who was on loan to Lancaster City three months ago) I would have laughed them out of court.

And so, finally, to the actual game. Despite some early Carlisle chances, Scunthorpe tended to dominate first-half possession and with five minutes to go to half-time I said to Adam that I'd happily settle for 0-0 at half-time. No sooner had I said that than Carlisle won a corner, the ball pinged about the six-yard box, and centre back Rod McDonald forced the ball home at the far end to cue wild celebrations amongst we 300 travelling fans.

The second half followed a similar pattern, with Scunthorpe dominating possession, but spending a lot of time passing the ball across the pitch rather than making real inroads. The longer that game went on, the more I felt that Scunthorpe were unlikely to score if they played until midnight, though I didn't voice that opinion for fear of tempting fate. As the game entered its final fifteen minutes, with Scunthorpe making increasingly desperate substitutions, the away support really began to believe that we were going to win and set up a constant barrage of songs and chants. I can hardly believe how invested I was in the game by the end, and the feeling of euphoria when the final whistle finally went. Two away wins on the bounce, and without a goal conceded, the first time since 2017.

The match statistics are quite telling. Despite Scunthorpe having twice as much possession as Carlisle, completing almost twice as many passes, and having more than twice as many corners, they managed only two more shots than us (16-14), and only half as many shots on target.

I feel like I reconnected today with the emotions that make me a Carlisle supporter in the first place, after so many recent disappointments, and I've got the sore throat and hoarse voice to prove it. I really hope our game at Harrogate on Tuesday isn't postponed due to Covid in the Harrogate camp.

Harrogate Town v Carlisle United. Tuesday 4 January 2022. The Envirovent Stadium (apparently). Papa John's Trophy round of 16.

We travelled to this game with some genuine expectation, rather than mere hope. We were coming off the back of two consecutive away wins, with clean sheets in both victories. It was also our second road trip in just three days, following the relative euphoria of our trip to Scunthorpe on Saturday. And Harrogate was just a short hop up the A1M from Wakefield.

Access to the ground was great. We were able to park just off Wetherby Road, with just a three-minute walk to the ground. That's when it started to get a little less impressive. With most Carlisle fans presenting e-tickets at the turnstile (note the singular!), it seemed to take an inordinate amount of time to admit us, given that Carlisle fans hadn't exactly travelled in their thousands (barely hundreds actually).

Once inside the ground, my first task was to message Lisa that we'd arrived safely. My description of the ground in that text message was 'a shithole'. We did have a good pitch side position, just three rows back from the touchline in the away seating section. However, that meant we were also just three rows from the back of said section! The terracing behind the goal nearest to us must have been all of two yards deep. Don't get me wrong, I admire and respect Harrogate's achievement in attaining League Two status, considering the level they were at when I lived in nearby Wetherby about twenty years ago, but when the crowd is less than a thousand, and the ground doesn't appear that empty, I think that says it all! I was surprised that the capacity is actually as high as 5,000. This was a new addition to my list of League grounds visited, and probably the most disappointing.

As for the game itself, we started with the same line-up that won on Saturday. Many fans have been eager that goalkeeper Mark Howard, only signed on a half-season deal, should be offered a contract until at least the end of this season. In only the seventh minute, he gave us reason to doubt that eagerness as he scuffed a kick to a Harrogate player just outside the penalty area who laid on an easy chance for a team-mate to score. Despite dominating possession in the second half, and a raft of attacking substitutions, our familiar failure to take chances meant that we left empty-handed. Just three games short of an appearance at Wembley, we had fallen short yet again.

Carlisle United v Bradford City. Saturday 8 January 2022. Brunton Park. EFL League 2.

I hate hindsight. With its benefit, Adam, Ben and I would have been at Brunton Park today for what was undoubtedly Carlisle's best performance of the season to date. When Adam mooted the possibility of going on Wednesday, I was quick to dismiss the possibility, feeling that after two relatively short road trips to away games in the last week, I really didn't fancy a much longer trip today for a home game. A further irony is that we had tickets for the original pre-Christmas fixture which was postponed due to a Covid outbreak in the Bradford City camp.

However, there was a bonus in that, unusually for a Saturday game in front of fans, the game was available to stream on i-Follow, so Adam and I were able to watch the entire game from the comfort of the sofa!

A bit of context before I get on to the game itself. It's been a busy week at Brunton Park. With the January transfer window open, two Premier League loanees, signed on season-long deals originally, returned to their respective parent clubs, Arsenal and Aston Villa. On Monday we signed right back Joel Senior from non-league Altrincham, who made a promising cameo debut coming on for the last ten minutes of Tuesday's defeat to Harrogate. On Wednesday we signed striker Tyrese Omotoye from Norwich City, on loan until the end of the season. Who? You might well ask, as I did at the time. He's a nineteen-year-old of Belgian/Nigerian heritage, who has been on loan at Orient during the first half of the season. Rumours also emerged on Twitter that we might be re-signing striker Omari Patrick, who only left in the summer for Burton Albion, also on loan until the end of the season. On Thursday it got much better when Patrick did re-join, but on an eighteen-month contract rather than on loan.

Despite all this transfer activity, there was only one change today from Tuesday's starting line-up, with Omotoye replacing fellow teenager Sam Fishburn, though the other new signings were both on the bench. The early signs were not good, with Bradford taking the game to Carlisle and creating a couple of chances. However, as the first half progressed, Carlisle began to assert themselves, and right-back Kelvin Mellor, a former Bradford player and the person with most to lose from Joel Senior's arrival, was having an absolute blinder of a game. Probably exactly the response manager Keith Millen wanted after his signing of another right-back.

Things got better on the stroke of half-time when Jordan Gibson, another former Bradford player received the ball on the left corner of the Bradford penalty area, slipped his defender with a neat turn, and curled a beautiful shot into the top right-hand corner of the Bradford goal. He was quick to share his celebration with the Bradford fans!

The second half was magnificent. The defence kept their shape superbly, and Omotoye led the line beautifully, constantly running at the Bradford defence. He departed after seventy minutes to a standing ovation, and eventually the man-of-the-match accolade. Jon Mellish was in barnstorming form, constantly chasing lost causes, to win throw-ins and corners he had no right to. When he's in that kind of mood he galvanises the whole team.

All that was missing was a second goal to consolidate Carlisle's superiority. That eventually came in the 86th minute, courtesy of the returning Omari Patrick, a seventieth-minute substitute and yet another former Bradford player! Receiving the ball in an unpromising position wide on the left he beat his marker, drove into the penalty area, beat another defender, and coolly side-footed the ball into the far corner. Like Gibson he was eager to celebrate in front of the away fans.

At the final whistle the Bradford fans were critical of their team, chanting "You're not fit to wear the shirt". Even though they were chasing shadows for most of the second half, they weren't that bad. They were made to look poor by a dynamic Carlisle performance that warmed the heart. Let's hope they can sustain this level of performance.

Carlisle United v Crawley Town. Saturday 15 January 2022. Brunton Park. EFL League 2.

This was something like a proper football weekend! I think both Adam and I were keen to go to yesterday's game, buoyed by last week's bravura performance, and the trip to Carlisle seems less onerous now that I'm not working Fridays and it therefore takes less of a chunk out of the weekend. So, while Ellie was in London hobnobbing with the likes of Wes Streeting, and Lisa took Imogen skating with some friends at Doncaster Dome, we headed North yet again. Our company this time was Sam (a Leeds supporter, but hey, nobody's perfect!). Ben was otherwise occupied with an athletics meeting.

Given the state of my back and knee, I'd seriously considered seats for the game, but Adam and my more primal instincts persuaded me to opt for standing in the paddock. It was a wise decision, because having arrived in decent time, we were able to secure a good position behind one of the crush barriers, meaning my back didn't bother me at all – until I moved.

Carlisle started brightly, clearly full of confidence after last week's performance, but with no end product, and Crawley weren't exactly passive participants. Disaster struck after about twenty minutes when centre back Morgan Feeney got the ball caught under his feet and was robbed by Ashley Nadesan who slotted home. To rub salt in the wound, Nadesan is an ex-Carlisle loanee. As the game progressed, it was clear that last week's mojo had gone missing. However, after about fifty-five minutes there was a tangible buzz in the crowd when last week's returning goalscoring hero, Omari Patrick, came on. Despite his best efforts, there was no end product, and the game looked to be slipping beyond Carlisle. With about twenty minutes to go Carlisle were denied an obvious penalty when three Crawley players and just one Carlisle player were left sprawled on the ground. You can guess which way the decision went.

I've made it almost a point of principle not to let this blog descend into a series of rants against incompetent referees. I realise that if your team plays in League Two, you're not going to get the best of officials. But yesterdays were particularly bad. If a Crawley player ever fell over, then it was obviously a free kick to them. If there was a tussle between attacker and defender, then it was obviously the attacker who had committed a foul. Add to that a linesman who carried a flag all afternoon, but apparently didn't realise that it was for him to use, and I began to feel that the odds were stacked against us. When will match officials realise that all professional footballers (excepting Carlisle players of course) are cheating conniving bastards?

A couple of minutes after Carlisle's non-penalty, my worst fears were confirmed when Crawley were awarded a penalty, for which the match highlights suggested was a blatant dive. Fortunately, Nadesan blasted it just over the bar.

A couple more attacking substitutions followed, and with growing vocal support, the team kept driving forward. But as we entered five minutes of added time, we remained a goal behind. To everyone's relief, a corner to the near post was met by a glancing header from substitute Lewis Allessandra (returning from an injury lay off), and we had achieved a draw that felt more like a win under the circumstances.

Carlisle United v Hartlepool United. Tuesday 18 January 2022. Brunton Park. EFL League 2.

This one shouldn't take long! The game was another streamed live on i-Follow, and we sat down with reasonably high expectations, particularly since Ellie had worked out how to connect the laptop to the TV, so we could watch on a decent size screen with a decent quality picture.

What a disappointment it turned out to be – two hours of my life I'll never get back (I think I may have said that before!). It was a game of relatively few chances with both teams struggling to break down the opposition defence. From Carlisle's point of view there were too many misplaced passes and too many instances of poor control from our supposed 'flair' players. Unsurprisingly it ended 0-0.

I really can't think of anything else to say, other than I'm glad we weren't there in person, as the weather looked pretty dismal. I can't even think of anything tangentially related to football with which to pad out this post! I considered a rant about the Prime Minister's party shambles, but I can't think of any way I can link that to football, and in any case I don't want him anywhere near a blog about my favourite football team.

Forest Green Rovers v Carlisle United. Saturday 22 January 2022. The Fully Charged New Lawn (yes, that actually is the name of a sponsor driven Football League ground – how bloody ridiculous). EFL League 2.

It has not been a good weekend. And when I say that I'm not referring to the fact that a significant part of

Saturday was spent disconnecting and disposing of a malfunctioning tumble dryer (never buy an Indesit!) and wiring and installing its replacement.

Carlisle travelled to Forest Green Rovers, currently leading League Two by a significant margin. I had a hunch, totally irrational I admit, that Carlisle might follow their traditional pattern of struggling against lower-positioned teams and pulling off surprise results against high flying teams.

It wasn't to be. We lost 3-0 and I felt strangely disengaged from the game, as I wasn't even able to check my phone that often for updates.

Carlisle United v Sutton United. Saturday 29 January 2022. Brunton Park. EFL League 2.

I did say from the outset that this journal wouldn't just be about football, that it might feature musings on matters only tenuously linked to football, or with no connection at all. Well, I think this is going to be one of those posts, with football featuring only peripherally in the weekend that's just coming to an end.

We didn't travel to yesterday's game (thank God, given the gales that were raging, of which more later) and it wasn't streamed on i-Follow, surprisingly given the fact that there were no Premier League games yesterday. In fact, a good part of the afternoon was spent dealing with the trampoline saga. We have a large (12ft) trampoline in the garden and as the gusts of wind reached their fiercest, we looked out of the lounge window to see the entire structure lifted off the ground and deposited two yards from its usual position. Not wanting to see it disappear over the fence into a neighbour's garden, we dashed out to secure the legs with any heavy objects to hand – large rock, big toolbox, lawn mower! I then struggled in the winds atop a stepladder to unscrew and lower the safety net, which was acting like a sail as the wind filled it. There followed a dash to B and Q for some pegs with which to secure the legs more firmly. All precautions remain in place, with another storm forecast for tonight, and winds already building.

As for the Carlisle game, they were 2-0 down by half-time, and that's the way it stayed. In the away game at Sutton we lost 4-0 at what was probably the lowest point of the season. Yesterday's result was the second defeat in a row, meaning that our mini revival is clearly over. I've not seen a match report yet, but a Carlisle News and Star headline suggested that a lacklustre performance was clear evidence of the need for a couple more signings before the transfer window closes.

FEBRUARY 2022

Salford City v Carlisle United. Tuesday 1 February 2022. Peninsula Stadium. EFL League 2.

It was a late decision to travel to this game, made at tea-time on Monday, aided by the facts that we already had tickets for the previously cancelled fixture over the Christmas period, and Salford is a relatively short hop across the M62. There was also the slightly perverse satisfaction on a weekday evening of saying "Sod the marking!" and heading off to watch some football.

Of course, it didn't turn out to be a short hop. A major delay between Junctions 29 and 28 meant that we arrived with precious little time to spare before kick-off. The Peninsula Stadium was another new League ground to tick off the list, and like Harrogate's ground it was a distinct disappointment. It was no more than eight rows deep on any side of the ground, whether that be terracing steps or rows of seats. Given our recent form, the travelling support was impressive, packing the away end, in contrast to the gaps on the other three sides of the ground. The post-match figures revealed that of a meagre crowd of 2,059, 958 were away fans.

The game came less than twenty-four hours after a day of feverish activity on the last day of the transfer window.

Keith Millen made five signings, four of them too late to be registered in time for Tuesday's game. That meant a total of nine new faces arriving during the transfer window (three of them on loan), a pretty damning indictment of the squad Chris Beech had assembled at the beginning of the season.

Unfortunately, the supporters didn't get the performance their loyalty deserved. Carlisle survived a torrid first ten minutes before establishing any kind of foothold on the game. We then proceeded to witness something I've never seen before – all three substitutions made before half-time, and all three due to injury. To make matters worse, none of the injured players are likely to be back for at least a month. One of them, Joel Senior, was signed as cover at right-back for Kelvin Mellor, who soon proceeded to incur his own long-term injury. God knows who'll play at right back in the next game. Given all that, it was a relief to reach half-time at 0-0, after six added minutes.

It couldn't last. A few minutes into the second half Jon Mellish handled in the penalty area, and Salford were ahead. Despite distinctly lacklustre performances from some Carlisle players, we got back into the game when Jordan Gibson was played in down the right (looking suspiciously offside) and his low cross was side-footed home by Omari Patrick in front of the away fans.

The prospect of a possible, and extremely unlikely, away win was short-lived. Within four minutes Salford restored their lead, and the rest of the game was a sad story of a lack of ideas, a lack of imagination, and in some cases a lack of commitment. I diverged from our usual practice of staying to acknowledge the players after the final whistle, saying to Adam and Ben that the players didn't deserve our applause after that performance. It transpired that when the manager and team did come over to salute the fans, they were roundly booed.

Predictably, the journey home was disrupted by lane-closure hold-ups as well. Given all that, I can't quite believe that Adam's persuaded me to take him and Ben to tomorrow's game at Rochdale! It might be something to do with Durkar not having a game this weekend. After Tuesday's performance by Carlisle, I think we can be pretty confident we'll see some of the new signings making their debut tomorrow.

Rochdale AFC v Carlisle United. Saturday 5 February 2022. Crown Oil Arena. EFL League 2.

Today's football jaunt came to a premature end at 2.00 p.m. as we approached the summit of the M62 on Saddleworth Moor – the game had been postponed due to a waterlogged pitch. It hardly came as a surprise; I was driving through some of the worst conditions I've experienced in a long time, and the game at nearby Salford had already been called off (a pity the Carlisle game there on Tuesday wasn't!). so off the motorway at the next junction, and back along the opposite carriageway. We couldn't even find a service station with a Greggs outlet for a sausage roll (a bit of a Saturday football ritual).

We knew as we set off that the pitch was being inspected, and we hadn't even reached the motorway when the news came through at 1.30 that there would be another inspection at 2.00. I appreciate that the referee was probably trying to give every opportunity for the game to go ahead, but it did seem to indicate a certain disregard for travelling fans who were a further half-hour away from home when the game was finally called off, and had an extra half-hour added to their return journey. That wasn't too bad for us, only travelling from Wakefield, but for the hundreds who were travelling from Carlisle, it meant a round trip of about five hours, all to no avail.

Carlisle United v Port Vale. Tuesday 8 February 2022. Brunton Park. EFL League 2.

I want to get this one out of my system quickly, less than two hours after the final whistle, while the pain is still raw!

The bare facts are that we lost 3-1 at home. The only two teams below us in the league table both won, meaning that we are only two points above the relegation zone, a slim buffer that will vanish if Oldham win their game in hand.

But in so many ways it was much worse than that. We sat down to watch the game on i-Follow with reasonable expectation that some of the new signings might feature and make an impact. Those hopes were quickly dashed as Port Vale scored in less than a minute, courtesy of an appalling pass by Joe Riley, so lauded by the Carlisle fans when he made his return as a substitute at Salford last week (more of him later). We did pull a goal back after twenty minutes, thanks to Owen Windsor, one of the new arrivals (on loan from West Brom), who was one of the few positives from the evening. Port Vale regained the lead just before half-time, and despite a few forays forward in the second half, Carlisle rarely looked like scoring before Port Vale put the game to bed with fifteen minutes left, courtesy of another bad defensive pass by Joe Riley.

Tonight, Carlisle were a team without organisation, without leadership, without ideas or imagination, and too often without fairly basic skills such as ball control. Corey Whelan, a natural defender, who barely knows how to make a forward pass, was played in midfield, while Joe Riley, a natural midfielder who can take on defenders and play forward passes, was played out of position at right back. Why manager Keith Millen didn't swap them around is beyond me. He doesn't seem to have any idea how to set up a team to play in a particular way, and I'm beginning to suspect he only got the job because he's a former teammate of our reviled director of football, David Holdsworth.

As for the new signings, Tyrese Omotoye made little impression in attack after his man of the match debut against Bradford. Central defender Dynel Simeu (on loan from Southampton) was quick and physical but a disaster waiting to happen. Up front we had Tobi Sho Silva (or Oluwatobi Fabian Shobowale Akintunde Sho-Silva to give him his full name!), a big target man for whom we actually paid a transfer fee. After weeks of putting crosses into the box with no-one getting on to the end of them, tonight, with a tall central striker, we seemed to have forgotten how to cross the ball. To describe him as statuesque would be unfair to sculptors, if the ball wasn't played directly to his feet or head, he appeared unwilling to move a centimetre towards the ball. I barely remember the commentator mentioning him, and how he was still on the pitch at the end defies comprehension.

It's just my luck that when I decide to keep a journal like this, my team embarks on its worst season for years! Paul Fisher (friend and Durkar U16s manager) posted today that he should be getting rid of his sling tomorrow, a fortnight after a shoulder operation. Would that I could shed my allegiance to Carlisle United as easily!

Colchester United v Carlisle United. Saturday 12 February 2022. Jobserve Community Stadium. EFL League 2.

Yet another ridiculous name for a League Two ground! A road trip to Colchester was beyond even Adam's persuasive powers, and video coverage wasn't being streamed on i-Follow, so we were reduced to the online Radio Cumbria commentary. In fact I didn't even manage that, being too busy with other tasks. A 0-0 scoreline at half-time suggested I'd made a wide decision not to listen!

The second half proved a bit more eventful. On the hour, Omari Patrick proved that while he may not be a great goalscorer, he is most definitely a scorer of great goals. A returning favourite, he's already proving to be the best of our transfer window signings. Unfortunately, two examples of Keystone Cops style defending meant we were staring down the barrel of a fourth consecutive league defeat. Thankfully, Tobi Sho Silva, who I condemned for his statuesque qualities on Tuesday night, found enough movement to stoop low and head home a late equaliser.

So, we remain just two points above the relegation zone, a buffer that will disappear if Oldham win their game in hand. Meanwhile, director of football David Holdsworth continues to remain missing in action, apparently exempt from any responsibility for the state of the club that employs him on a salary I can only dream of. Would that my job involved so little accountability!

Carlisle United v Swindon Town. Saturday 19 February 2022. Brunton Park. EFL League 2.

Storm Eunice let me down badly this weekend. A few more vicious gusts on Friday might have caused some serious damage to an increasingly dilapidated Brunton Park, and led to yesterday's game being called off on health and safety grounds. That would have saved us the journey for what was one of the worst days I have experienced in my near fifty-four years as a Carlisle United supporter. I was going to make bad officiating the focus of this blog, but things have got much more serious than that.

The portents weren't promising, to be honest. Adam, Ben and I set off at 11.30 in steady drizzle, which had become heavy rain by the time we joined the A1M near Pontefract. Driving was awful, with surface spray making overtaking hazardous to say the least. And

I was doing this with very limited expectations of a positive outcome to our journey! Conditions did ease slowly as we headed North, but the first time the windscreen wipers were turned off was when we stopped at Scotch Corner Services for the obligatory Greggs' sausage rolls. Once we continued our journey along the A66 the wipers were turned off briefly. However, once we passed Bowes, and began to climb to the summit of Stainmore, the snow on the ground was soon matched by the soggy snow (otherwise known as sleet) against the windscreen. As an English teacher, I should probably be making some sort of contrived quip about pathetic fallacy at this point, but right now I really don't have the wit, imagination or motivation!

Surprisingly, once we left County Durham, and began the descent into Cumbria, conditions changed dramatically. The skies cleared and we were bathed in bright sunshine. As we approached Penrith we were treated to the magnificent sight of the snow-coated Lakeland fells, with Blencathra particularly impressive. We arrived in good time to secure a place near the half-way line in the Paddock, behind the all-important crush barrier, essential for one with a dodgy back and gammy knee!

A little bit of context now, for what is to follow. We beat Swindon on their own patch earlier this season, a rare moment of away success – in fact just a rare moment of success. Yesterday marked the return to Brunton Park of one Harry McKirdy, who spent a season at Carlisle two years ago. All you need to know is that even before he left the club, he'd managed to alienate the supporters with some of his posts on social media. It was interesting that as we listened to 'The Brunton Bugle' (a podcast by a couple of Carlisle fans) the Swindon supporter they had on gave the distinct impression (though he never said as much) that he thought McKirdy was an immature wanker, and that it was only a matter of time before he alienated the Swindon supporters with his Instagram posts.

All this meant the atmosphere was quite febrile even before kick-off. However, I chose to focus on the positive in the bright sunshine and, as I told Adam, remembered and re-visualised the Chris Balderstone penalty at the Waterworks End that took us to the top of Division One in 1974, as well as the legendary Jimmy Glass goal at the same end in 1999. Why did I deceive myself?

Once the game kicked off, every touch of McKirdy's was greeted with boos, every misplaced pass or tackle on him greeted with loud cheers. Those cheers increased to a crescendo after fifteen minutes when he started limping after a tackle. We should have known better – just after twenty minutes he did the thing everyone had been dreading and scored against us on his return to Brunton Park. If players can receive a yellow card for taking off their shirt in celebrating a goal, God knows why this little prat didn't receive a red card for his gestures in front of the home supporters.

Interestingly Keith Millen, our manager, thought that the game was relatively even up to half-time. I wish I'd been watching the same game as he was. In the second half, two Swindon goals in three minutes around the hour mark ensured that the atmosphere in the ground turned truly toxic. Our defenders continued to lump balls forward to our new 'target man' Tobi Sho-Silva, who must be one of the worst strikers I have seen in a Carlisle shirt. On the rare occasions he actually challenged for a ball forward, he invariably lost the challenge, and his commitment off the ball was negligible. God knows which idiot thought he was worth paying a transfer fee for – and we're stuck with him for eighteen months. The fact that he was the last player to be substituted speaks volumes for the incompetence of our manager. It's pretty rare for a player to be booed when he's substituted.

The final, meaningless half-hour was played out with two pitch intrusions by disillusioned supporters, each greeted with ironic chants of 'Sign him on.' I'm really surprised the reaction of the fans at the final whistle wasn't more vitriolic.

As for our wonderful Director of Football, David Holdsworth, he'd vacated his seat in the Directors' box well before the end of each half, obviously eager to avoid being the target of supporters' wrath. 'That clown needs to clear out or the club will never move forward!!' Not my words, but those of Adam Collins, a goalkeeper with over two hundred appearances for Carlisle, and a former club captain.

As we walked back to the car after the game, we were regaled with chants from fellow Carlisle supporters of 'Hello to the National League', and I really can't see how that fate can be avoided.

There was still time for things to get even worse. Today a video has appeared on social media of a Carlisle player involved in a violent altercation in the city centre yesterday evening, apparently in response to a racist slur, and the club confirmed today that two players had been spoken to by police. Whoever thought it was a good idea to allow the players a night on the lash after yesterday's woeful performance should be looking for alternative employment.

Day Zero (Wednesday 23 February 2022)

Never mind match days being the focus for each post, today was much more important, a potentially pivotal day in the recent history of Carlisle United. It's difficult to explain feeling euphoric when your team sits next to bottom of League 2, in very real danger of losing their Football League status, but I'll give it a go!

If you bother to read these posts, you'll probably recall that the most recent one was full of doom and gloom, "one of the worst days I have experienced in my near fifty-four years as a Carlisle United supporter" and stuff like that. Why the sudden transformation? Bear with me as I attempt to explain.

At about ten o'clock this morning it was announced that Keith Millen, our hapless manager for the last four months, had left the club 'by mutual consent'. We all know what that means! Less than half an hour later came the further announcement that David Holdsworth, the real villain of the piece, had 'stepped down' from his role as Director of Football. At this point I sense an

English lesson on the use of euphemism in the making! Much fist pumping and punching of the air ensued, with the sense of joy being akin to that when a late winner is scored in a vital cup-tie or promotion game.

I commented to Adam at this point that all that remained was to appoint a new manager by lunchtime to give him a couple of days to prepare the team for Saturday's away game at Leyton Orient – who coincidentally also parted company with their manager today. Adam asked me who my ideal replacement would be, and I had no hesitation in naming Paul Simpson. In reality I fully expected the new boss to be a shouty, old school bully type of manager in the mould of Derek Adams, who just happened to be available, in contrast to the two previous 'nice guy' managers.

But no, it got even better. At about midday it was announced that the new manager, at least until the end of the season, was indeed Paul Simpson, probably the ideal choice in the circumstances.

For those of you who don't share my extensive knowledge of lower divisions trivia, Paul Simpson had a respectable playing career at clubs like Wolverhampton Wanderers, Manchester City, Derby County and Blackpool. His managerial career included spells at Preston North End, Shrewsbury Town, Stockport County and most impressively managing England U20s to World Cup glory in 2017. He has also been assistant manager at Bristol City, Derby County and Newcastle United.

But, and here's the rub, he's a native of Carlisle, supported the club as a boy, and has had a previous spell as club manager. He joined the club as a player-coach during the 2003-2004 season. He took over as player-manager when the club were fifteen points adrift at the foot of League Two. Despite promotion level form in the second half of the season, he was unable to save us from relegation to The Conference (now re-branded as the National League). Fortunately, he chose to stay on and retained most of the playing squad, who proceeded to win promotion back to the Football League at the first attempt, via the Conference play-off final at Stoke City's Britannia Stadium, now known as the Bet365 Stadium (no comment tonight about football's murky association with the gambling industry). I was there! I was there again a year later, as Simpson steered Carlisle to a second successive promotion at Mansfield's Field Mill ground, before we were promoted as League Two champions. At that point Preston North End came calling for Simpson, and although we had two or three good seasons in League One, making the play-offs at least once, it's largely been downhill since then.

So I hope you'll understand the sense of the returning hero and saviour. Reaction on social media has been uniformly positive, and apparently the ticket office at Brunton Park has been besieged by requests for tickets for next Tuesday's game against Rochdale, which will mark Simmo's homecoming. Adam has been dropping hints all day about the possibility of going, despite it being a midweek evening fixture. I'm playing hard to get at the moment, but the truth is 'try to keep me away!'. The place will be bouncing, it feels like we've finally got our club back, and I want to be there! Tomorrow can wait!

Leyton Orient v Carlisle United. Saturday 26 February 2022. The Breyer Group Stadium (really?). EFL League 2.

Yeeeeeeeeeeeeeesssssssssssss!!!!

If anyone had told me at this time last week that my own mood, and the whole vibe surrounding my club, could be so utterly transformed I would have laughed them out of court, and probably reported them to the police.

I've recounted the desolation after last Saturday's fiasco, and the euphoria after Wednesday's seismic changes in my last two posts. A Board of Directors who had got so many things wrong for too many years finally had a moment of clarity and got three massive decisions right in as many hours. The departure of the two people who were primarily responsible for the club's dire situation would have been good enough, but to then immediately appoint the person best suited to deal with that situation, was inspired.

However, no matter how positive the aura that was created by Paul Simpson's appointment, the reality remained that we were still in the bottom two of League Two and staring relegation in the face. I've spent the last three days deliberately lowering my expectations, reminding myself that another defeat today was likely and that a draw would be a good result in the circumstances.

An impressive 700 Carlisle fans made the 600-mile round trip to Leyton Orient, a number no doubt boosted by the positivity generated by Paul Simpson's appointment.

Orient, who have been in free-fall recently, also dismissed their manager this week, but have only appointed a caretaker replacement. Simpson's starting eleven was pretty much what I would have chosen, going for experience rather than potential. Prayers were answered after just five minutes when Omari Patrick scored the fourth goal since his recent return to the club. Thereafter it was a performance of grit and determination, holding on through six minutes of added time at the end of the second half to clinch our first win in eight games.

Adam had got me to pay for the radio commentary, and it was brilliant to hear the enthusiasm and sheer volume of the travelling support after the final whistle. It makes the homecoming of Simmo the Saviour on Tuesday evening an even bigger event. Brunton Park will be rocking, and the atmosphere will be electric! Biggest crowd of the season?

MARCH 2022

Carlisle United v Rochdale. Tuesday 1 March 2022. Brunton Park. EFL League 2.

This was a real rarity – a journey up to Carlisle for a midweek game under floodlights during a working week. As I said to Adam and Ben as we travelled north in beautiful late afternoon sunshine, the last time I could remember doing this was for a League Cup second round second-leg tie against Tottenham Hotspur, sometime in the Nineties. So long ago that David Ginola was still appearing for Tottenham, rather than being reduced to appearing in 'I'm a Celebrity'! That evening was also the last occasion I met the legendary Chris Balderstone in person, and he actually remembered me!

This was a massive night for Carlisle United. They had started the Paul Simpson era (Mark 2) with a much-needed away win at Orient on Saturday, but was this just a case of new-manager bounce, a set of players desperate to prove themselves to the new boss? In Simpson's first home game, would they revert to the disastrous selves that were on show just ten days ago against Swindon?

The club had obviously gone out of their way to build up a sense of occasion, with club legend Peter Murphy introduced to the crowd before kick-off, following the renaming of one of the club's bars in his honour. He has the second highest number of appearances in the club's history. There was also an audio compilation of some of the club's greatest moments played over the P.A., including the Jimmy Glass goal, and our first EFL Trophy win at the old Wembley Stadium.

I thought that rather more fans might have turned out for The Saviour's return to Brunton Park, but the five thousand plus who did attend were fully committed. Simmo's starting line-up was the same as Saturday's and exactly what I would have picked. Where Millen picked Jamie Devitt and Kristian Dennis, two seasoned professionals but not 100% match fit, on the bench, and brought them on for late cameos, Simmo gave them the chance to stamp their mark on the game for an hour plus, before replacing them with fresher legs for the closing stages.

It worked really well. Although Dennis didn't get a lot of service or have many chances, he worked tirelessly, a great example of what Simmo calls 'defending from the front', constantly closing down defenders and the Rochdale goalkeeper. Jamie Devitt scored some great goals from free kicks in his first spell at Carlisle. On this occasion he turned provider. He delivered a teasing free kick into the six-yard box, close enough to the goal to force the keeper to come out, but just far enough away for him to be unable to take the ball cleanly. He palmed the ball to the feet of Omari Patrick who gleefully slammed the ball into the roof of the net for his second goal in four days, and his fifth since his recent return to the club. I described him recently as a scorer of great goals rather than a great goalscorer, but he's beginning to suggest he might be both.

Rochdale played some nice football, lots of neat passing, but not a lot of end-product. When they did pierce the Carlisle defence they found Carlisle keeper Mark Howard in magnificent form, a series of saves earning him the man of the match award. To be honest it could have gone to a number of players: Omari Patrick for his pace and skill; centre-half Morgan Feeney for his willingness to throw himself in the way of anything that might threaten the Carlisle goal; fellow centre-half Dynel Simeu for winning just about everything in the air, despite distinctly dodgy positional sense.

Simeu is interesting. He was signed on loan from Southampton for the rest of the season just before the transfer window closed. Apparently, Southampton paid £1.5 million to Chelsea for him, which is difficult to believe when he's earning his first football league appearances at a club fighting to retain their league status. But his commitment is ferocious. A particularly good sliding tackle was celebrated with a massive fist-pump, and his celebration of the second goal was something to behold. He went to two sides of the ground, punching the air and thumping the Carlisle badge on his chest. He's only played five games for us, and he's only on loan!

The other contender for man of the match was Jon Mellish. Signed as a central defender, last season he was reinvented as a goalscoring midfielder.

On occasions this season he has been played as a striker. On this occasion he reverted to his original role, as a third central defender. He was magnificent! His tackles were timed to perfection, and he made some incisive surges forward out of defence. In the 89th minute he ran the ball away from danger towards the Carlisle corner flag, before launching a long punt upfield. His long clearance was met on the half-way line by substitute Tobi Sho-Silva, who for once managed to retain the ball. I was scathing about his performance against Swindon in our last home game, but he was about to redeem himself. Having won the ball, he started to make inroads into the Rochdale half, accompanied all the way by an equally tall and physical Rochdale defender. He held him off all the way into the penalty area before taking a couple more turns and slotting home what was probably the most wildly celebrated goal of Carlisle's season.

So, Saturday wasn't a flash in the pan. The Simmo redemption is under way, as last night's result took us three places up the league table. Next up are Oldham, who number two former Carlisle players and a former manager amongst their staff. Victory on Saturday would be particularly satisfying. We'll be there!

It was particularly gratifying to look up at the directors' box last night and see an empty seat where former director of football David Holdsworth used to sit. As a Carlisle United podcast put it, there is a need for directors of football, but not when you've got the worst one in the country.

Oldham Athletic v Carlisle United. Saturday 5 March 2022. Boundary Park. EFL League 2.

This was just magnificent. This was the stuff of which dreams are made. This was the kind of day that makes the years of defeats, disappointment and disillusionment seem worthwhile.

And it was a game that really mattered. Before the game Oldham were in the bottom two, just three points behind Carlisle but with a game in hand. Victory for Carlisle would open up a reassuring six-point gap, but defeat would leave us equal on points and back in the mire. It was what cliché-ridden pundits like to refer to as a 'relegation six-pointer'.

There were all sorts of interesting contexts to this game. Both clubs have been experiencing problems both on and off the pitch. Both clubs have sacked their manager recently, a little longer ago in Oldham's case. Both clubs have turned to a former manager in a last-ditch attempt to avoid relegation. Oldham have re-employed John Sheridan and his assistant, Tommy Wright, for the umpteenth time. Carlisle have called on Paul Simpson who led the club to successive promotions sixteen years ago. To add further spice, Sheridan and Wright spent half a season in charge at Carlisle.

Each manager has made a good start. Oldham were unbeaten in seven games under Sheridan, a run that Oldham fans laughingly referred to as 'The Shezurrection'. After eight games without a win before his appointment, Simpson had steered Carlisle to victory in his first two games back in charge. Was this a false dawn, or the beginning of something special?

As if that weren't enough, Oldham featured two former Carlisle players in their line-up, 'striker' Hallam Hope and winger Nicky Adams. After Hope had missed a particularly easy chance during his Carlisle days, a wag in the crowd close to us was heard to opine "You couldn't finish a fucking book Hope!". However, he did score one impressively cheeky goal against Notts County. Adams was a crowd favourite during his time at Carlisle, but his every touch in this game was met with predictable boos.

Thirteen hundred Carlisle fans had travelled to Boundary Park, making it a raucous away end. I love it when the Carlisle support is so noisy that you can see that the home fans are chanting and clapping, but you can't actually hear them! For us it was an easy trip across the M62, a change from the lengthy trek up to Carlisle. Time for lunch before we left, and home in good time for tea!

Fortunately, the game itself lived up to the pre-match hype. An early Carlisle appeal for a handball penalty was rejected by the referee, before he awarded Oldham a penalty for what seemed to be a much less obvious handball – well, much less obvious to us Blues fans! The subsequent confrontation between opposing players was an early sign that the referee was struggling to impose his authority on the game. When the penalty was finally taken, it was struck down the middle, and keeper Mark Howard, who had dived to his left, was able to flex a trailing leg sufficiently to clear the ball. The follow-up shot went narrowly wide of the post, and we celebrated like we'd just scored ourselves!

Not long after, tempers boiled over again when Hallam Hope lunged in with a late challenge on Howard. Cue more 'handbags' between the players and a yellow card for Hope, though later photos of the challenge clearly showed it should have been a red card. There was some consolation when Nicky Adams also received a yellow card for protesting at the one for Hope.

But for the second time in a fortnight, a former player was to come back to haunt us. On the stroke of half-time the ball pinged around the Carlisle penalty area before Hallam Hope got the final touch to poke it home. Predictably he celebrated wildly and aggressively in front of the Carlisle fans, and predictably he was roundly abused for doing so.

It took only three minutes of the second half for parity to be restored. Jordan Gibson won possession in the Oldham half, and moved the ball on to Kristian Dennis, who played a beautifully judged through pass to Omari Patrick. He still had plenty to do, but advanced and calmly side-footed the ball just inside the right-hand post for his third goal in successive games, and his sixth in twelve since returning to the club.

Patrick was superb in the second half, tormenting his opposing full-back, but as the clock ticked down none of the chances went in, and a draw looked the likely outcome. Seven points out of nine since Simpson's return would still represent a very impressive return.

Deep into time added on, substitute Tobi Sho-Silva made one last surge forward, drawing a foul from Oldham not far outside their penalty area. Simmo subsequently revealed that when the free kick was awarded, he heard the fourth official tell the referee via his radio that there were ten seconds of playing time left. Callum Guy floated the ball into the six-yard box, where defender, and new cult hero, Morgan Feeney, timed his run to perfection, heading home via the post. Cue bedlam! It might not have quite been on the level of Jimmy Glass's historic goal, but it wasn't far behind. I've not experienced many goal celebrations like this one.

When the final whistle went, just seconds after the restart, the Oldham fans quickly streamed out of the ground, with the 'Shezurrection' having come to a grinding halt. But we were going nowhere! Fired-up players and fired-up fans celebrated for a good ten minutes after the final whistle and as we finally walked back to the car, we were still struggling to take in what we'd just witnessed. And even better, all the significant action of the game happened at the away end. This was one of the most memorable games in my many years as a Carlisle fan.

Next up are high-flying Northampton at Brunton Park on Saturday. Will we be there?

Carlisle United v Northampton Town. Saturday 12 March 2022. Brunton Park. EFL League 2.

Of course we were there!

As with the previous two games, I've allowed two or three days to pass in order to let the dust settle and gain some perspective on yet another remarkable match. This one was a real test. Our previous three wins under Paul Simpson had all come against teams in the lower half of the League Two table. While that meant the wins had added value in terms of the relegation battle, it meant our new resolve hadn't been tested against a 'good' team. Northampton represented just that, travelling to Brunton Park holding down one of the automatic promotion places.

We travelled in expectation of a decent crowd, thanks to a cheap tickets promotion – another sign of the club finally getting things right. One wonders why this kind of thing wasn't done sooner. It makes sense, doesn't it? A new manager and three wins on the bounce – let's capitalise on that by reducing ticket prices and getting a bumper crowd for the next game. Maybe our former director of football might be responsible for that lack of common sense. 'The Brunton Bugle', an unofficial Carlisle podcast, commented on David Holdsworth's record in scathing terms in its first broadcast following his sacking three weeks ago. The presenters then promised that his name would never be mentioned again. On the brief occasions since when reference has been made to him, he is simply referred to as 'he who shall not be named'.

Incidentally, listening to 'The Brunton Bugle' on the way to home matches has become just as much of a ritual as the obligatory Greggs sausage roll at Scotch Corner services.

We arrived in good time to secure a reasonable parking spot, though not early enough to get a place behind a crush barrier once we entered the ground, to ease my creaking back and knee. I know I could go for a seat, but the constant standing up and sitting down again is even worse. At Oldham last week the whole away end was seating, but the only time most of us sat down was at half-time! The actual attendance was about 8,500 (approximately 300 away fans), representing almost double the number who witnessed the horror show against Swindon just three weeks earlier.

As we walked along Warwick Road to the ground, I pointed out to Adam that I'd made the same walk at his age with my own dad to watch Carlisle play in what was then Division 1. If you'd told me than that almost fifty years later, I'd be making the same walk to watch them in League Two (Division 4 back then) and having travelled 135 miles from Wakefield rather than just 30 for the pleasure, I might have been a touch sceptical. A pity my dad's no longer with us – he'd have loved hearing about the recent upturn, even if unable to attend matches any more.

I was a bit disappointed by the atmosphere in the first half. I'd expected the crowd to be a bit more raucous and vociferous. It was almost as if people didn't quite believe yet another win was possible. Nonetheless, we went in at half-time at 0-0, with the feeling that we'd pretty much matched a decent opposition.

The starting line-up had been unchanged for the fourth game in a row, and as the second half wore on, the substitutions followed their usual pattern. Jamie Devitt was replaced around the hour, and fifteen minutes later

Kristian Dennis was replaced by super sub Tobi Sho-Silva. I think this is brilliant tactics by Simpson. Dennis is a diminutive player who spends about seventy minutes scurrying round, pressing defenders and the goalkeeper, creating space for Omari Patrick. He is then replaced by a big, tall and physical target man, meaning defenders have to adjust to a totally different scenario.

It worked to perfection on this occasion. Brennan Dickenson, also a substitute after returning from injury, and whose work off the ball does not impress me at all, battled hard to win a header, brought the ball under control, and played a superb through ball to Sho-Silva, who slotted the ball home with his very first touch of the ball. Ecstasy on the terraces, as a scarcely credible fourth successive win beckoned. We were soon brought back to earth, as Northampton equalised within five minutes. Still, a draw against a top three side would represent a very reasonable result.

As full-time approached, the sense of déjà vu from last week's Oldham game became increasingly strong. First of all, there was the same five minutes of added time. As that time ticked away, Sho-Silva battled against a defender and won a free-kick out on the right, just like last week. Once again captain Callum Guy floated the ball towards the far post. This time, instead of meeting the head of an onrushing Morgan Feeney, it made contact with the arm of a Northampton defender who had inexplicably lost his bearings and balance. After what seemed like an eternity, the referee pointed to the penalty spot. After some inevitable delay, Jordan Gibson did the honours, and drove the ball into the left-hand side of the goal. It was Oldham all over again, but this time in front of 8,000 fans rather than 1,300.

The final whistle brought more wild celebrations, with very few leaving the ground until the team had finished acknowledging the supporters. As we walked back to the car along Warwick Road, I was sporting my Kefalonia smile, the inane grin that covers my face every time we arrive at Kefalonia Airport, and we walk across the tarmac to the terminal, knowing that I'm back in one of my two favourite places on Planet Earth (the other being Brunton Park of course!). We were largely speechless, struggling for the second week in succession to process the last-minute drama we'd just witnessed.

We even got a shout-out on 606, the Radio 5 Live football phone-in hosted by Chris Sutton and Robbie Savage. In the intro, alongside the usual focus on the Premier League, Sutton called on Carlisle fans to get in touch about the club's remarkable revival under Paul Simpson. That might have had something to do with the fact that Sutton's dad used to play for Carlisle, back in my early days of supporting the team.

This sequence of wins will come to an end, but for as long as it continues it's a bloody marvellous feeling!

Carlisle United v Newport County. Tuesday 15 March 2022. Brunton Park. EFL League 2.

I stated in my last post that Carlisle's winning run would come to an end, and unfortunately the end came sooner rather than later. Not only did Tuesday night mark the end of a glorious run of victories, but also the end of what felt like a long sequence of live attendance at matches. This post will probably be briefer than recent ones, but mainly because we weren't there, rather than because I'm sulking!

For the first time since his return, I disagreed with Paul Simpson's team selection. Four changes to a team that had won four successive games seemed a bit drastic. Admittedly, one of those changes was due to injury, and another to personal circumstances, but the other two didn't make sense to me. Tobi Sho-Silva was rewarded for his impressive contributions from the bench with a place in the starting line-up. Unfortunately, he produced a performance more in keeping with his last starting performance in the disaster that was the defeat against Swindon, the last game before Simmo took over. Mitchell Roberts, a West Brom loanee came in at left wing-back and didn't really do anything to suggest why he'd been preferred over previous incumbent Jack Armer.

The first half displayed too many of the traits that had landed us in relegation trouble in the first place – particularly lack of shape, and poor decision making. We were probably lucky to be only one goal down at the interval, against another team in an automatic promotion place. When we went two goals down, I feared the worst, but that seemed to galvanise the team. Substitutions and changes to formation led to an Omari Patrick goal that continued his hot scoring streak since returning to the club and demonstrated some very deft penalty area control.

That left enough time for a possible equaliser, but despite Carlisle pouring forward in the closing stages, it wasn't to be. At least our winning run came to an end against a decent team, who we ran close in the final stages.

And so, it's on to a local Derby at Barrow, a game at which Carlisle's support will be woefully underrepresented, due to Barrow's poxy little ground and the limited allocation of away tickets.

As for Adam, he chose not to watch the game with me on i-Follow, instead going to Elland Road to watch Leeds United U23s play Liverpool. His driver was informed that Judas Iscariot had already eaten his last supper prior to departure.

Barrow v Carlisle United. Saturday 19 March 2022. The Dunes Hotel Stadium (another laughable one!). EFL League 2.

This was the first Cumbrian derby in front of fans at Holker Street (the ground's proper name) since the 1960s. Holker Street must be the worst ground in League Two, though it has some pretty tough competition from the likes of Harrogate Town and Salford City, to name but a couple. It's frustrating when a team with strong travelling support has that support limited by the ability of their opponents to accommodate them. I suppose they wanted to avoid the scenario that occurred a couple of years ago, when Carlisle played another derby game at Morecambe, and the away supporters outnumbered the home contingent!

A crowd of nearly eight thousand had turned up for the reverse fixture at Brunton Park earlier this season.

We were treated to a stultifying 0-0 draw between two very mediocre sides. This time, a crowd of about 4,500 was Barrow's biggest for a home league fixture in over fifty years! Unfortunately, we couldn't get tickets, nor was the game available to stream on i-Follow. Fortunately, those who were able to attend were treated to a rather better spectacle than the previous game.

The bare bones are that Carlisle took the lead around twenty minutes, through an excellent low Jordan Gibson angled drive from the edge of the area. That lead was increased, and the points looked secure around seventy-five minutes, when Kristian Dennis poked home an opportunist effort that just trickled over the line, following indecision from Barrow goalkeeper Paul Farman, who was playing for Carlisle this time last year. Barrow struck back almost immediately, but despite a nervy last few minutes, Carlisle held on to record their fifth victory in six games, and to move twelve points clear of the relegation zone – a scenario that was unimaginable just four weeks ago.

At this point I should mention a feature of Carlisle's media coverage called Pitchside Blues. It's quite simple. A pitchside cameraman captures the pre-match preparations, and the match action from a pitch-level perspective, which is then edited down to about ten minutes without commentary. It's brilliant for re-creating the buzz of the moment if you were there, or for giving a sense of the atmosphere if you weren't. For instance, it captures the moment Kristian Dennis launched himself into the crowd to celebrate his goal yesterday, before re-emerging safely about a minute later.

Carlisle United v Bristol Rovers. Saturday 26 March 2022. Brunton Park. EFL League 2.

As is becoming increasingly common on a Saturday morning, we climbed into the car at about 11.15, and set forth. Except on this occasion "we" wasn't Adam, Ben and me, it was Lisa and myself, and we weren't heading north to Carlisle on the A1M, we were heading south to Birmingham on the M1 to watch Ellie in a dance show!

That meant a second weekend in a row without attending a Carlisle game. Not only that, but I also wouldn't be able to watch the game on i-Follow – since it's an international break, the game was available for live-streaming. This was a big test too. Bristol Rovers and Carlisle were the two form teams heading into this game, each with five wins from the last six games. The one difference was that Rovers were battling things out at the top end of League Two, while Carlisle were fighting to pull away from the bottom of the division.

So, my engagement with the game was reduced to surreptitious glances at my phone during the dance show, but not so often that I appeared uninvolved with the dance! I cheered silently when Kristian Dennis scored in the 72nd minute to give us the lead, and then, as the dance show built to its climax, experienced a double dose of tension as a seemingly interminable seven minutes of added time played out at Brunton Park, before the final whistle blew on a 1-0 victory. The dance show was superb by the way, well worth missing a Carlisle game for, if it isn't heretical of me to admit such a possibility!

Obviously, I can't give you chapter and verse on this game, despite Adam giving me some details after watching the live stream. So, I'm going to deluge you with statistics instead. Five weeks ago, after the dreadful Swindon defeat, we were in the relegation zone. Now, just seven games later we are an unbelievable fifteen points above said relegation zone. A win on Tuesday night will mean we will be closer to the promotion play-offs than to relegation. Five weeks ago, the bookmakers' odds on Carlisle being relegated were 6-5. Now they have lengthened to 150-1. Six wins in his first seven games means that Paul Simpson now holds the record for the most successful start ever by a Carlisle manager. Ironically, he also holds the record for the worst ever start by a Carlisle manager! When he was in his first spell at the club, having joined as player-coach, he took over a team in dire straits (nothing new there then!), and proceeded to oversee six defeats in his first six games. Following the inevitable relegation, he then secured two successive promotions. One final statistic – Tuesday's opponents are Rochdale, whose recent form has seen them lose five and draw two of their last seven games, compared to Carlisle's six wins and one defeat. Ironically, Rochdale's winless run began at Brunton Park, less than a month ago.

Rochdale v Carlisle United. Tuesday 29 March 2022. The Crown Oil Arena (yes, another one!). EFL League 2.

We were back on the road for this one, an easy trip just across the Pennines. And at least we made it all the way, rather than having to turn back at the top of Saddleworth Moor when the game was called off, as happened in

February. We arrived in good time and were able to find street parking just a couple of minutes from the ground.

Spotland (to give the venue its proper name) is a tidy little all-seater ground, with a capacity of 10,000. It's also embedded in the heart of the local community, rather than adjacent to an out-of-town retail park, as are some relatively new builds such as Scunthorpe and Doncaster. It's deserving of a better crowd than the paltry 2,160 who attended last night's fixture. Even more worrying for a club that were in League One last season, is that a travelling contingent of over five hundred made up almost a quarter of the attendance.

It was an odd evening in some ways. We lost 2-0 yet it was still a quite enjoyable evening! Carlisle were nowhere in the first half. We went behind to an early soft penalty and were never really on the pace. The drive of recent performances was missing, and it was a relief to reach half-time at only 1-0. The second half saw an improvement, helped by a couple of substitutions on the hour, but a goal disallowed dubiously for a challenge on the goalkeeper, and a late breakaway from Rochdale as we pushed forward for an equaliser meant we lost 2-0, only our second defeat under Simpson's management, and the first time under his current stewardship that we'd failed to score.

I think the enjoyment came from the fact that despite losing, there was quite a feisty atmosphere among the Carlisle fans, provoked by some dreadful decisions by the referee, and his assistant on our side of the pitch. It was telling that at the final whistle, the rest of the ground emptied almost immediately (well, it doesn't take long for 1,600 people to vacate a 10,000-capacity stadium), while most of the Carlisle supporters waited patiently as Simpson conducted his on-pitch post-match huddle, before saluting their defeated team.

As with our previous defeat under Simmo, against Newport County, I would take issue with a couple of his team selections, the only two games where I would question his judgement. Our two most influential midfielders, Jamie Devitt and Callum Guy, are out injured for the rest of the season. Both are playmakers, and both good at delivery from set pieces.

My main concern is over the selection of Brennan Dickenson. He tends to play in a wide midfield role and is capable of impressive moments – a raking cross-field pass or bursting past a defender and getting away a shot. Unfortunately, his play is more often characterised by poor set-piece delivery and being too easily dispossessed. He's one of those players who appears to be working quite hard out of possession, but on closer examination the truth is rather different. He runs towards opposition players quite a lot, giving the impression that he's working hard, but all too rarely actually makes a challenge. When he does, they're generally ineffective, as evidenced by his ineffectiveness in the build up to Rochdale's second goal. The conclusion to this is obvious – Simmo should sack Gavin Skelton and install me as his assistant!

Dickenson is out of contract at the end of the season – I wouldn't offer him a new one.

Before I finish, another mention for our loanee from Southampton, Dynel Simeu. He gave another commanding performance in central defence. It's great when high balls are played forward, and you can feel almost entirely confident that your defender will win the challenge. Not only that, but he is also highly motivated, celebrating successful tackles with a fist pump, and always looking to rouse and applaud the fans. Adam tells me that today he's been visiting a local school to make a speech. That's the sort of behaviour you might expect from a club captain, not a half-season loan signing from a Premier League club who only turned twenty last week. Simmo should bust a gut to get him on a full season loan for the next campaign. However, I suspect that, given his success at Carlisle, Southampton will want him to gain further experience at a League One or Championship club.

APRIL 2022

Tranmere Rovers v Carlisle United. Saturday 2 April 2022. Prenton Park (credit to Tranmere for no inane ground sponsorship!). EFL League 2.

This was just another humdrum day in the current experience that is supporting Carlisle United – eleven yellow cards, two red cards and a 97th minute equaliser.

This was one of our longer road trips for an away game, though still not as long as the journey to home fixtures! After yet another journey across the M62, and then a long haul along the Wirral Peninsula we arrived in good time and found street parking just a minute's walk from the ground. Initial impressions were favourable – like Rochdale's ground, Prenton Park is situated in the heart of the local community. On entering the ground, impressions were equally favourable: an all-seater ground, with two substantial stands, it's probably the best ground we've visited all season. Sadly, it gives off the vibe of a club that has seen better days. Time was that Tranmere were vying for promotion to the topflight under John Aldridge's management and contesting League Cup semi-finals. Time was that as good a player as Pat Nevin turned down untold wealth and luxury at Galatasary to sign for Tranmere Rovers.

Tranmere are in the battle for play-off places, so this was no easy assignment. Paul Simpson rang a few changes, with Danny Devine earning a well-deserved starting place, and Kelvin Mellor making his first start after a lengthy absence through injury. Jon Mellish moved from defence into midfield, and Corey Whelan was dropped to the bench. Unfortunately, Brennan Dickenson was still in the starting eleven at left wing-back and was hopelessly at sea when Tranmere scored the first goal after a cross from their right. As one considered critic in the Carlisle end shouted, "It's a footballer we're looking for Dickenson, not a fucking bodybuilder!"

Things really took off about five minutes before half-time when a Tranmere player was sent off for a knee-high challenge on Kelvin Mellor. As he left the pitch he decided to indulge in some further verbals and it all kicked off – handbags at high noon! When the melee was finally subdued, two players from each side received yellow cards, as well as the respective managers. Interesting that in the second half Mellor was repeatedly booed by the Tranmere fans, presumably for being on the receiving end of a potentially career-ending tackle!

Carlisle made their numerical advantage count just ten minutes into the second half. Following a short corner, Omari Patrick cut in from the left, and curled a shot into the top right-hand corner, aided by a deflection. It was largely one-way traffic after that, until the 76th minute. From a free kick, Morgan Feeney's header was brilliantly saved by the Tranmere keeper and the ball was cleared long. The Tranmere striker broke clear of our final defender and bore down on goal, keeping a calm head to slot the ball home.

Despite having four strikers on the pitch in the closing stages the equaliser would not come, despite numerous chances. A minimum of six minutes of added time were indicated, and the excitement had yet to begin! Just a minute into added time a Tranmere player went in with a high boot as Rod McDonald stooped slightly to make a header, and rightly received a red card. In the following minutes we witnessed some shameful time-wasting by both the remaining nine Tranmere players and also by their supporters. When the ball went out for a throw-in, one Tranmere fan spent about a minute booting it high into the stand in an attempt to run down the clock. How fitting that Carlisle equalised in the further time the referee added for such blatant gamesmanship! How stupid that Tranmere fan must have felt when the goal was scored!

In the dying seconds, Jordan Gibson hit a superb shot from about twenty-five yards that cannoned into the air off the right-hand post. In what felt like slow-motion, it eventually fell to supersub Tobi Sho-Silva, who calmly headed home. The crowd reaction was anything but calm – I have the scars on my right shin to show from the fan who fell onto us from a couple of rows back! It was another of those games when an equaliser so close to the end makes it feel more like a win than a draw. Remarkably, Dynel Simeu, who had been substituted a few minutes earlier, was one of the first players to reach Sho-Silva to celebrate!

Gaining a result in the dying seconds usually happens one, maybe twice, a season. This must be about the sixth time it's happened for us this season, mostly in the last six weeks. In post-match interviews manager Paul Simpson was highly critical of the abuse the Carlisle bench suffered from Tranmere fans, and even more critical of the failure of stewards and police to take any action.

For some strange reason, the car satnav set us on the way home by a totally different route, taking us through the Birkenhead tunnel, for my second ever visit to Liverpool. The first visit was in 1975, to see Carlisle play at Anfield, a game which, if my memory serves me right, confirmed our relegation from Division 1.

Carlisle United v Exeter City. Saturday 9 April 2022. Brunton Park. EFL League 2.

This was another stern test against a team riding high in one of the automatic promotion places, having lost only one game in the last seventeen. After trips to Birmingham (twice), Tranmere and Rochdale during the previous week, I'd elected to give myself a break from driving duties. However, thanks to Adam's ingenuity, we were still able to stream the game live.

To the game itself. Exeter thrashed us 0-0 in the first half! They dominated possession, were quick and incisive going forward and created numerous chances. Their inability to put away those chances was the only reason Carlisle reached the interval on level terms. A number of the faults of the bad old days were in evidence – bad positioning and decision making in defence, and the failure of the midfield to provide decent service to the forwards.

Carlisle did come into the game a bit more in the second half, creating a handful of chances of their own, and as the clock ticked down it looked like we were going to snatch an undeserved point from a disappointing performance. Slack marking from an Exeter corner led to an unchallenged header and an 89th minute winner for Exeter. For once the late drama belonged to the opposition! Suddenly we've only gained one point from the last possible nine.

I want to have a little beef about League Two grounds, their capacities, and the allocation of tickets to away fans. Of the twenty-four grounds in the division, less than half (eleven) have a capacity of over 10,000. Ten have a capacity of less than 8,000, and five less than 6,000. Harrogate are in last place with a meagre 3,800 capacity.

This leads to some pretty paltry allocations of tickets for away supporters. For instance, Carlisle were given just 600 tickets for the recent local derby at Barrow's Holker Street, less than half the number of Barrow fans who were able to attend the corresponding fixture at Brunton Park. The Carlisle allocation for this Friday's game at Walsall was initially only three hundred, though I think this has subsequently been increased to about 450 (we've got ours!). Walsall's capacity is 11,300. I very much doubt the remaining 10,850 seats will be filled by Walsall fans! Are some clubs unwilling to stump up the stewarding and administrative costs to allow all the way fans to attend who wish to, even though they have the capacity to accommodate them? The Carlisle game at Harrogate on Saturday week is another case in point. The allocation is so small that season ticket holders have been given priority for ticket purchase, meaning that I'll have to be on the phone the minute the ticket office opens for general sale tomorrow, in the hope of securing three of any tickets that might remain. It'll be far easier to secure tickets for the Easter Monday home game against Mansfield, though that will involve us travelling about five times further than to Harrogate!

I know that certain minimum ground requirements exist, because when Harrogate were promoted to League Two they had to replace their 3G artificial pitch, a valuable community resource, with a grass pitch. Surely such requirements should extend to overall capacity and the ability to accommodate away supporters?

Walsall v Carlisle United. Friday 15 April 2022. The Bescot Stadium. EFL League 2.

We (that's Adam Ben and me, not Carlisle United) are ending this season as we began it, with a flurry of in-person match attendances – four out of the final five games, and five out of the last seven. Today's Walsall jaunt will be followed by our final trip of the season to Brunton Park on Easter Monday to watch Carlisle play Mansfield, with short hops to Harrogate Town and Bradford City to follow.

We were slightly later joining the bank holiday traffic than intended, due to one or two problems with the paperwork for Lisa's new car, but eventually hit the road around midday. Apart from a slight detour around Sheffield our journey was mercifully free of traffic delays. Walsall was new territory, both in terms of visiting the town itself, and the football club. Impressions were favourable – dedicated parking for away fans (at a price) just a couple of minutes' walk from the ground and extremely friendly and helpful stewards. The ground itself is a tidy all-seater with room for about 11,300. Over six hundred Carlisle fans had made the journey, well over 10% of the total attendance.

The game itself was a distinct anti-climax. The buzz that was evident in the first few weeks after Paul Simpson's return seems to have dissipated, among both the players and the supporters. It was a poor performance, with too much indecision in defence, a lack of shape and control in midfield, and the forwards left to feed off scraps. I honestly can't recall either goalkeeper having to make a serious save from a shot or header on target. It was probably fitting that the game was settled by a scrappy Walsall goal on the brink of half-time, following panic in the Carlisle defence and a repeated inability to clear the ball. We're still not mathematically safe from relegation, and only one point from the last twelve is rather worrying.

Brennan Dickenson did nothing today to change my opinion that he's very lucky to make his living as a professional footballer!

Bizarrely, just as with the Tranmere game a fortnight ago, the satnav chose to bring us home by a very different route from the one we arrived by. Having travelled south via

Derby and Burton on Trent, we travelled back on the M6 initially, which took us through the centre of Birmingham!

Carlisle United v Mansfield Town. Monday 187 April 2022. Brunton Park. EFL League 2.

This was our last trip to Carlisle for a home game this season. We travelled in the knowledge that a win would guarantee our safety. In fact, if Oldham lost today, we would survive irrespective of our result. Oldham were up against league leaders Forest Green Rovers, while we faced Mansfield, who were looking to consolidate a play-off place, sitting in sixth place.

Despite a couple of Bank Holiday traffic hold-ups en route, we arrived in time to collect our tickets before kick-off – or so we thought. Apparently, the ticketing software couldn't cope with the fact that when I bought tickets last Wednesday, I asked for the tickets for Saturday's game at Harrogate to be posted out, and today's tickets to be sent as e-tickets. When they failed to appear in my in-box, I phoned, and the ticket office said they'd print them out for collection this afternoon. Having arrived, we were initially directed to the wrong window, and when we got to the right one, we discovered that only two tickets had been printed. we were referred to yet another window where they had a printer that could actually produce the missing ticket. The upshot was that we missed the first seven or eight minutes of the game, though fortunately no significant incidents.

Mansfield looked good in the first half, quick and slick passing, moving the ball forward rapidly, though with a tendency to over-elaborate when they got into dangerous areas. Carlisle were a bit sluggish, appearing to be suffering a bit of a hangover from Friday's disappointing performance, though they did have the best chance of the half when a Simeu header was cleared off the goal line.

At half-time we made the unusual decision to move our position, from the right-hand section of the paddock to the left-hand section, so we were closer to the Waterworks End which Carlisle were attacking in the second half. What a wise move it proved to be. Carlisle were a team transformed in the second half, with wave after wave of attack. We only had a single Omari Patrick goal to show for our dominance, but there could have been four or five more. We hit the woodwork twice, Patrick had a second goal chalked off for a ridiculous offside decision, and Joe Riley almost scored the goal of this, or any other, season. Playing at right wing-back, he picked up the ball ten yards from his own line, and embarked on a run, via a one-two with Omari Patrick, that ended with his shot being blocked away for a Carlisle corner.

After a frankly incomprehensible five minutes of added time, the final whistle blew, and we were able to celebrate securing safety with three games to spare, an outcome that appeared almost impossible two months ago after our dreadful home defeat to Swindon left us in one of the relegation places. As Paul Simpson took the crowd's applause and disappeared down the tunnel, he wore the smile of a man well pleased with a job well done. According to Adam, his post-match interview was very positive, raising hopes that he'll be with us in the longer term.

As it happened, Forest Green Rovers did the business, and duly beat Oldham, who are now in serious danger of relegation to the National League. I'll be quite happy to see John Sheridan managing in the National League again, though knowing his lack of loyalty to anyone who isn't called John Sheridan, he probably won't hang around beyond the end of the season, because everything will have been someone else's fault. Having said that, I'll be sorry to see a club with a history and ground like Oldham's disappear from the Football League. I know that those factors don't entitle a club to League status, but some of the grounds we've visited this season have been shocking. League One is welcome to Forest Green Rovers next season. While they are going to be playing at the likes of The Stadium of Light and The University of Bolton Stadium, their opponents will have to endure the dubious comforts of The New Lawn.

We're not quite done for this season though. Despite having guaranteed safety, our last two away games are our two shortest trips of the season, to Harrogate Town and Bradford City. Although there's no longer anything at stake other than pride, we'll be at both games to bring down the curtain on what has been a pretty remarkable season, though not always for the right reasons.

Harrogate Town v Carlisle United. Saturday 23 April 2022. The Envirovent Stadium (that's another joke!). EFL League 2.

This was not how today was meant to be. After safety was secured on Monday, with a vibrant second half attacking display against Mansfield, this should have been an afternoon in the sun. The shackles were off, no need to play with any inhibitions, and for some players whose contracts expire in the summer, this was an opportunity to either state their case for a new contract or put themselves in the shop window. Add to that the fact that we were up against a team that had lost eight of their last ten games, and we had one of our shortest trips for the season, and everything seemed set fair.

The feel-good factor was increased as we approached the ground and bumped into Dean Walling, an iconic Carlisle centre-half from the nineties. I was able to shake hands and exchange a few pleasantries. This was my second meeting with Deano, the other occurring in a layby on the A1M. the circumstances surrounding that meeting are far too complicated to recount, and probably of no interest to anyone other than myself.

I've ranted previously about how crap Harrogate's ground is, but I'd forgotten just how bad it is until we actually entered it. The away ticket allocation had been limited to 600, but there was still space in the away section for plenty more. To add further insult, the crowd was a meagre 2,700, well below the capacity of even this tiny ground. And Carlisle supporters constituted almost a quarter of that total.

The game itself saw an abject display from Carlisle. Harrogate were rubbish, but still managed to score two first-half goals, each from unchallenged headers. At least a couple of players probably destroyed their chance of a new contract, and Brennan Dickenson continued to give the worst impersonation of a professional footballer

I've ever seen. I'm not the only supporter who's noticed that he's invariably the first player to disappear down the tunnel at full time, and that he rarely comes over to the fans to properly salute them.

I think that the problem today was that Ben wasn't with us. On the odd occasion when he hasn't been able to go to a game, and Adam has invited another friend along, we've witnessed the worst performances of the season, namely today, and the 3-0 home defeat to Swindon a couple of months ago that prompted the sackings that led to Paul Simpson's return and our eventual survival. Come back Ben, all is forgiven!

Day Zero Mark 2

I used the term Day Zero just over two months ago when the Carlisle board finally acted decisively and sacked the then manager and director of football, bringing in Paul Simpson as manager to the end of the season, in the hope that he could rescue us from the looming prospect of relegation. 18 points from a possible 21 in his first seven games in charge pretty much banished that demon, though it took a little bit longer before supporters could finally relax.

This evening came the news that every Carlisle fan has been hoping for but didn't dare expect. Paul Simpson has signed a contract to manage Carlisle United for the next three years! I can't imagine many, if any, League Two managers are offered a contract of that length. I don't think any other club in the EFL, or the Premier League for that matter, has a World Cup winning manager in charge. Okay, it was the U20s world cup, but it sounds good!

Every season that Paul Simpson has started as Carlisle manager, the club have won promotion, so based on that precedent we'll have just got into the Premier League by the time his contract is up for renewal!

Now that he's committed to the long term, it'll be fascinating to see who he releases, who he retains, and who he brings in over the next two or three months, both on the pitch and off. He's made it clear over the last few weeks that he'd only commit to the job in the longer term if the set-up off the pitch is right, so it's massively encouraging that his demands have apparently been met, to the extent that he's committed to upping sticks and moving back to Carlisle. Right now, the future looks rosy!

Carlisle United v Stevenage. Saturday 30 April 2022. Brunton Park. EFL League 2.

And so the season draws towards a close. With safety assured two games ago, and nothing at stake in this game, I'd decided this was one 270-mile round trip we didn't need to make. However, when Lisa pointed out that she was going to a poetry launch at which she was reading one of her poems, and that her and Imogen were going to see Jinx Monsoon at Leeds City Varieties in the evening, there was a last-minute change of heart and tickets were bought online. It would be good to be at the game to celebrate Simmo's appointment as manager for the next three years, and to salute the players after the last home game of the season.

I have fond memories of the one previous occasion I've seen Carlisle play Stevenage. That was in the Conference (now National League) play-off final in 2005, played at Stoke City's Britannia Stadium (now the Bet 365 Stadium) during Simmo's first spell as Carlisle manager. A 23rd minute goal from Peter Murphy ensured that we returned to the Football League at the first attempt. That would be followed a year later by a second successive promotion as we became champions of what was then known as Division 3.

We had none of the ticket problems of our previous trip to Brunton Park, and were in position by half past two, safely ensconced behind a crush barrier to give some relief to my troublesome back and knee! Simmo had decided to give youth player Jack Ellis a debut at right back, and he proceeded to give an impressively assured performance, fully justifying the two-year full contract he has been awarded.

To be honest, the first half had a distinctly end-of-season feel to it. Carlisle created some half-chances, but some sloppy defending gave Stevenage more chances than the quality of their play deserved. Fortunately, things looked up in the second half. On fifty-five minutes, Joe Riley scored with an excellent low drive from just outside the right-hand corner of the penalty box, though he overstretched in the process and had to be substituted shortly afterwards. About ten minutes later a beautiful passing move that started in Carlisle's right back position took the ball the length of the pitch before Lewis Allessandra slid home Jack Armer's superbly measured pass from the left from just inside the six-yard box. Despite Stevenage scoring from an inexplicably awarded penalty with five minutes to go, the final result was never really in doubt.

There followed the obligatory end-of-season lap of honour by players, their families and club officials. I wonder how many of those we enthusiastically applauded will be reporting for pre-season on 22nd June. There remained time for a visit to the club shop and the purchase of a t-shirt commemorating Carlisle's 3-2 victory over AS Roma at the Olympic Stadium fifty years ago in the Anglo-Italian Cup.

As we travelled home and listened to Final Score on Radio 5, I realised that at this stage of the season, my interest in promotion and relegation issues has nothing to do with the merits of the teams involved, and everything to do with Carlisle's fixture list next season. Therefore, I'm happy to see Exeter and Forest Green Rovers be promoted to League One, as they're well out of range, and I'd probably like to see them joined by Bristol Rovers and Sutton United. Similarly, I welcome the relegation to League Two of Crewe Alexandra and Doncaster Rovers. The ideal scenario in The National League would be for two of Stockport County, Notts County and Halifax Town to get promoted!

Yesterday's crowd was a respectable (for us!) 5,700, including 98 travelling fans. I appreciate that Stevenage to Carlisle is a bit further than Carlisle to Bradford, but next Saturday we will be taking 1500-2000 travelling fans to a similarly meaningless end of season game at Valley Parade.

MAY 2022

Bradford City v Carlisle United. Saturday 7 May. 2022. Valley Parade. EFL League 2.

I'm writing this on Sunday evening, which is appropriate as 8 May is St Jimmy's Day, the 23rd anniversary of Jimmy Glass's iconic goal, possibly the most significant in Carlisle United's history.

Remarkably this meaningless end of the season League Two game, with nothing at stake, drew a crowd of well over eighteen thousand. The sizeable away following could be ascribed to the desire to celebrate the remarkable revival that was sparked by Paul Simpson's return as manager. 'Hello to the National League' has been replaced by 'Simmo's at the wheel!' Far more importantly, this was the first time in three years that Bradford fans were able to commemorate in person the fifty-six victims of the Valley Parade fire disaster. What a shame that one idiot chose to break the one-minute silence, and by doing so tarnished the reputation of Carlisle United and all of us supporters who were present. Fortunately, the minute's applause on fifty-six minutes was supported by everyone.

The game itself was unremarkable. Bradford took the lead in the first half, but the game turned on one minute in the second half. Carlisle were denied a blatant penalty when Kristian Dennis was dragged to the ground. The referee, who was abysmal throughout, waved play on, and predictably Bradford broke forward and scored at the other end.

And so a remarkable season comes to an end. I'll reflect more fully on the whole season in a later post, but I'm not too upset by yesterday's result. Following the remarkable run of six wins from seven that effectively ensured our survival, the last few games have been a timely reminder of the weaknesses among the playing staff and the issues off the pitch, both of which need resolving if we are to make progress next season. Tomorrow will be very interesting, with the announcement of a new head of recruitment, and the publication of the list of players who have been released or offered a new contract. According to Simmo, one of the players he intends to offer a new contract has already been illegally 'tapped up' by another club.

I've not yet decided where to close the door on this year's season, and start next season's journal, but it won't be just yet. What I can say is that season tickets for 2022-23 have already been purchased, the first time in over fifty years of supporting Carlisle that I've made such a commitment.

Close season Day 1 – 9 May.

The season may have ended, but there's been plenty of activity today before anyone heads off on holiday. The day has been a combination of drawing a line under the past season, and putting the first blocks in place as the club starts to build towards next season.

First came the release of the retained/released list. There were no major surprises though the departure of goalkeeper Mark Howard just a day after his impressive accumulation of end-of-season awards was a little surprising. He's in the twilight of his career, so his age probably counted against him, but I think he could have done a good job for at least another season. I'm disappointed that Brennan Dickenson has been offered a new contract – I can only hope that either Simmo has spotted something in him that I've missed, or that he gets a better offer! I was pleased that Joe Riley had also been offered new terms, but he's just posted on Twitter that he'll be moving on.

Equally, if not more significant are the additions today to Simpson's backroom staff. First came the news that Greg Abbott has returned to Brunton Park as head of recruitment. Abbott was Carlisle's longest serving manager since the turn of the century, and also the last Carlisle manager to win a trophy with the club. We now have the two most successful managers of the last two decades back at the club. Secondly came the appointment of Paul Gerrard as goalkeeping coach. Gerrard has been at the club on a short-term basis since Simpson returned, and it's been obvious from the paddock that his influence on the touchline extends well beyond the goalkeepers. Despite having other offers, it's very encouraging that he's decided to commit in the longer term. When you have someone of Paul Simpson's stature and experience in charge, it's gratifying to see the quality of person he can attract to work at the club.

15 May 2022

And so the last game of the season has been played. I know there are still trivia like European finals and promotion play-offs to be settled, but for the Falshaw family the watching and playing is over for 2021-2022. I'll probably do an overview of Carlisle's season in a few days' time, but otherwise it's probably time to draw this journal to a close. We know which Carlisle players have been released and offered new contracts, appointments to Simpson's backroom team have begun, and the first pre-season friendlies have been announced, so from this point, subsequent events belong to the narrative of the next season rather than the one just concluded.

Reflections – Thursday 19 May 2022

The day on which Carlisle made their first signing of the close season seems an appropriate point at which to indulge in a brief retrospective and then draw a final line under the 2021-22 season.

The season started with the usual optimism that it was a fresh start and that anything was possible. That feeling was bolstered by the number of early season games that we were able to attend in person. However, by late September reality was beginning to bite, as it became obvious that few, if any, of the summer recruits were up to scratch. A run of poor results led to the regrettable but inevitable departure of manager Chris Beech, as he appeared incapable of reversing the collapse that had destroyed our previous season.

He was duly replaced by Keith Millen. Who? Oh yes, the man with no experience of club management, who just happened to be a former team-mate of our Director of Football. During his brief tenure he never really showed any signs that he was capable of reversing the fortunes of the club, even though hope shone briefly after a 2-0 defeat of Bradford City, featuring two excellent goals from former Bradford players. With hindsight, that result was far more due to Bradford's woeful performance on the day than any resurgence by Carlisle.

The nadir was reached on 19 February, with the horrendous 3-0 defeat at home to Swindon, when I really feared for the future of the club. Incredibly, that woeful day was followed just four days later by the day that transformed the fortunes and the prospects of the club. Manager gone, Director of Football gone, and a club legend, Paul Simpson back in the hot seat until the end of the season.

There followed a remarkable transformation. In the relegation zone when Simmo returned, Carlisle proceeded to win six of his first seven games in charge, a run that virtually, but not quite, ensured survival. Not only that, but they were also games packed with incident, last-minute winners and equalisers, most of which we were there to witness. To be fair to Keith Millen, he did make some decent signings in the January transfer window, but it took Simpson's arrival to galvanise them.

Results and performances then tailed off somewhat, a timely reminder to both fans and Paul Simpson that there is much work to be done at the club. I read that newly appointed Head of Recruitment Greg Abbott is planning to recruit a network of part-time scouts to report to him and feed into the process. Now that would be the perfect part-time job with which to embark on my retirement!

A final postscript, with vague relevance to Carlisle. In my post on the dreadful Swindon game, I posted about reviled ex-player Harry McKirdy returning and twisting the knife with a goal and two assists. He was playing tonight in Swindon's play-off semi-final against Port Vale. The tie went to penalties, then to sudden death. When McKirdy finally stepped up to the mark as Swindon's seventh penalty taker, he blazed his effort high and wide. In the aftermath all he could do was grin inanely like an idiot as he walked back to the half-way line. Swindon proceeded to lose. According to Adam, Twitter was almost instantly buzzing with fans revelling in his embarrassment – not just Carlisle fans, but fans of all League Two clubs. Karma!

I enjoyed blogging about Carlisle United's 2021-22 campaign so much that I've decided to subject my Facebook friends to more of the same for the 2022-23 season! However, the landscape has changed in two fundamental respects. Firstly, with retirement imminent, I've taken the plunge and bought season tickets for Adam and myself. After fifty-four years I'm finally a season ticket holder. Ironic that it only happens when I live 135 miles from Brunton Park! Using that 270-mile round trip as a gauge, we should be able to make more than half of the away fixtures as well, leading to an attendance rate at league fixtures of over 75%. And I suspect that when we play London teams such as Wimbledon and Orient, the train might take the strain and extend our range!

2022–23 season

23 June 2022 – Pre-season Post Number 1

Is it that time already? My last post for the previous season was in May, and I'm posting for the new season a week before the end of June. Gone are the days when a footballer like Chris Balderstone could go off to play cricket for Leicestershire and England, before returning for pre-season training! I'd originally decided to start this season's journal on the day that the players reported back for training, namely yesterday, but Heckmondwike Grammar School's open evening put paid to that. However, a day's delay means that I now have a new signing, the newly published fixture list and the newly revealed kit to comment on.

Most of the close season has been remarkably quiet. Manager Paul Simpson had already got his backroom staff in place. Of four out-of-contract players who were offered new terms, two decided to move on. One who has accepted new terms spent the second half of last season on loan at Gateshead. I am a vocal critic of the other, who I would have been happy to see leave Brunton Park for good. Adam thinks he will surprise people this season, but I remain to be convinced. Simmo signed Owen Moxon, a midfielder from Annan Athletic, early in the transfer window, and then everything went quiet for about three weeks. Then, about a week ago, Tomas Holi, a 6ft 9ins goalkeeper from the Czech Republic, joined on a two-year contact.

Things have really taken off this week though. Our signing of a 6ft 9in goalkeeper was followed by the signing of Sonny Hilton, a 5ft 6ins Fulham midfielder on a season-long loan. I look forward to seeing those two stood next to each other in the pre-match line-up! Today we signed Ryan Edmondson, a 21-year-old 'traditional' centre forward from Leeds United. It's pointless speculating on the potential of these new signings until I've seen them play. For now I'm happy to trust Simmo's judgement, based on the signings he made in his previous spell as Carlisle manager, and bearing in mind the impact he had on a struggling squad of players when he returned to the club in February.

My initial response to the new kit was underwhelming. The home kit, a dark navy-blue, looked more like a typical away kit, and there's a long-standing superstition that we never have a good season when we play in blue shorts. Last season would support this view! The away kit is a bit better, though I'm never that keen on red.

Finally, our draw in the first round of the Carabao Cup was equally underwhelming. Given that the first-round draw is made on a regional basis, we couldn't have had a much longer journey than Shrewsbury away!

JULY 2022

Sunday 10 July – Pre-season Post Number 2

Two and a half weeks on, we're still experiencing the phoney war that is pre-season. This season's shirts have arrived, the season tickets are in the post, but the season is still almost three weeks away. There's only been one addition to the playing staff since I last posted – Ben Barclay, a defender from Stockport County, on a season-long loan. It's not a squad that's suited for a long League Two season yet, but at this stage I'll trust Paul Simpson's judgement in not panic-buying.

Three pre-season friendlies have taken place, against significantly inferior opposition, resulting in seventeen goals for and just one against. Given that the opponents were Penrith (5-1), Kendal United (9-0) and Workington (3-0), I'm not getting carried away!

Monday 18 July – Pre-season Post Number 3

The pre-season phoney war continues to tick away nicely. The sequence of friendly matches continues to develop well, with four wins and a draw. One should never read too much into these games, but the most recent and encouraging was a 3-1 win over Bolton Wanderers, one of the favourites for promotion from League 1. We've made one more loan signing, a full back from Nottingham Forest, who appropriately goes by the name of Fin Back. Less appropriately, his father Neil Back was a member of the England team who won the 2003 rugby union World Cup – as a forward.

Most importantly, the replica shirts arrived about a week ago, and even more significantly than that the season tickets have come in the post, along with a 'personal' letter from Paul Simpson.

Friday 29 July – Final pre-season post

The wait is almost over! In just thirteen hours Adam and I will be embarking on the first of many journeys to Brunton Park and other venues over the coming months. I've already said to Adam that I need to start acting my age. I'm 64 and newly retired, yet I probably feel as excited on the eve of the new season as I ever have in my fifty-four years as a supporter – with the possible exception of the 1974-75 season in Division 1!

The final third of last season was insane, with Paul Simpson rescuing the club from the clutches of the National League with a remarkable run of results, frequently featuring incredible last-minute dramas. The mood as the new season beckons is a little more sanguine. The late season adrenaline rush that saw the club to safety will not sustain it through a full season. There have been several departures, and not as many new faces as one might have hoped as the season begins. But we have a manager who's with us for the long-haul now, with the backroom team that helped achieve survival having also signed up for longer. And that team has been strengthened by the appointment of former Carlisle manager Greg Abbott as Head of Recruitment.

I think there's a feeling that the dramatic change in mood around the club brought about by Simpson's appointment and the surge to safety will be carried over into the new season. A decent crowd and a good result tomorrow would help sustain that positivity.

While I'm a little concerned about the thinness of the playing squad, I'm pleased that Simpson hasn't rushed into hasty buys simply to bolster numbers. With a month to go until the end of the transfer window, I'm confident that the necessary additions will be made. It'll be good to watch new signings in the flesh for the first time and assess their abilities in person, rather than relying on match reports.

Here we go!

Saturday 30 July. Carlisle United v Crawley Town. Brunton Park. EFL Division 2.

I didn't realise how invested I was in this game until just before kick-off. I've been looking forward to the game for weeks, but it was only when I was standing in the familiar stadium, joining in the minute's applause for staff and supporters who have left us in the last year, that I appreciated how much the start of the new season meant to me, bolstered by the knowledge that we'll be at every home game and many away fixtures.

Ben is on holiday, so Sam Hardy stepped in as a willing back-seat substitute to keep Adam company. This was not a good omen as the last game joined us for was a woeful 3-0 defeat at Harrogate Town at the back end of last season. The journey north consisted mainly, for me at least, of listening to 'The Brunton Bugle', the Carlisle United podcast. The main feature of the first episode was an interview with manager Paul Simpson. It was immensely reassuring to hear what a considered, rational and realistic man we now have in charge. He's disarmingly honest about himself and the club and is happy to discuss all aspects of the management of the club.

Having arrived in good time, an iconic moment was reached when we got to the turnstile and, for the first time in fifty-four years, I presented my season ticket rather than the usual one-off ticket or cash. Once inside the ground, we found a crush barrier for me to lean against to rest my weary knee and watched the latter stages of the pre-match warm-up. The minute's applause was particularly moving this year, featuring Clive Middlemiss, a former manager, and Frank Clarke, a hero of the Division 1 team, both now sadly departed.

With five debutants on show, the start of the game couldn't have gone much better. After some early pressure, Kristian Dennis scored the opener after just five minutes. I'd dreamed of such a start but hadn't dared believe it would happen! For the next fifteen minutes Carlisle continued to create chances and although the score remained 1-0, after twenty minutes the stadium was rocking.

The game continued in a similar vein. Crawley have been taken over by a consortium of American crypto-currency speculators, who broadcast an embarrassing video about why everyone hates Carlisle a couple of days before the game. It was so bad that Crawley fans themselves were apologising. Despite investment in a couple of highly rated strikers, they made little impact on the Carlisle defence. Yesterday evening Adam tweeted that Carlisle captain and central defender Morgan Feeney had emptied his pockets – in them he found a wallet, two sets of keys, and two Crawley strikers.

How the score remained at just 1-0 defies belief. Carlisle continued to create chance after chance but failed to apply the finishing touch. I'll quote the ITV highlights programme voiceover to support my case- "Carlisle were utterly dominant" and "Carlisle created enough chances to win the game many times over". Nonetheless, with only a one goal advantage, there remained the possibility that a momentary lapse could cost us two points. Fortunately, that didn't happen, and Carlisle were able to celebrate a rare opening day win. Not only that, but the performance was also really encouraging – a defence that kept their shape impressively, a midfield that frequently broke up opposition moves and drove forward with real penetration, and strikers who never allowed the Crawley defence a moment's respite. The performance was even more encouraging than the result.

Post-match I popped into The Blues Store to buy a new training top and a copy of 'Jack's Shirt, Deano's Bottoms', a Carlisle United memoir written by acquaintance and fellow retired English teacher Tim Pocock. I'm slightly miffed that Tim has got there before me, as I'm hopeful that these journals might find a publisher, but really pleased that Tim's got out there and look forward to reading his book.

The England Women's team were in action this evening. I'll be absolutely honest and say that given a choice between a Carlisle win yesterday and an England win today, I'd go with Carlisle every time. But having got the three points yesterday, I was fully invested in tonight's Euros final. And what a delight to celebrate the first England success in a major football tournament since I was eight years old!

AUGUST 2022

Saturday 6 August. Colchester United v Carlisle United. Jobserve Community Stadium. EFL Division 2.

Quite a lot has happened since the last post. The Falshaw family have had a short break at Seahouses in Northumberland, on the stretch of coast that is one of my favourite places on Planet Earth. A pity Carlisle didn't have a midweek fixture at Brunton Park – it would have been a significantly shorter journey than the slog from Wakefield!

Before I get to yesterday's game, quite a lot has been happening off the pitch, including a couple of events that preceded last week's game.

Firstly, Jamie Devitt accepted the offer of a one-year contract. Devitt had a successful previous spell with Carlisle before re-joining the club on a short-term deal in the January transfer window. A bit of a midfield maestro, his free-kick expertise had made him something of a fans' favourite. He was not offered a new contract in the close season but was invited to attend Carlisle's pre-season schedule to prove his fitness and earn a new contract offer. That done, and the new contract signed, he promptly caught Covid and was unavailable for last

Saturday's fixture! He was an unused substitute for yesterday's game.

Secondly, we signed a back-up goalkeeper in Michael Kelly, who joined from Irish part-time club Bray, the signing announced as we travelled to last weekend's game. Apparently, he was so excited at the prospect of full-time football that he paid for his own flight to join the club for training and said Paul Simpson could have put whatever salary he liked on the contract, and he'd have signed it!

Two further signings have followed. On Tuesday midfielder Jayden Harris joined from National League Aldershot, being offered something of a rarity in League Two, a three-year contract. Simpson must be impressed by what he's seen. Finally, striker Jack Stretton joined from Derby County on a season-long loan. Another defender, and I think we might just about be there.

Finally, winger Brennan Dickenson has suffered an ACL injury that means he'll be out for most of, if not the entire season. If you were paying attention to last season's posts, you'll realise that for me this is not the disaster it might appear to be! I was less than impressed by Dickenson's performances last season and was quite surprised when he was offered a new contract. Adam had already appealed to me, before the injury, to go easy on Dickenson and give him less abuse from the paddock. His absence for the next few months will make it easy to co-operate with that request!

And so, finally, to yesterday's game. After the drive home from Northumberland on Friday, the prospect of the long haul to Colchester yesterday did not appeal, quickly putting paid to any fanciful notions of attending every game this season! However, thanks to I-follow we were able to watch the game streamed live.

Carlisle picked up where they'd left off in the previous game, creating three or four clear chances in the opening twenty minutes, but failing to convert any of them. Perhaps predictably, a defensive lapse gifted Colchester an undeserved lead. Carlisle continued to press, and just before half-time Kristian Dennis headed home his second goal in a week, which was the least we deserved.

The second half performance was less impressive. The team struggled to keep their shape and created fewer chances. Simpson rang the changes, but Omari Patrick made little impact, largely due to a lack of decent service. New boys Stretton and Harris featured late on, but it would be unfair to form any judgements on such limited game time.

Adam, with a glass half-full approach, is of the view that a point from a long away trip, and four points from a possible six, represents a decent start to the season. I, with a glass half-empty approach, am of the view that we really should have taken all three points against a mediocre Colchester team.

Tuesday 9 August. Shrewsbury Town v Carlisle United. The New Meadow. Football League Cup, Round 1.

I've made a conscious decision not to buy into any of the commercial sponsorship bullshit that surrounds professional football, following my rant about ridiculous names for grounds last season. So, tonight's game was played at The New Meadow, not The Montgomery Waters Meadow, and the competition was the Football League Cup, not the Carabao Cup!

The games start to come thick and fast now, with just three days since the last game. My friend and former colleague Kevin Kehoe, who I met for coffee this morning, urged me to take the trip to Shrewsbury this evening, but a painful right leg and the prospect of drives to Carlisle and Grimsby in the next seven days persuaded me otherwise. We didn't even have the option of a live stream, having to listen to the audio commentary on Radio Cumbria.

There were several changes to the starting eleven, though it was far from being a second-string side. This was proved on 13 minutes when Ryan Edmondson scored his first goal for the club to give us a 1-0 lead. Shrewsbury went ahead in the 75th minute before Kristian Dennis scored his third goal in three games to level the scores again. Shrewsbury scored the winner in the 86th minute.

I can't say I'm too upset by tonight's defeat. A good cup run is always enjoyable, but invariably ends in disappointment. The only regret will be if Shrewsbury get a plum draw in the next round. They beat us in Round 2 of the F.A. Cup last season and proceeded to get drawn against Liverpool at Anfield. Now that would have been a day out!

The above was written shortly after yesterday's final whistle – a postscript is required. Today Carlisle united announced the signing of defender Paul Huntington, who has played in the Championship for Preston North End for ten years, amassing over 300 appearances for the club. He was born and brought up in Carlisle, and, according to the publicity machine, turned down better money and opportunities to play at a higher level to sign for his home-town club. Apparently, the clinching factor was the opening match of the season, which he attended as a spectator. He was impressed by the style of football played, and by the passion and atmosphere generated by the supporters.

I hesitate to be sentimental and superstitious, but experienced central defenders have been central to previous Carlisle United successes. Derek Mountfield, formerly of Everton and Aston Villa, was a lynchpin of the Carlisle team in the nineties that won Division 4 and reached Wembley for the first time. A decade later, Captain Fantastic Kevin Gray led the team to promotion from the Conference via the play-offs, and a season later to promotion as League Three Champions. Could Huntington be the final piece of the jigsaw? At the risk of repeating myself, Paul Simpson has won promotion in every season he has started as Carlisle manager!

Shrewsbury have been drawn at home to Burnley in Round Two of the Football League Cup. So that softens the blow of last night's defeat!

In an interesting footnote, apparently former Carlisle United owner Michael Knighton is about to front a hostile takeover bid of Manchester United. I think we have been here before. Having failed in a previous bid to take over the club, he set his sights lower and planned to take Carlisle United to greater things. After initial success, a lack of investment led to the club languishing in League Two as it still does. A word of warning to Manchester United supporters – however bad you think the Glaziers are, don't let this charlatan screw up your club the way he screwed up my club.

Saturday 13 August. Carlisle United v Swindon Town. Brunton Park. EFL League Two.

I'm getting in early with this one. It's a day before kick-off, but tomorrow is loaded with significance. The corresponding fixture last season was one of the worst afternoons I have spent at Brunton Park. A dismal performance was compounded by the fact that a pathetic former player, Harry McKirdy, scored the first goal and provided assists for the other two in an appalling 3-0 defeat. However, that was also the game that finally prompted the club's board to take decisive action, sacking hapless manager Keith Millen and removing inexplicable director of football David Houldsworth, before bringing back club legend Paul Simpson as manager.

Now that Simpson has signed up for the long-term, following last season's remarkable rescue act, I hope that Carlisle fans will respond to Simpson's call to ignore McKirdy – well at least until we are four goals up! Don't give him anything to feed off!

Looking a bit further ahead, it will be nice to have adult company for the Grimsby game next Tuesday.

As well as having Adam and Sam for company, I will also be joined by John Clarke, with whom I share the distinction of being both a retired English teacher and a Carlisle United supporter. I think I should set up a Whatsapp group for retired English teachers who support Carlisle, given former teacher Tim Pocock's recent publication of a Carlisle United memoir!

Supporting a football team should always be like this! A glorious sunny and cloudless day, with the only protective gear required being a baseball cap and sunblock. The roads were a bit busier than usual due to the ASLEF strike, but a few minutes delay on the road is as nothing compared to the fight for a decent living wage. And we had the glorious sight of the Lakeland fells in the distance as we approached Penrith, by way of compensation.

As for the game itself, it followed a very similar pattern to last week's game at Colchester, though three of last week's starting eleven were missing, with a significantly re-shaped central defensive unit. Carlisle started strongly, creating early chances, being denied an early penalty appeal, and having a goal chalked off for offside. And then, just like last week, we gifted the opposition their opening goal, when Callum Guy tried to dribble out of defence rather than just clearing the ball. He lost possession, and the rest was sadly predictable. Nonetheless, Carlisle continued to make chances and Omari Patrick was guilty of a particularly glaring miss from all of two yards out. And then, just before half-time, and just like last week, Kristian Dennis pounced to restore some much-needed parity to the scoreline.

The second half was relatively even with chances at both ends, but Carlisle goalkeeper Tomas Holi was in fine form to ensure Harry McKirdy had no opportunity to celebrate his latest return to Brunton Park. Carlisle substitute striker Jack Stretton was guilty of a bad miss at the other end, before the game ended in a 1-1 draw.

There is much to feel positive about. To be unbeaten after the first three league games of the season is always encouraging. Kris Dennis today became the first Carlisle player in over sixty years to score in the first four games of the season. The strength in depth of the squad is infinitely greater than a year ago.

However, a couple of minor doubts remain. The injury list is becoming worryingly long, particularly in defence, which means that Simpson's selection options are limited. In the two drawn games we have gifted the opposition their goal, and despite creating numerous opportunities have failed to finish that one that would turn a draw into the win. The teams we have faced so far have ranged from mediocre to average, and I only hope that we do not regret the failure to turn these draws into victories later in the season.

I bumped into my friend Tim Pocock at half-time and was able to congratulate him on the publication of his Carlisle United memoir, as well as getting some useful advice on getting published myself.

Entertainment on the journey home was provided by the commentary on Brentford's stunning 4-0 defeat of Manchester United! Q: When do Manchester United kick off against Brentford? A: about every five minutes.

Reading the post-match interviews, Paul Simpson seems pretty pleased with the performance, and confident that the goals and results will come, so perhaps I should start subscribing to the glass-half-full camp. I've started reading Tim Pocock's Carlisle memoir, and it's a great read so far, partly because I was present at many of the events he describes. It's probably of limited interest to non-Blues fans!

Tuesday 16 August. Grimsby Town v Carlisle United. Blundell Park. EFL League 2.

This could only happen to Carlisle United! An early-season game, at the end of a heatwave, is abandoned in mid-August because of a waterlogged pitch!

On Saturday, at Brunton Park, the referee paused the game after twenty-five minutes so that the playing staff of both sides could take on water. Last night, at Blundell Park, the referee paused the game after twenty-five minutes so that the Grimsby Town ground staff could take off water from the pitch! Two minutes after the restart, he called the captains together and gave it up as a bad job!

A new first saw me accompanied by another adult to a Carlisle game for the first time in years, with the aforementioned John Clarke joining Adam, Sam and myself on the journey to the East Coast. We'd just turned onto the M180 when the heavens opened, with a scenario reminiscent of the opening lines of The Jam's 'A-bomb in Wardour Street'. It's the line about 'cataclysmic overtones' that I'm thinking of! I jovially suggested that we'd probably soon drive through it, mindful of the fact that Adam and Sam hadn't had the foresight to put a coat in the boot of the car. All that happened was that the downpour abated slightly as we neared Cleethorpes. It should be pointed out that Grimsby Town are the only Football League team that play all their matches away from home. Their Blundell Park ground is actually situated in the neighbouring town of Cleethorpes.

The coats that John and I had taken proved to be of minimal benefit. By the time we'd parked and walked the half-mile or so to the ground, we were all thoroughly soaked to the skin and my feet were so wet I'm surprised I haven't suffered trench-foot today. We eventually found our way to a dry spot in the away end, and having spotted Tim Pocock a few rows away, I was able to verify that three retired English teachers, within a ten-yard radius, were supporting Carlisle United on a wet Tuesday evening in Grimsby (sorry, Cleethorpes). That must be some kind of first.

The surface water wasn't visible from where we sat, but soon became evident as well-hit passes stalled just a couple of yards from the point where they were made. John commented to me after just five minutes that if the rain didn't ease, we'd be lucky to see the game completed. And so it proved. After a five-minute break during which the ground staff did their best to remove standing water, the game resumed for a couple of minutes before the referee accepted the inevitable and abandoned the game.

The reaction of the crowd was remarkably tolerant. The Grimsby fans applauded us, I suspect for both having made the journey in the first place, and for accepting the inevitable with good grace. That positive spirit was re-enforced as we left the ground with both stewards and police wishing us well and a safe journey home. Very few of my journeys to Blundell Park have had enjoyable outcomes, but despite the inconclusive end result, this felt like one of the more positive visits!

To compound the evening's frustration, we were hit by closures on the M62 on the way home, meaning we experienced what seemed like endless detours through Eggborough and Knottingley before we finally arrived home.

To finish on a positive note, the Carlisle directors have pledged to fund the travel costs for the re-arranged fixture for all the Carlisle fans who travelled by coach yesterday. We didn't!

Saturday 20 August. Stevenage F.C. v Carlisle United. Broadhall Way. EFL League 2.

Stevenage was a touch too far to travel. And I'm glad we didn't because it wasn't Carlisle's finest hour. What's been encouraging in the games so far has been the way Carlisle have imposed their style of play on the opposition, both in and out of possession. Yesterday they came up against a team who did exactly the same to them and were found wanting.

Stevenage's pacy direct approach had Carlisle struggling in the first half and the home side were 2-0 up as half-time approached. Predictably, given the last two completed games, Carlisle scored on the stroke of half-time, as Kristian Dennis became the first Carlisle player since the 1950s to score in each of the first five games of the season. The last man to do so was one Alan Ashman, who later became the manager who led Carlisle all the way from the Fourth Division to the First Division, albeit in two separate stints.

Carlisle upped their game in the second half, but neither the creation nor finishing of chances was enough to salvage a point. It's not necessarily a bad thing to get the first defeat of the season out of the way fairly early on. It can stop players and supporters becoming preoccupied with remaining unbeaten, rather than winning games.

What is a cause for concern is the injury list. As well as a couple of long-term absences (months rather than weeks), four key players who played important roles in the first couple of games were missing from yesterday's starting team. It's to be hoped that the current spate of injuries is simply down to bad luck, rather than an over-demanding pre-season.

Saturday 27 August. Carlisle United v Gillingham. Brunton Park. EFL League 2.

It's starting to become pleasantly routine, setting off to football late on a Saturday morning! Not that we've done it for an away game yet – the only one within range so far was the waterlogged and abandoned Tuesday night game at Grimsby. The games that we can attend start to come thick and fast over the next three months, with only a couple of League games we can't attend.

This trip involved a slightly earlier start, taking a circuitous route to Wetherby to avoid Leeds Festival traffic. Last year, heading for Northumberland, it took us well over four hours to travel from Wakefield to Wetherby, as we got caught up in the thousands leaving the festival on Bank Holiday Monday morning! Leeds Festival was also the reason for Ben's absence (again – I'm beginning to doubt his commitment!). No traffic issues this time – we took our place in The Paddock just under half-an-hour before kick-off. Although not quite as hot as a fortnight ago, it was shirt-sleeve order again in a sunny Brunton Park.

Following relegation from League 1 last season, Gillingham are already struggling this season, with just one win, one draw and one goal from their opening five fixtures. With central defender Paul Huntington starting his first game, and midfielder Owen Moxon returning from injury, Carlisle fielded a stronger starting eleven than last week, and Gillingham rarely threatened Tomas Holi's goal. Unfortunately, the same was true of Carlisle at the other end! A couple of players were having probably their poorest forty-five minutes so far this season (step forward Jordan Gibson and Omari Patrick) and too many passing movements broke down without achieving any penetration.

I thought Gillingham's problems could be seen in the way they emerged for the second half. They were late, walked out in dribs and drabs, and did no warm-up drill. They appeared unmotivated and disinterested.

A few criticisms could be heard on the terraces, but the Carlisle supporters largely remained behind the team as they made a brighter start to the second half and were rewarded after fifty-five minutes when Jon Mellish bundled home a rather messy goal – they all count.

Thereafter, there were a handful of further Carlisle chances, but it was largely a case of game-management, seeing out the rest of the game, with an encouraging twenty-minute cameo from Fulham loanee Sonny Hilton. He at about 5' 6" and Kristian Dennis at about 5' 10" must be the smallest strike force to lead the Carlisle attack in many a season!

It was a messy and unspectacular game won by a messy and unspectacular goal. At the risk of indulging in cliché, it's a result that was less then convincing, but may prove to be valuable in hindsight, three points gained from a mediocre performance. It was a shame that Kristian Dennis's scoring streak came to an end but pleasing that someone else has now registered a League goal. I have a feeling that Kristian Dennis could be pivotal to our success or otherwise this season.

Referee Marc Edwards had an excellent game, one of the best refereeing performances I've seen at this level for some time. He was quick to spot and penalise some of the defenders' dark arts, offences that often go unpunished in League Two. His only mistake was not to show Gillingham defender David Tutonda a second yellow card for scything down wing-back Fin Back on the edge of the penalty area. Gillingham manager Neil Harris admitted as much by substituting Tutonda almost immediately.

Tuesday 30 August. Carlisle United v Manchester United U21s. Brunton Park. Papa John's Trophy group stage.

This won't take long! The generic name of the Papa John's Trophy is The Football League Trophy. It was originally devised as a knock-out competition for League One and Two teams, offering smaller clubs the chance to experience the glamour of a Wembley appearance should they make the final. Carlisle United have certainly seized that opportunity, making a record six appearances in the final, two at the old Wembley, two at the Millenium Stadium (as it was called at the time) and two at the new Wembley, winning the competition twice.

Unfortunately, the competition lost most of its credibility a few years ago when Premier League and Championship clubs were allowed to enter U21 teams, even though they can't progress to the latter stages of the competition. Just what is the point? I worry that it prefigures a time when top clubs will be allowed to field a nursery/feeder team in the lower divisions.

The crowd was surprisingly good, well over 3,000, when I thought it might struggle to reach four figures. The game offered an opportunity for a couple of players returning from injury to gain useful game time, some squad players to show their worth, and the chance to try out a couple of positional changes.

In an interesting if trivial by-line, probably only of interest to Kevin Osborne and myself, Saturday's Carlisle matchday programme previewed tonight's game with a photospread from a 1978 F.A. Cup third round tie between the two clubs, watched by a crowd of 25,000. Kevin and I were both present that day, as opposing fans, though it took another forty years to meet each other and discover that fact! Carlisle, then in the old Division 3, gained a creditable 1-1 draw against the then cup-holders, before losing the replay 4-2 at Old Trafford, a game I also attended.

I half-watched the last half-hour of the live stream of tonight's game. We lost 2-1 by the way.

SEPTEMBER 2022

Saturday 3 September. Carlisle United v Rochdale. Brunton Park. EFL League 2.

I think three should be the motif for this particular post: three of us travelled from Wakefield to Carlisle yesterday; the result was a 3-3 draw, which was Carlisle's third draw of the season; it was the first time Carlisle have scored three goals in a league game since May 2021; the goals were scored by three different players; three was the margin of victory for Brentford over Leeds and Brighton over Leicester; Manchester United scored three against Arsenal today; there were three particularly controversial VAR reviews over the weekend. I could go on if it wasn't for the fact that it's already become boring!

Ben joined us at Brunton Park for the first time this season. Where Ben once seemed to be the harbinger of bad results, his presence these days seems to be a near guarantee of an exciting game! I splashed out and spent £3 parking closer to the ground as a concession to my arthritic knee.

A couple of players, captain and defender Morgan Feeney and striker Ryan Edmondson were making their first start after injury. Unfortunately, Edmondson didn't last long, being substituted immediately after Rochdale's 22nd minute opener. His loss of possession led to the goal, though his departure was due to injury rather than his mistake. Carlisle scored a barely deserved equaliser in the 36th minute when centre-back Jon Mellish scored for the second game in succession, this time with a bicycle kick. Could this be the start of another prolific scoring streak by Mellish, like the one he went on two seasons ago when playing in midfield?

The wheels really came off in a two-minute spell early in the second half when the Carlisle midfield went inexplicably AWOL, and Rochdale scored twice. Thankfully Paul Simpson acted instantly, switching to a back four, enabling the wingbacks to focus on defensive duties. Mellish moved into midfield to provide more aggression, and playmaker Jamie Devitt came on to provide more vision. I'd have played him from the start. Five minutes later, Devitt provided a superb long-range pass to send Jordan Gibson racing down the right wing. His centre eventually fell to 'fox in the box' Kristian Dennis whose instep touch had just enough force for the ball to cross the goal-line, though it required an anxious glance to the linesman for confirmation.

Twenty minutes later another central defender, Paul Huntington scored with a towering header from a corner, and it was truly game on. Despite numerous chances, neither team managed to score again, but the journey home was a lot more cheerful than appeared likely at ten past four! After a day's reflection, it was a game that was high on excitement but fairly low on quality.

I was fulsome in my praise of the referee last week. Yesterday's was absolutely diabolical. Don't expect objectivity from me on this, but he appeared perfectly willing to stop play whenever a Rochdale player feigned injury as a promising Carlisle attack developed. Not only was he oblivious to the dark arts of defending, but he was also seemingly incapable of spotting a player being wrestled to the ground less than ten yards away from him.

Tuesday 13 September. Mansfield Town v Carlisle United. Field Mill. EFL League 2.

It's been a little while since the last football post, due to the rather mystifying decision by the EFL to cancel all last weekend's fixtures, unlike the vast majority of other sports. Did they really think that we football fans were incapable of acknowledging the Queen's passing in an appropriate manner? Last night the minute's silence to commemorate the Queen was impeccably observed – you could have heard the proverbial pin drop. Not all fans joined in the singing of the national anthem, but I can understand and probably share their reasons for not doing so.

On an infinitely more trivial matter, we arrived in good time, and I was delighted to be able to park in the car park behind the main stand at Field Mill, albeit at a cost of £5. It meant we only had a 200-yard walk to the top corner of the car park, and through a gate, to reach the away end turnstiles. With my dodgy knee, I was less impressed when we emerged from the ground after the game to find the same gate locked, which necessitated a walk of at least three quarters of a mile to get back to the car. I was in considerable discomfort by the time I finally made it, so much so that I was minded to e-mail Mansfield Town today to express my displeasure, until I realised that only sad retired people do that sort of thing!

The game itself was relatively forgettable, a 0-0 draw, the first game we've failed to score this season. Despite good build-up play and dominating possession, there was little end product from Mansfield. Despite having twice as many shots as Carlisle, both teams had the same number of shots on target, and the Carlisle ones were probably better chances. Carlisle's best chance came in the opening minute of the second half. A superb 60-yard pass from central defender Paul Huntington found Jordan Gibson in acres of space on the right wing. His early cross found goal machine Kristian Dennis perfectly, only for him to put his shot a couple of yards over the bar. A couple of Carlisle players were worryingly anonymous, but I'll give them a bit more time to redeem themselves before I name and shame! As seems common after disappointing midweek 0-0 draws away from home, our return journey was blighted by night-time motorway closures and diversions.

Given the sombre prelude to the game, it was ironic that the comedy moment of the season so far came halfway through the first half. A shot into the side netting by a Mansfield player caused part of the net to become detached from the post and crossbar. The referee halted the game while the ground staff were summoned. I have to say they looked like a comedy act doing their own version of Monty Python's 'Ministry of Silly Walks'.

After much stroking of chins, one was despatched to find some gaffer tape and another to get a stepladder. The gaffer tape arrived first, and the stepladder soon proved redundant as Carlisle's 6ft 9in goalkeeper grabbed the gaffer tape and completed running repairs himself without any need for artificial elevation!

Saturday 17 September. Carlisle United v AFC Wimbledon. Brunton Park. EFL League 2.

I've got a fair amount of time for AFC Wimbledon. I'm old enough to remember non-league Wimbledon taking the then mighty Leeds United to an F.A. Cup replay in 1975, which Leeds only won 1-0. Over the next few years Wimbledon earned Football League status and rose rapidly through the divisions to join the old First Division. Hard to believe now, but in 1988 they beat reigning League Champions Liverpool to win the F.A. Cup. A rapid subsequent decline led to the club being moved to Milton Keynes in 2003, being renamed MK Dons in 2004, in what was widely regarded at the time as a disgraceful example of franchise football. Disgruntled supporters formed AFC Wimbledon in 2002, and the regenerated club fought its way through the non-league tiers to regain league status and reach League One before relegation at the end of last season.

All that respect counted for nothing yesterday. A win would make it a good week following the draw at Mansfield on Tuesday, so no room for sentiment! The trip to Carlisle is becoming a doddle now, though 270 miles, a day after clocking up 230 miles taking Ellie back to Birmingham University, wasn't ideal for back or knee.

The weather was beautiful, and it struck me that it might well be the last time for a few months that we make the journey in such lovely conditions, with no need to wear a coat for the game itself.

As on Tuesday evening the minute's silence in memory of the Queen was observed perfectly. As a non-royalist I opted not to join in the singing of the national anthem. It was a touch disturbing to hear a shout of "No surrender!" from a few rows behind us as the national anthem finished – an uncomfortable reminder that football has a tendency to attract right-wing extremists from the lunatic fringes of society. I suspect it may have been Jacob Rees Mogg!

Carlisle started the game brightly, dominating possession, and creating a couple of good chances. The game went a bit flat after about twenty-five minutes with Wimbledon offering little threat but Carlisle struggling to thread their way through midfield. All that changed on the stroke of half-time when midfielder Callum Guy hit home a left foot shot from the edge of the penalty area. It was his first goal for Carlisle, in his 97th appearance, and only the second senior goal of a 175-game professional career. He was quite pleased, and I was quite pleased as he was one of the players who I had regarded as anonymous on Tuesday evening.

The other was Omari Patrick, who had a fairly quiet first half yesterday apart from one moment of magic. He pushed the ball past the right back, had the pace to outflank him and regain possession and had to be hauled to the ground to prevent further progress. Patrick is a player who thrives on receiving the ball to feet, rather than having to contest high long balls forward, which was the case for much of the first half. In the second half he started to receive the sort of service he thrives on and gave his full back a torrid time. On occasions he cut inside and fired in a shot on goal, on others he went wide before whipping in a cross.

Wimbledon equalised in the 59th minute when the Carlisle defence went missing, and a through ball was efficiently dispatched. It was from a Patrick cross that Carlisle scored the winner. Armer flicked it on, and Kristian Dennis was at the far post to nod it home, despite a defender desperately trying to tug him back by his shirt. I wonder if the referee would have given a penalty if Dennis had missed the target?

I doubt it very much. He'd already failed to award a penalty for a blatant handball by Wimbledon, taking the easy option by giving Carlisle a corner. On three occasions when Carlisle had set pieces, there was ridiculous holding and pushing in the Wimbledon penalty area. Each time he delayed play to speak to the players involved, who promptly continued to do exactly the same thing. On no occasion did he take punitive action against any player. By the end of the game, he'd pretty much lost control of the players, taking no action when a Wimbledon player shouted "You're shit" at him. He's the worst referee we've had this season, and that's saying something. Adam summed him up pretty well when the officials were going through their pre-match warm-up – "I hope the middle one isn't the referee. He looks almost as old as you."

Match Day Number 12. Tuesday 20 September. Carlisle United v Fleetwood Town. Brunton Park. Papa John's Trophy group stage.

I've waxed cynical previously about this competition, so this won't be a long post. Last night saw Carlisle face Fleetwood Town, a test against a team from the division above us, though both sides fielded vastly different teams from last Saturday's league games, so it's debatable how genuine a test it was.

Neither Adam or I were interested in making a five-hour round trip for a relatively meaningless midweek game, so we relied on the live stream for our coverage of the game. Or rather Adam did. I was more interested in preparing our meal, washing up and such like. I did take in odd moments of the game and the most telling reaction was that reserve goalkeeper Mike Kelly looks a vary able deputy should Tomas Holy suffer a loss of form or fitness.

The bare bones are that Fleetwood took the lead early in the second half before Carlisle equalised a couple of minutes into injury time. That meant, that under the arcane rules of the Papa John's Trophy, the game went to a penalty shoot-out with a 'bonus' point at stake. Despite Jordan Gibson missing Carlisle's first spot-kick, the other penalty-takers held their nerve and Carlisle won the shoot-out 4-2, keeping alive the possibility of progressing to the knock-out stage of the competition.

Saturday sees an away trip to Newport. A quick check on Google Maps confirms that that is one journey we won't be making this season!

Saturday 24 September. Newport County v Carlisle United. Rodney Parade. EFL League Two.

I felt largely detached from yesterday's events in South Wales. As previously mentioned, we'd made the decision not to travel to this one, and with a number of domestic tasks to do I passed on the rare opportunity to stream a Carlisle game (a consequence of the international break). I was therefore reduced to regular checks of my phone for score updates.

It turned out to be a weekend of 1-1 draws. Newport took the lead in the 36th minute and Carlisle equalised with about fifteen minutes left. Despite eight minutes of time added on neither team could find a winner, so the point moves us up one place into the top half of the table. According to Paul Simpson, neither team played well enough to deserve all three points, though he described it as the sort of game Carlisle should be winning. There's not much else to say about a game I didn't attend, didn't watch, and haven't even seen the highlights of yet.

Tuesday sees us head to Grimsby for the rearranged game that was abandoned due to heavy rain last month. It marks the beginning of a long sequence of games both home and away that we can get to, petrol prices allowing!

Tuesday 27 September. Grimbsy Town v Carlisle United. Blundell Park. EFL League Two.

Q. Which EFL club plays all its fixtures away from home?
A. Grimsby Town, because their Blundell Park ground is actually in Cleethorpes.

The above fact has given rise to some stunning examples of terrace wit in chants from Carlisle fans. They include such gems as "You're just a bus stop in Cleethorpes", "You only sing when you're fishing" and "You're shit, and you stink of fish".

Tuesday's fixture was the second attempt to play the August 16 fixture that had to be abandoned due to a waterlogged pitch. The Wakefield Blues sallied forth yet again, though this time Leeds supporter Sam Hardy was replaced on the back seat by True Blue Ben Smith. I love Sam's dry sense of humour, but he's a bit of a fellow traveller when it comes to Carlisle United! There was a worrying flashback to August when the heavens opened just as we joined the M180, but fortunately we emerged from the downpour a few minutes later and were able to walk along dry streets to the ground.

Grimsby had failed to win a home game before Tuesday evening but were above us in the table despite us losing only one league game to date. That suggested that Carlisle should expect to win, but historically Carlisle have a record of helping opposition teams to end unenviable runs of results!

The portents in the abandoned game had not been promising. Carlisle had very much been on the back foot, and the weather probably did us a favour that evening. This time nerves were settled as early as the seventh minute, when midfielder Owen Moxon became the third player in successive games to score his first goal for Carlisle, and the second to score for his hometown club. If the sequence continues, then defender Fin Back should be on the scoresheet on Saturday! Moxon scored with a low drive from the edge of the area after excellent approach work from Jack Stretton.

Grimsby dominated possession for the rest of the half but much of the movement was sideways rather than forwards, and things got even better on the stroke of half-time when Kristian Dennis seized on a loose back pass and slid the ball home from a narrow angle for his eighth goal in ten games this season. It was at the opposite end of the ground for us, and the ball seemed to take an age before it eventually crossed the line, during which time I fully expected a Grimsby defender to slide in with a last-ditch clearance. Watching it on the highlights everything seemed to happen much quicker!

I can't remember the last time I was at a game where Carlisle went into the break with a two-goal advantage! It was a very enjoyable half-time. Grimsby had a period of intense pressure in the second half as Carlisle tended to stand off them and concede possession too easily. They eventually pulled a goal back, but Carlisle weathered the storm that followed and gradually took the heat and pace out of the game. In the last ten minutes the main entertainment was watching Kris Dennis winding up the Grimsby fans he used to play in front of! As an away fan it was particularly gratifying to see the home fans leaving the ground in droves as the game headed into time added on.

At the final whistle the 144 of us who'd made the journey vigorously celebrated a win that was out first away victory of the season and leaves us just one place and one point outside the play-offs. This was the evening a solid start to the season became a good start. Victory at home to Crewe on Saturday will make it a very good start.

OCTOBER 2022

Saturday 1 October. Carlisle United v Crewe Alexandra. Brunton Park. EFL League Two.

This was a distinctly underwhelming event. A win would have taken us into the play-off places, and we travelled with both hope and expectation after Tuesday night's hard-earned away victory at Grimsby. Alas, it wasn't to be. Recently relegated Crewe were a very poor team. Their defence included two players who Carlisle deemed surplus to requirements at the end of last season, and their performances yesterday did nothing to suggest that Paul Simpson was wrong to let them go. Like Grimsby, much of Crewe's movement was sideways rather than forward, and they conceded possession far too easily and often. It was something of a surprise to reach half-time with the score still at 0-0.

Unfortunately, Carlisle lacked the guile or imagination to break down Crewe's mediocrity. I'd be hard-pressed to name a Carlisle player who had a bad game, but only man-of-the-match centre-half Paul Huntington could be said to have had a good game. He's giving Adam a glimpse of what football at a higher level can be like! There was no spark or cohesion about Carlisle's performance, and as the game wore on, rather than hoping for a Carlisle goal, there was the possibility that Crewe might snatch a late and undeserved winner.

I shouldn't be too downbeat. We didn't lose and have still only lost one league game out of eleven this season. We're in ninth place, which we could only have dreamed of a year ago, and Adam and I have yet to see them lose a game in person. I've spent the last couple of months loving the fact that we're able to travel to so many games, racking up the miles with a smile on my face. Yesterday was the first occasion I've even vaguely questioned my sanity in doing so!

Saturday 8 October. Hartlepool United v Carlisle United. Victoria Park. EFL League Two.

As part of the preparation for Saturday's trip, I started typing 'Victoria Park Hartlepool' into Google Maps, to ascertain how long it would take us to get there. Before I'd finished typing, I was being offered 'The Suit Direct Stadium' as a search result. It's reassuring to know that Google's algorithms are so closely aligned to commercial priorities! I'll resist the temptation to make any references to 'The Fast Show' and camp, suggestive gents' outfitters.

This was a glorious afternoon. After we won at Oldham last season with a goal in the dying seconds, I waxed lyrical about those days that make all the misery and disappointment worth it. This wasn't quite as significant, but it was damn close.

Like the Oldham game, there was plenty of context. The fixture is regarded as a bit of a local derby, despite the journey from Carlisle to Hartlepool taking two hours, as manager Paul Simpson discovered when he went to check out Hartlepool last Tuesday evening. At that point Hartlepool had failed to win a game all season, so there was the nagging fear that Carlisle would revert to type and provide a struggling team with the end to a dismal run. Fortunately, Hartlepool beat Doncaster, to remove that particular elephant from the room. To add extra spice, Hartlepool's interim manager is Keith Curle who spent three seasons in charge at Brunton Park.

As we approached the ground, we were held up for a few minutes as a coach of Carlisle supporters received a police escort to the ground. Having parked, Adam commented that I was brave to don my Carlisle United baseball cap. I replied, "No, just loyal." I blogged last season that the proximity of core home and away supporters make for a cracking atmosphere, and so it proved once again. And once again we found seats directly behind the goal at the away end. Victoria Park may have a capacity of less than eight thousand, but that means that a relatively small crowd can generate real passion. Just under seven hundred Carlisle fans were there, a number which could probably have been much higher were it not for the meagre allocation of away tickets.

The match stats show that Carlisle dominated the first half, so it was something of a shock when Hartlepool took the lead from a set-piece in the 43rd minute. I remained confident that the team could turn the game around, and everything was set fair for the second half with Carlisle playing towards their own fans.

In the 53rd minute midfielder Owen Moxon received the ball about ten yards inside the Hartlepool half. He surged forward, took on and beat a defender, and placed his low shot precisely and perfectly just inside the right-hand post. We had a perfect view as well. Cue bedlam as Moxon celebrated in front of the Carlisle fans. Moxon is a Carlisle-born lad who was a van driver for UPS a few months ago, while playing as a part-timer for Annan Athletic. He used to support Carlisle from the Brunton Park terraces, and some of his mates were in Saturday's crowd. It must have been music to his ears as the chant of "Owen Moxon, he's one of our own" rang out.

As the half progressed Carlisle surged forward ever more frequently and threateningly. In the 75th minute Moxon sent a searching pass to second-half substitute Omari Patrick, wide on the left. He approached the corner of the penalty area. As he ran across the front of the area, he three times shaped to shoot before taking the ball a couple of paces further. His eventual low shot unerringly found the middle of the net.

Things got even better seven minutes later. Goalkeeper Tomas Holi made a long throw out to Jordan Gibson, playing in an unaccustomed right wing back role after Fin Back went off injured. He looked up and launched a long pass towards the edge of the penalty area. Patrick's first touch controlled the ball on his chest. His second touch steered the ball into the goal. Route One football? Nah, far too much vision and skill involved for that. Holy ran the length of the pitch to join in the goal celebrations! Asked in a post-match interview what he was thinking at the time he replied "Thinking? I wasn't thinking! Just enjoying the moment."

One of the things that has impressed about Carlisle this season is their ability to manage the latter stages of a game, to take the intensity and pace out of the situation, and to secure a result. There was never any real likelihood of Hartlepool getting back into the game. For the second away game in a row, it was particularly gratifying to see the home fans leaving in droves well before the final whistle!

We weren't going anywhere though! Once the immediate post-match handshakes and formalities were complete the Carlisle players and staff headed to our end for five minutes of joyous celebration. It's moments and days like this that are what being a football supporter is all about. And all the key moments happened right in front of us at the away end. It was right up there with the celebrations of the win at Oldham last season.

As we finally left the ground the Kefalonia grin was back on my face (see March's post on the home game against Northampton Town). On the way back to the car I was hailed by Eric Hornsby, who lives in Orton, the Cumbrian village where I grew up. Eric's commitment to Carlisle United far outstrips mine. He once spent his summer break from work following the team on a pre-season tour of Ireland. When I commented that Paul Simpson has taught the team how to see out a game, Eric's sincere and unhyperbolic response was "He's a god!"

With the benefit of hindsight, Carlisle's dismal performance in last season's corresponding fixture marked a turning point. It was the beginning of the end of the Chris Beech era at Carlisle United. It's just possible this season's game might prove to be another turning point – the moment when players and fans began to believe that this team might do something special this season.

Saturday 15 October. Carlisle United v Doncaster Rovers. Brunton Park. EFL League Two.

It just keeps getting better!

When Lisa suggested that we got season tickets for this season, I knew it was going to be good getting to see so many matches, but I never imagined it would be this good this soon. We've been to ten matches so far and we've yet to see them lose. That may be something to do with the fact that Carlisle have only lost one of their thirteen league games to date. Only one other team in League Two can match that, and that team is Leyton Orient. Carlisle's next game is at home to Leyton Orient!

The weather certainly wasn't getting any better though. We walked to the ground in heavy rain, under very dark skies. This week we were accompanied by Aden, the latest of Adam's friends to be introduced to the dubious pleasures of Brunton Park and watching Carlisle United. Remarkably, just half-an-hour later, as the game kicked off, the sun was out and the sky was blue. Things stayed that way for most of the match, but as the final whistle approached the storm clouds were gathering again. At the very moment we arrived back at the car, hailstones hammered down, accompanied by gale-force winds. The journey home is always pleasant after a win, but yesterday's weather made it slightly less so.

Paul Simpson said that the game would be a good test for Carlisle, as both teams started the day on the same number of points, and Doncaster are recently relegated from League One. By the end of the afternoon Carlisle had passed the test with flying colours. They now sit in sixth position, while Doncaster have dropped to twelfth.

Last week at Hartlepool was about passion and fervour. This game was about quality and dominance. The pre-match omens weren't good. Leading scorer Kris Dennis was out injured, as was right wing-back Fin Back, possibly this season's outstanding player to date. Not to mention two-goal substitute Omari Patrick's absence. In came Ryan Edmondson after a lengthy injury absence to lead the line with mobility and aggression, and Back was replaced by Jack Ellis, a local teenager making just his fifth first team start. Ellis was so good that Fin Back will have a battle to win back his starting place, and I'll forgive Edmondson his penalty miss in injury time for the overall commitment of his performance.

Carlisle were surging forward from the start, obviously buoyed by the victory at Hartlepool the week before. Nonetheless, it took a world-class save from Tomas Holi half-way through the first half to keep the score even. Wrong-footed and diving to his right, he managed to thrust out his left hand and parry the ball for a defender to clear. Just before half-time Callum Guy, who had taken ninety-seven games to score his first Carlisle goal, repeated the trick just four games later with a low drive from about twenty-five yards.

The result was settled in a period of about ten minutes early in the second half. Following a surging run by

Jon Mellish, the ball ricocheted around the Doncaster penalty area before a Jordan Gibson shot was deflected into the net off Jack Stretton. Stretton is a youngster on loan from Derby County and has worked his socks off in his last four or five starts, putting in a huge shift, closing down the opposition when out of possession, as well as running at defences with real threat.

A few minutes later the same three players were again involved. A stupendous defensive tackle by Jon Mellish saw the ball break to Jordan Gibson just inside the Carlisle half. He took the ball forward, looked up and threaded a beautiful pass down the inside-right channel for Jack Stretton to run onto, carry forward, and coolly finish into the bottom corner.

That was effectively game over. To be honest (and completely objective!) the score could easily have been doubled. The statistics tell their own story. Carlisle had twenty-three shots with eight on target. Doncaster has seven shots, with only one on target. I would have had no argument with any of the Carlisle team being named man of the match, an accolade which eventually went to Jack Stretton. This was a performance to sit back and luxuriate in, definitely the best performance of the season so far. And this was with a team and squad that is ravaged by injuries. Who knows what they can achieve when everyone is available.

A couple of footnotes. We've been drawn against Tranmere in the first round of the F.A. Cup, which means we'll be playing them twice in succession at the end of the month. And while I would never celebrate someone being made redundant, there's a certain twisted satisfaction in seeing your most recent opposition dismiss their manager after a bad defeat to Carlisle.

Tuesday 18 October. Barrow v Carlisle United. Holker Street (not the SO Legal Stadium!). Papa John's Trophy group stage.

This will be a brief post, as befits such a joke of a competition. The sponsorship of what is officially called the Football League Trophy says it all. Over the years a third-rate competition has attracted third-rate sponsors. The Papa John's Trophy doesn't have quite the ring that the Pizza Hut or Domino's Trophy would have. Likewise, the Johnstone's Paint Trophy didn't have the cachet of the Dulux or Crown Paints Trophy. The only thing to be said in its favour is that once a year it provides the players and supporters of two lower league clubs with a grand day out at Wembley.

The bottom line is that we lost 2-0, ending our interest in this year's competition, and bringing an end to our unbeaten run. I hardly even acknowledge the end of the unbeaten run, as all that matters this season is performances in the league. Manager Paul Simpson took responsibility for the defeat, owning up to mistakes in his selection of the team.

The main talking point of the evening came in the early minutes of the game, when a moronic Barrow supporter threw a firework onto the pitch, which exploded just yards away from Carlisle goalkeeper Mike Kelly. A seventeen-minute delay ensued as the referee consulted police and safety officials, resulting in all home fans in that end of the ground being moved elsewhere.

Saturday 22 October. Carlisle United v Leyton Orient. Brunton Park. EFL League Two.

Well, it had to come to an end at some point. By 'it' I mean both Carlisle's unbeaten run in the league, and mine and Adam's record of not having seen Carlisle lose in person this season. At least both records lasted longer than Liz Truss's period as Prime Minister!

We were spared last Saturday's apocalyptic pre-match downpour and post-match hailstorm. It was mild enough to wear merely a jacket over the replica shirt – for the last time this year I suspect!

Things couldn't have got off to a much worse start. Orient cut through a Carlisle midfield and defence that were still asleep to score in the second minute. Fortunately, it took just fourteen minutes to restore parity. Ryan Edmondson headed home strongly a Callum Guy corner, to score his first league goal for Carlisle. We had barely finished celebrating when Jon Mellish slipped while in possession on the edge of the Carlisle penalty area. There followed what must be the very rare sight of our giant goalkeeper being lobbed!

It got even worse just minutes later. After the referee (of whom more later!) had turned down a blatant Carlisle penalty for handball, Edmondson overreacted to some petty provocation from an Orient defender. He raised a hand to him, and the defender also overreacted, flinging himself to the ground in dramatic fashion. The inevitable red card followed. No excuses for Edmondson. After a strong start to the game, he let his team-mates and the supporters down badly. Meantime midfielder Owen Moxon, possibly the player of the season to date, had suffered a head injury that required stitches, and was duly substituted.

With their backs against the wall, the last thing Carlisle needed was another bad decision by the officials. That duly came when the linesman in front of us failed to flag for a clear offside. Carlisle defender Corey Whelan hesitated, fully and understandably expecting to see the flag go up. It didn't, and Strinan strode forward to put Orient 3-1 ahead.

From that point you would not have thought that Carlisle was the team with only ten men. They continued to battle, and drive forward, and received their reward when Jordan Gibson pulled one back on fifty-six minutes. Despite the team's best efforts an equaliser wasn't forthcoming, but what was impressive was the grit and determination shown by the players to salvage at least a draw, and the strength of the support and encouragement from the terraces. Given a needless sending off and two defensive errors that each led to Orient goals, it wouldn't have been surprising if some supporters had become a bit critical. But in an indication of the positive mood that now prevails at the club, they were roared on for the last half-hour and the ovation they received at the end was almost as good as the one they received for last week's superb win over Doncaster.

And so to the referee! His officiating was an absolute disgrace. It's his first season as an EFL referee, and I fervently hope it's his last. In ten games, including yesterday's, he has shown fifty-three cards, three of them red. At an average of over five cards per match, that reeks of a referee who struggles to control the games he's in charge of. Paul Simpson was scathing of the officiating in his post-match interview, and he's not usually prone to having a pop at referees. The club subsequently received an apology from the EFL over the penalty and offside that weren't given. The apology was meaningless – the points had already gone.

My overall feeling is that despite the disappointment of defeat, there were extenuating circumstances, there was plenty to praise about the performance, and the mood among the supporters remains upbeat. I suspect this will prove to be a blip, rather than an early sign of the wheels coming off.

A busy week ahead, with road trips to Stockport on Tuesday and Tranmere next Saturday.

Tuesday 25 October. Stockport County v Carlisle United. Edgeley Park. EFL League 2.

This game saw a couple of firsts. It was the first time I've been to Edgeley Park, so that's another League ground ticked off the list, though I doubt I'll ever complete the full set of ninety-two. It was also the first time I've taken three Durkar players to a Carlisle game, the victims this time being Adam, Ben and James.

We travelled in real hope that the team could bounce back from Saturday's 3-2 defeat to Orient, where the side showed real fight and spirit, despite being down to ten men for an hour. Adam was worried about Stockport's Paddy Madden, an experienced, well-travelled and fairly prolific lower divisions striker who spent a couple of unspectacular seasons at Carlisle early in his career. I reassured him that Paul Huntington, with his years of Championship experience, would have him in his pocket. When the line-ups were announced, it was rather discouraging to learn that Huntington was missing with a thigh strain. With Edmo suspended following Saturday's red card, we were left with a diminutive strike force of Denno and Gibbo (yes folks, it's lazy football nicknames time – if in doubt stick an 'o' on the end!).

A travelling contingent of 1,150 made for a vibrant pre-match atmosphere. Unfortunately, Carlisle's performance failed to match it. This was probably the most disappointing performance of the season to date. Stockport were superior in every area of the pitch, and the 2-0 scoreline probably flattered Carlisle. We briefly threatened to get back into the game in the second half, but Stockport's second goal killed off that revival. The squad is ravaged with injuries and the strain is beginning to tell on those still standing. We currently have a full team missing through either injury or suspension. We've dropped out of the play-off places to tenth, which doesn't worry me unduly. The time to be at the top end of the table is April and May, not late October, and I think Carlisle have shown the potential to be there.

Another rant about referees, though this is a general one rather than aimed at Tuesday's official. I've already lost count of the times referees have delayed corner kicks to admonish defenders for holding attacking players. The moment the lecture is over, the defenders immediately resume the same holding. Don't just wag a finger at them, brandish a yellow card – they'd soon think twice!

I'm going to stop Adam taking new people to Carlisle games – we invariably lose!

Saturday 29 October. Tranmere Rovers v Carlisle United. Prenton Park. EFL League Two.

This was a really good one! And it was much needed after three defeats in a row, two of them in the League. There was much to be encouraged by in last Saturday's 3-2 defeat to Orient. Down to ten men for an hour the team battled impressively against thirteen men (when we include the referee and his assistant on our side of the pitch!) and gave one of the best teams in the division a real fright. Tuesday at Stockport was less impressive. There was a real lack of sparkle about the performance, and perhaps a sense that suspensions and a ridiculous injury list were beginning to have their impact on what has been a really encouraging start to the season.

Given that, Tranmere weren't the ideal opponents for yesterday's game. They were on one of the best runs of results in the division. The corresponding fixture last season was full of incident – two sending-offs, eleven yellow cards and a 97th minute equaliser for Carlisle that felt like a winner, as it sustained our remarkable run of results as we pulled away from the threat of relegation. Yesterday's team was strengthened by the return of Paul Huntington in defence, but further depleted by the absence of Jordan Gibson through suspension and Fin Back through illness. There was a real sense that the squad was down to its bare bones.

Having set off in good time and pre-booked parking right next to the ground, we took our seats with relatively little time to spare, thanks to heavy traffic in Liverpool and match-day road closures around the ground which made it difficult to find our way into the car park. For the second time in five days around a thousand Carlisle fans made the trip to an away game, approximately 20% of our usual home support. A four and a half hour round journey on Tuesday evening was followed by a five hour one yesterday. Unsurprisingly there was a vibrant pre-match atmosphere.

The atmosphere became much more vibrant immediately after kick-off. Tranmere started the game by going long before Carlisle won possession and moved the ball through midfield. A long searching ball found Jack Stretton racing down the right, and his low centre was clinically dispatched by Kris Dennis, ending his brief goal drought. Just thirty-nine seconds had elapsed since the referee started the game! I don't think I've ever seen Carlisle score a quicker goal in person. It took a moment to realise that the ball had actually gone into the net rather than narrowly wide. Joy unconfined in the Cowshed, as the away end at Prenton Park is unflatteringly named.

That set the tone for the rest of the afternoon. Carlisle absolutely bossed Tranmere, being stronger in the tackle, quicker to break forward, and winning the vast majority of defensive headers. All this was accompanied by raucous away fans, who barely stopped singing and chanting for the whole ninety minutes – perhaps partly from a sense of relief that the team had got its mojo back. The imbalance between the teams is highlighted on the Pitchside Blues video when, as Carlisle create yet another chance, a Tranmere fan can be distinctly heard complaining, "How fucking easy is this?"

Further reward came early in the second half when the referee awarded Carlisle a free kick wide on the right for the kind of shirt-pulling that frequently goes unpunished. The ball was whipped into the penalty area, where a Carlisle player went tumbling to the ground, and the referee awarded a penalty for the kind of skullduggery that again often goes unpunished. Kris Dennis did the business again from the penalty spot to take his league goals tally into double figures, with barely a third of the season's games gone.

From that point Carlisle didn't really need to 'manage' the rest of the game, as Tranmere rarely threatened, and the only question really was whether Carlisle might score a third. They didn't, but the celebrations at the final whistle were loud and prolonged, both on and off the pitch. In recent weeks Carlisle-born Owen Moxon has been hailed by supporters as "one of our own" but for this game he was joined in the starting line-up by three other Cumbrian-born players in Paul Huntington, Taylor Charters and Jack Ellis, the first time in seven years that four home-grown players have started a game for Carlisle. Senior pro Paul Huntington made sure that the quartet featured in a post-match photo. For the second time this season Ellis, barely nineteen, was deputising at right wing back for Fin Back, one of our standout players of the season to date, and the biggest compliment I can pay Ellis is to say that Back's absence was barely noticeable.

This wasn't a particularly pivotal game in terms of the season as a whole, though it did return us to the play-off places. Nonetheless it was a great day – a magnificent performance from a threadbare squad, and a brilliant atmosphere in the stand.

NOVEMBER 2022

Saturday 5 November. Carlisle United v Tranmere Rovers. Brunton Park. F.A. Cup Round 1.

Same team – different venue and competition. It was Tranmere Rovers again, but this time at Brunton Park and in the F.A. Cup Round 1. After Carlisle took almost a thousand fans to Prenton Park last week, Tranmere responded with a paltry 260 traveling fans this week. However, the home support numbered just under 4,000, a reduction of over a thousand on normal league gates. I can only assume that this is a reflection on the declining allure of the F.A. Cup.

Although we could travel with reasonably high expectations after last week's convincing performance at Prenton Park, a part of me worried that it couldn't be so easy for a second week in a row, that Tranmere would have figured out a way to counter our style of play. Those nagging concerns were heightened when the line-ups were announced and both last week's strikers were missing with injury niggles – Kristian Dennis who scored both goals, and Jack Stretton who assisted both goals. That meant a first start of the season up front for Tobi Sho Silva, who got injured in pre-season, and a return from suspension for Jordan Gibson. Jack Ellis deservedly retained his place at right wing back despite Fin Back being fit and available again.

I needn't have worried! For a good 75% of the game Carlisle were just as dominant as last week. They were strong in the tackle, winning first and second balls and creating numerous chances, though not always very clear ones. Fortunately, one of them was converted in the 30th minute. Following a run by Sho Silva, the Tranmere keeper could only parry his shot and Jordan Gibson gleefully slammed the rebound into the roof of the net.

Having run himself into the ground, Sho Silva was replaced by midfielder Jayden Harris, meaning that for a spell we didn't have a recognised striker on the pitch. No matter. Just five minutes later Harris was played through into the penalty area, rounded the goalkeeper, and was just able to force the ball home at the near post from a tight angle. It transpired later that if the ball hadn't crossed the line Carlisle would have been awarded a penalty and the Tranmere defender who handled the ball in trying to prevent it crossing the line would have received a red card. The defender in question was one Dynel Simeu who spent the second half of last season on loan at Carlisle and became something of a cult hero as the team made their dramatic escape from the threat of relegation. He's now on a season-long loan at Tranmere. It's fair to say that he received a more generous response from the Brunton Park crowd than he did from the Carlisle travelling support at Tranmere the week before!

Teenager Nick Bollado, who only turned eighteen about three weeks ago, came on for the last quarter of an hour, which at least meant we had a striker on the pitch. I hesitate to call him a recognised striker, as his Football League experience is currently measured in minutes rather than appearances!

Carlisle went to sleep in the 82nd minute allowing Tranmere to head home from a free kick, which made the last ten minutes a little more fraught than they should have been and the scoreline a lot closer than the balance of play merited. But the team saw out the game to earn – a second round trip to glamorous Walsall. This means that similar to Tranmere we'll be playing them twice in three games.

What was really encouraging about this performance was the fact that, despite a squad even more threadbare than the week before, the players called into action stepped up to the mark and delivered the goods (two cliches in one sentence!). We didn't have enough players to name a full bench, and the aforementioned Nick Bollado doesn't even feature in the first team squad on the club website, only found in the youth squad. Jack Ellis put in another massive performance, deservedly winning the man of the match award. He's already earned the soubriquet "the Kendal Cafu'! Fin Back may well be one of our best players this season, but he faces a real struggle to win back his place in the team.

Tuesday 8 November. Harrogate Town v Carlisle United. Wetherby Road. EFL League 2.

"I hate coming to Harrogate!"

Thus spoke Tim Pocock, fellow Blue and fellow retired English teacher when we encountered each other as we were leaving the ground last night. And this was from someone who used to live and work in Harrogate! To be fair, he was speaking in a strictly footballing sense. I know what he means! Before last night's game, Carlisle had played Harrogate five times since their promotion to the Football League, losing four and drawing one – the definition of a bogey team. Last season's two visits to Wetherby Road were eminently forgettable. In January we spent a freezing evening watching a 1-0 defeat in the first knock-out round of the Papa John's Trophy. In May we visited again in the League when survival was almost guaranteed. A 3-0 defeat was a dispiriting reminder of times and displays before Paul Simpson's second coming.

Up front Kristian Dennis returned from injury and Ryan Edmondson from suspension, and Corey Whelan stood in for the suspended Jon Mellish in defence. Following illness Fin Back replaced Jack Ellis at right wing-back which I felt was harsh on Ellis, following his two superb displays against Tranmere. To be honest I felt that Back struggled defensively for much of the game, though he did redeem himself in the final quarter of as he pressed forward.

A 3-3 draw does not indicate that the bogey has been laid. I would argue otherwise. A point from this game was probably more than Carlisle deserved. From the outset Harrogate did what Carlisle had done to Tranmere in the previous two games, and totally imposed their game on ours. It was therefore something of a surprise when Carlisle took the lead in the twelfth minute in what was probably their first attack worthy of the name. Taylor Charters curled home a beautiful shot from 28 yards to give Carlisle a lead that was totally against the run of play.

However, Carlisle's shortcomings were all too evident as Harrogate were invariably first to second balls and repeatedly made inroads down the Carlisle left. It was no surprise when they equalised, and we were somewhat lucky to be on equal terms at half-time. To be fair to Paul Simpson he recognised that things were amiss and switched to a four-man defence after half-time, replacing Corey Whelan with Jordan Gibson, to give us a bit more penetration going forward.

The tactical switch appeared to have worked in the 50th minute when Carlisle regained the lead. A superb cross from the left by Jack Armer (man of the match for Carlisle) was met by a powerful header from Ryan Edmondson in front of the travelling fans. However, the flaws from the first half remained as Harrogate equalised with an unchallenged header from a corner, and then took the lead when defenders stood off a Harrogate player as he drove forward and buried a shot that Tomas Holi should maybe have saved.

In the final fifteen minutes Carlisle drove forward in search of an equaliser, with both Morgan Feeney and Paul Hutchinson heading narrowly over from corners. Nonetheless, it took until the final minute of time added on for Carlisle to equalise. A corner from Owen Moxon led to a sequence of penalty-area ping-pong before Moxon himself headed home from a narrow angle. It might have only been a draw, but the last-minute drama made it feel like a win. I'd have been interested to hear and see the crowd reaction had we not salvaged a point, because there were some fairly vocal critics close to us.

To be fair, for a team to salvage a point from a sub-standard performance could be seen as a strength. Successful teams tend to grind out results even when not at their best. This game could fit into that category, but a good performance against Walsall on Saturday is needed to make this a good week.

I know I banged on about this last season, but Wetherby Road really is an appalling little ground. Rarely can have such a nice town have had such a crap football ground. On most sides the terracing stretches back a mere six steps. Last night's attendance was a paltry 2,147, of which six hundred (almost 30%) were away fans. When the attendance was announced a Carlisle fan commented, "Oh, that's so adorable.", his voice laden with irony. I can't argue with Harrogate's performances on the pitch, but they do strike me as a club without the infrastructure or support to sustain League football.

I also liked the description from the away terraces of Harrogate's screeching midfielder as being "like a fucking chiwawa."

Saturday 12 November. Carlisle United v Walsall. Brunton Park. EFL League 2.

Our faces appeared in a picture on Carlisle United's official social media pages on Saturday morning as part of the build-up to yesterday's game against Walsall. I briefly considered marching into the club office on our arrival at Brunton Park in the afternoon and banging on about image rights and demanding payment for unauthorized use of our faces, but quickly settled for being quietly pleased at forming part of the club's social media profile! The red away shirt and hoodie, plus the smiles, suggest that this was taken at the away fixture against Tranmere a fortnight ago, which means that poor Ben has unfortunately been cropped from the image!

Surprisingly, given that we're well into November, we travelled to Carlisle and watched most of the game in bright sunshine. I did point out to Adam that despite experiencing some pretty bad weather on our journeys to and from Brunton Park this season, most games have been played in lovely weather. I suggested that this might mean that someone up there was shining down on us this season!

Jon Mellish made a welcome return to the defence following suspension and Jordan Gibson started the game after being a second-half substitute on Tuesday night. Kris Dennis was fit enough to be on a strong-looking bench. Following Tuesday's rather fortunate draw at Harrogate, a win was needed for this to be regarded as a good week.

Unfortunately, it wasn't to be, and this time we didn't have the consolation of six goals to temper the loss of two points. For the second time this season we witnessed a 0-0 home draw. Carlisle pressed much better than on Tuesday, and Walsall didn't offer a great threat, but once again the spark was slightly missing, and relatively few good chances were created. The best one came in the closing moments of the first half, when Taylor Charters was beautifully set up for a strike on goal. After his superb goal in the previous game, I would have put money on him dispatching this one, but he blazed it inches over the bar. I said to Adam at the time that I hoped we didn't look back and regret the miss, but so it proved to be. Carlisle huffed and puffed in the second half, but to no end. Jack Stretton's impact as a very late substitute suggested he should perhaps have been brought on earlier.

The result means that we've dropped to eighth place, just outside play-off qualification. I can't say I'm too worried. We want to be making headlines next April and May, not this November. Two years ago, we topped League Two going into the New Year, and didn't even make the play-offs. If you'd told me at the start of the season that we'd be in eighth place and in the second round of the F.A. Cup, despite having a squad ravaged by injuries, I'd certainly have taken that. What's been really impressive is the way that supposed 'fringe' players in the squad have stepped up to the mark and performed superbly when called on. I'm thinking particularly of Jack Ellis and Taylor Charters.

The officiating was predictably dire. I don't expect FIFA qualified referees every week, just a basic level of competence. It was interesting to read Chairman Andrew Jenkins comments about refereeing in yesterday's programme. I quote him in full.

"I understand that after the recent game against Leyton Orient, we were invited to write to the powers that be to highlight if we had any problems regarding the officiating of the game that day.

This was done, and an apology was subsequently received when it was acknowledged that clear handball and offside decisions weren't given. It's obviously good to get a response, but these decisions led to a player being sent off directly after the handball, meaning a three-game suspension, and also the loss of three points to the club.

"We all know that it isn't easy for officials, but I feel huge efforts have to be made to improve the standards at all levels. It will only help all aspects of the game if this is achieved."

I rest my case.

On a nostalgic note, I was quite touched when the P.A. played Van McCoy's "Do The Hustle" during the half-time interval. Back in the Seventies that was the song that was always played as the fans were leaving the ground, and it brought back a lot of memories for an old lag like me!

Saturday 19 November. Salford City v Carlisle United. Moor Lane (forget all this Peninsula Stadium crap!). EFL League 2.

John Clarke took me to task over the lack of cliches in my last post, so this week I'm determined to *step up to the mark* and *go the extra mile*.

Appropriately John joined us for this jaunt across The Pennines, having recently returned from a rather more spectacular jaunt to Atlanta U.S.A. he was also attempting to claim talismanic status, having yet to see Carlisle lose this season.

This was a special afternoon. Another of those days (at least two this year) that make all the heartache and disappointment worthwhile; a day when you stand on the terraces grinning broadly and thinking "It doesn't get much better than this!". So, this could be quite a long post!

The initial portents were not good. Steady rain in the morning brought fears of a repeat of the Grimsby farce, when the game was abandoned after twenty-five minutes, or even worse, last season's abortive trip to Rochdale, when the game was called off as we were crossing Saddleworth Moor on the M62. We needn't have worried. Despite persistent rain as we drove west, once we'd reached the summit of the M62 the clouds cleared, and the sun came out. Another case of the sun shining on Carlisle United this season?

I'd set the car's satnav for a reported park and ride scheme, wanting to avoid a lengthy walk. When we reached Salford, it quickly became evident that said park and ride scheme was a figment of someone's imagination. A quick reset of the satnav for the ground enabled us to find street parking just ten minutes from the ground, on Moor Lane from which the ground takes its name.

Carlisle had sold out the entire away ticket allocation of almost 1,400. To describe Moor Lane as a compact little ground would be an understatement. It's marginally larger and definitely smarter than Harrogate's woeful

Wetherby Road ground, but not by much. The floodlights are so low they must be a dazzle hazard to traffic in the surrounding area! This meant that the away section was packed and heaving. It also hosted another convening of the Yorkshire-based, Carlisle supporting, retired English teachers' group, with Tim Pocock just a few yards further along the terrace from us. We were on the front row of the tiny away terrace, directly behind the right-hand post of the goal, with a crush barrier in front of us enabling me to take the weight off my dodgy back and knee. These things must be considered when you're my age!

I love games when the Carlisle support is so loud and vibrant that you can't tell whether the home supporters are actually making any noise. The away end was bouncing prior to kick off, prompting me to turn to Adam and say, "With this level of support we could do with another Tranmere start.". For those of you with short memories, about a month ago, with similarly passionate support, Kristian Dennis scored the opening goal after just 39 seconds. We had to wait a little longer this time, but after just three minutes an off-balance Owen Moxon sent a superb pass down the *inside right channel* for right-wing back Fin Back to run onto. His shot was parried but fell conveniently to Kris Dennis, in *acres of space* in the six-yard box, who gleefully side-footed home. Cue bedlam in the away end.

The remainder of the first half was worryingly reminiscent of last season's game at Moor Lane, when we had used all our substitutes by half-time due to injury. That led to a performance so abject that I refused to stay behind to acknowledge the players at the final whistle. First centre-back and captain Morgan Feeney departed through injury, shortly followed by Fin Back, though not before he'd come close to doubling the lead when his shot hit the post. Despite Salford dominating possession, they had little penetration, and Carlisle went into the half-time break with a deserved 1-0 lead.

It proved to be the proverbial *game of two halves.* Salford came out for the second half fired up and dominated the early minutes before scoring an equaliser on 52 minutes. Carlisle weathered the onslaught that followed, and then, attacking the away end, struck three times in thirteen glorious minutes. On 67 minutes, following a Carlisle corner, the ball pinged around the penalty area before falling to Callum Guy just outside the box. As we all screamed "Shoot!" he did exactly that, a superbly hit low volley *skimming the turf.* We were directly in line to see the ball heading for the net, and although we didn't see it enter the net, we did see *the net bulge!* Guy took 97 games to score his first Carlisle goal, and now he just can't stop! One of the great things about away games is the celebration between players and fans when Carlisle score at the away end.

Just five minutes later a short-corner routine led to a cross which was *powerfully headed home* by Corey Whelan, who had replaced Morgan Feeney as both centre-back and captain in the first half. As we celebrated wildly, we knew that the three points were secure but didn't realise that even better was to come. On eighty minutes a cross from Jon Mellish was deflected and looped up for Kris Dennis, perfectly positioned on the edge of the six-yard box, to *head home*. On the way back to Wakefield we waxed lyrical about his ability to be in the *right place at the right time*, a real *fox in the box*. Dennis rather undermined that point of view in his post-match interview when he admitted that he was suffering from cramp, was waiting to be substituted, and simply stood there in the hope that the ball might come his way. Fortunately, it did!

At this point the Salford supporters started streaming towards the exits, which led to the inevitable chant of "Is there a fire drill?". There could have been a couple more goals in the final ten minutes, but no-one really cared. I think it's the first time I've seen Carlisle score four goals away from home, and Paul Simpson rated it the best performance since he returned as Carlisle manager in February. Adam rates it in the top three Carlisle games he's seen.

After the post-match formalities, the Carlisle squad went into a huddle before heading to the heaving away end to celebrate, while the rest of the ground was already completely empty. One of the chants that could be heard was "And now you're going to believe us, the Blues are going up!". A bit premature perhaps but indicative of *the current mood in the camp*. Regarding chants, I think the number of bespoke Carlisle chants is an indication that the club is on the up. The generic chants like "Salford's a shithole, I want to go home" and "Is this the library?" are all well and good but what is really impressive is the number of chants about individual players and staff. At least half of the starting line-up either have their own chant or are featured in one. The current Carlisle anthem, chanted repeatedly at the end of away victories like this one is,

"We've got super Paul Simpson,
He knows exactly what we need.
Feeney at the back,
Dennis in attack,
Carlisle are going up the football league."

As a recently retired English teacher I would argue that this bears a passing resemblance to the limerick form, in terms of metre if not rhyme!

This was one of those games where you were reluctant to leave the ground and leave behind the joy of the moment. Once we'd exited the gates, the experience was already a thing of the past, rather than the visceral buzz of the instant.

Saturday 26 November. Walsall v Carlisle United. Bescott (Poundland) Stadium. F.A. Cup Round 2.

This is quite an important fixture as victory means entry into the draw for the third round of the F.A. Cup and the possibility of being drawn against a team from the Premier League or the Championship, who only enter the competition at this stage.

But before I get into the real grist of this post, a slight digression. On Friday Adam messaged me to tell me that a particular Carlisle replica shirt, known as the deckchair shirt, is now worth £250. He obviously doesn't have enough to keep him busy at 6th form college! Having checked that I am indeed in possession of said shirt, I noted that it also has embroidered on it "Wembley '97" to mark the club's achievement in reaching the final of, and indeed winning, the Football League Trophy that season. That should add a few further pounds to its value. I've also got another vintage replica shirt that is worth £50. Cash in now, and that's next season's season ticket paid for, particularly as I'll be due a further discount for being over 65!

Adam and I are also in possession of a genuine Carlisle United shirt, not a replica but a real one as worn by Carlisle United legend Chris Balderstone in the early seventies. There's a story behind this, which you know I'm about to tell you! As a dual sportsman, in the early seventies Chris Balderstone was awarded a joint cricket benefit/football testimonial season, in recognition of his services to both sports. Having actually met Balderstone after a friendly fixture against York City, my dad agreed to try and sell as many of Balderstone's testimonial brochures as possible. Having done so, Chris Balderstone's thanks included a copy of his testimonial brochure with every photograph signed by the person who appeared in it, and one of the actual Carlisle shirts he wore when he played at Number 9. There's no sponsor's name on the shirt (different times), but there is a laundry mark at the top of the Number 9. I'd love to know how much that is worth!

When Chris Balderstone finally retired from professional cricket at the age of 42, he became a first-class cricket umpire. Whenever he was umpiring a game in the north of England, he would let dad know that there were a couple of complimentary tickets available for him at the ground, and that he would meet him for a drink after the day's play was concluded. I still have some of the letters he wrote to Dad about his experiences as a cricket umpire, and his reflections on the ongoing fortunes of Carlisle United. He died at the sadly premature age of 59. They really don't make them like that anymore.

Anyway, it looks like we chose a good game to miss. After eleven games in a row that we'd attended in person (if we disregard the meaningless Papa John's Trophy), we decided that the Wakefield Blues were going to have a rare Saturday off. There wasn't even the consolation of watching the game on iFollow. Adam streamed the audio commentary, but I was reduced to regular checks on the score on my phone. Having said that, Carlisle took the lead through Ryan Edmondson in the 29th minute and the scoreline remained unchanged for the next hour of playing time.

In the meantime, I'd gone to Asda to pick up a couple of items. On getting out of the car I checked my phone to see that the score remained 1-0 to Carlisle after 88 minutes. When I emerged from the store five minutes later and checked my phone again Walsall were 2-1 ahead! And this time there was to be no last-minute drama from Carlisle. The equaliser was down to an absolute howler by Carlisle keeper Tomas Holi, the stuff of nightmares.

It appears that all sorts kicked off after the final whistle. There are reports of a Walsall player goading the Carlisle fans, confirmed reports of Carlisle substitute Jamie Devitt receiving a black eye from an unidentified

Walsall player, and Paul Simpson condemned the way the fourth official spoke to the Carlisle staff as 'a disgrace', a view that he claims was shared by the match referee. Mind you, Simpson's view of the referee wasn't exactly flattering!

"I don't think the referee showed any cards from that situation. I think he carried on at the end of the game in the same way he did for other 90 odd minutes. He hadn't got a clue what was going on."

The shenanigans were sufficiently bad for Walsall manager Michael Flynn to make some of his players go into the Carlisle changing room to apologise for their behaviour.

DECEMBER 2022

Saturday 3 December. Carlisle United v Sutton United. Brunton Park. EFL League 2.

It seemed that we'd been away from Carlisle United for too long. It was in fact only two weeks since the coruscating 4-1 away win at Salford City, and just a week longer since we'd last visited Brunton Park for the lacklustre 0-0 draw against Walsall.

We had an earlier start than usual as kick-off was at 1.00 p.m., the timing having been moved forward to allow for the possibility of England finishing in second place in their World Cup qualifying group and playing their round of sixteen game later in the day. The precaution proved unnecessary, even more so after seeing the ease with which England dealt with the challenge of Senegal to reach the quarter finals. However, the early kick-off did have some benefits, of which more later.

Given that Bradford, who were immediately above us in the table, were playing top of the league Orient, and that Barrow, who were two places above us, had been thrashed 5-0 by Stevenage the previous evening, a win against a team from the lower reaches of League Two would do Carlisle no end of good. Only Adam and

I travelled this weekend, though we were joined in the paddock before kick-off by John and Julie Clarke who were visiting family (or so they claimed!) in Carlisle. John has one over me in that he is a born and bred Cumbrian, rather than an adopted son like me.

The first half seemed relatively straightforward. Carlisle strung together some slick passing moves without finding an incisive finish, while Sutton appeared to have very little to offer. Carlisle duly took the lead on the half-hour. After a couple of attempts on goal from outside the area, Owen Moxon opted instead for a lofted pass into the box and Ryan Edmondson comfortably headed home. So far, so good. A lapse in concentration led to a Sutton equaliser just before half-time, but the general view seemed to be that with patience and persistence Carlisle would secure all three points.

That was the problem. As Paul Simpson rightly identified in his post-match interview, there seemed to be a belief amongst both supporters and players that because we were a team in the play-off positions facing a team in the bottom third of the table, the win would eventually happen. It wasn't to be. Neither players or supporters could generate any momentum or passion in the second half, and we had to settle for an insipid 1-1 draw. The officiating was, predictably dire. At the end of the game the supporters were much more focused on booing the referee and linesmen than acknowledging their own team. Apparently, it was only the referee's second game in charge of an EFL fixture. It showed.

Things weren't quite as disappointing as they felt at the final whistle. Bradford duly lost to Orient, and the point we gained meant that, thanks to our good goal difference, we moved up a place to fifth in League Two. If you'd offered me that in February, when we were in the relegation places, I'd have bitten your hand off! To put things in context, as we said our goodbyes, I suggested to Julie Clarke that what we'd seen would probably deter her from coming to another game for a while. She replied, "Oh no, that's the first time I haven't seen them lose in about five years."!

One advantage of the early kick-off was that it meant that Adam and I didn't have to miss out on the Durkar Devils Christmas do. Rather than the usual ten-pin bowling, this year saw us going to watch Sheffield Steelers take on Cardiff Devils in the Elite Ice Hockey League. Just three and a half hours after leaving Brunton Park in Carlisle we were in our seats at Sheffield Arena ready for a seven o'clock face-off.

The close proximity of the two events didn't do the ice-hockey any favours. My only previous experience of British ice-hockey was in the late Seventies when, as an undergraduate, I would sometimes go to watch Durham Wasps. At the time Wasps were one of the pre-eminent teams in British ice-hockey and went on to dominate the sport in the Eighties. In 1996 the team was purchased by Sir John Hall as part of his grand scheme to establish a centre of sporting excellence on Tyneside, comprising Newcastle United, Newcastle Falcons rugby union team (formerly Gosforth), Newcastle Eagles basketball team and the Wasps. Wasps were taken to Newcastle and renamed the Newcastle Cobras. In the next few years they changed owners and names from the Cobras, to the

Riverkings, to the Jesters, before the team finally folded. An early example of franchise sport in the UK?

Whatever the case, the fare on offer in the late Seventies was very different from the sanitised, commercialised product on offer on Saturday evening! The level of skill was indisputable, but it was all the off-rink distractions that got in the way. That, and the fact that there seemed to be relatively little variety, particularly in methods of scoring. Goals were the result of either an excellent slapshot from distance, or a frantic goalmouth melee before the puck was forced home into a tiny goal past a goalkeeper of ridiculous bulk, due to all the protective padding he has to wear to protect himself against a piece of vulcanised rubber being smashed towards him at ridiculous velocities!

Compare that with the multitude of different ways in which a try can be scored in rugby, or a goal in football. However, one thing that did impress me was the speed of substitutions, or 'interchanges' as I think they're known. It made a pleasant change from substitutions in football, which are frequently used as a method of time wasting. One of the few good things about the current tainted football World Cup has been the addition of realistic amounts of added time to counter the time-wasting chicanery that goes on during normal time.

Time for a slight digression!

On 8 May 1999 Carlisle United faced oblivion. Less than 25 years after briefly topping the First Division they were bottom of the Football League on the last day of the season, needing to better Scarborough's result to ensure survival. Scarborough manged to draw, but the Carlisle game lasted considerably longer, due to a serious injury to a Plymouth player just before half-time. After Plymouth took the lead in the second half, Carlisle managed to equalise, but as time ticked away everyone knew that a draw was not enough. As the game reached ninety minutes, the fourth official indicated four minutes of additional time. By this time fans at Scarborough were already on the pitch, celebrating what they realistically believed was their survival.

In the final moments Carlisle won a corner. I checked my watch to see that the four additional minutes were just about complete. Coach Nigel Pearson urged the Carlisle goalkeeper Jimmy Glass to go up for the corner. Glass had been signed as an emergency loan from Swindon Town and had only played two previous games for Carlisle. The corner was swung in, and a powerful goal bound header was parried by the Plymouth goalkeeper. It fell at the feet of Glass, who swept the ball home from about eight yards. Cue pandemonium and a massive pitch invasion! When the pitch was finally cleared the referee blew to restart the game, and a second later blew again to indicate full-time. It really was that close.

Jimmy Glass never played for Carlisle again, but he was subsequently awarded the freedom of the city. He has become a club legend, because without his goal Carlisle would probably have been consigned to the oblivion that engulfed Scarborough following their relegation from the Football League.

On Saturday he was back at Carlisle United to mark the renaming of one of the ground's bars in his honour. Adam and I got to the ground early enough to be in the fan zone behind the main stand when Glass came out to meet the fans. It was a very special moment to shake his hand and tell him that he'd provided my best ever experience in 55 years of supporting Carlisle. Adam, in a masterpiece of understatement, simply said "He's told me quite a bit about your goal."

Saturday 10 December.

Well, that was the football weekend that wasn't! Carlisle's 'local derby' against Barrow (Opposite ends of the county but that's as local as it gets for us) was called off by Friday lunchtime due to a frozen pitch. Add to that the fact that England's World Cup hopes disappeared due to an abysmal refereeing performance and Harry Kane's inability to hit the target from twelve yards, and it's been a pretty dismal couple of days. I wonder if Kane will be subject to the same degree of online trolling as was experienced by Bukayo Saka, Jayden Sancho and Marcus Rashford after the same failing in the Euros final?

But refereeing is the main focus of this short post. The performance of the referee in England's game was barely on a level with League Two refereeing, and believe me, that's a pretty low bar. In contrast to the referee in the Argentina-Holland game, who basically gave a yellow card to anyone who moved, this referee was notable for his reluctance to punish any wrongdoing. Blatant fouls repeatedly went unpunished, he displayed a marked reluctance to reach for his yellow card, and it took a

VAR review to persuade him to give a penalty for the most blatant foul imaginable.

I fully appreciate that refereeing is a thankless task and I respect those who are willing to take on the role at every level of the game. The best referee I have seen in the last couple of years was for an U16's game, where the official had to send off two players for fighting, and deal with all sorts of touchline antics. He stopped the game for about fifteen minutes to talk to the players in question and to consult with the respective coaches. Having finally restarted the game, he had the balls to send off a third player just five minutes later for a dangerous and late challenge on a goalkeeper. He was barely eighteen, and apparently was far from a model pupil when at school.

Obviously, most of my current experience of referees is at League Two level, and equally obviously I tend to see refereeing decisions through Carlisle-tinted spectacles. However, I've invested quite a lot in Carlisle this season, and I mean financially as well as emotionally. Season tickets for Adam and myself don't come cheap, and that's before you factor in the significant fuel costs of travelling to both home and away fixtures. Given that investment, I think I have a right to expect at least a competent level of officiating at the games I go to watch. I accept that mistakes will be made, but when mistakes materially affect the outcome of a game, as a couple of decisions in the Carlisle v Orient did a couple of months ago, it's simply not acceptable.

Ok. Rant over.

Monday 12 December.

Yesterday's rant about inadequate refereeing requires some further elaboration.

One assumes that the responsibility for appointing match officials for World Cup games lies with FIFA, the governing body of the world game. Was there ever an organisation less fit for purpose? After the corruption of the Sepp Blatter era, aided and abetted by Michel Platini, his counterpart at Uefa, we now have Gianni Infantino, a man who is apparently happy to be photographed sitting between Vladimir Putin and the Crown Price of Saudi Arabia.

Don't get me wrong. International football means far less to me than club football. If someone had said to me on Saturday evening that if Harry Kane missed England's second penalty Carlisle would be guaranteed promotion, I'd have replied, "Thank you very much and goodbye England's World Cup prospects." I'm far more invested in the team and players that I watch most weekends than I am in a bunch of grossly overpaid 'elite' players.

The last two World Cups have been hosted by two of the less tolerant and democratic nations on the political spectrum in Russia and Qatar. How long before North Korea or China is awarded the World Cup? After all, China has already hosted the Olympics!

I think it's time the F.A. and equivalent bodies in other major footballing nations established a breakaway organisation. Not a profit-driven entity such as the aborted European Super League, but a body that would restore an element of integrity and morality to world football and would eventually become the de facto governing body of the world's most popular sport.

Saturday 17 December.

It's been another non-event of a weekend from a footballing point of view. For the second week in a row Carlisle's game was postponed by Friday lunchtime due to a frozen pitch. I can't say I'm too bothered. Much of yesterday was spent driving to Birmingham and back to bring Ellie home for the Christmas break. Roadworks and accidents meant that I spent over seven hours on the road for a round trip that normally takes about four and a half hours. Even the drive from Ellie's flat to the university library probably took longer than it would have done to walk. So, the prospect of heading down the M1 for the second day in succession didn't exactly fill me with enthusiasm!

The game at Northampton has rapidly been rearranged for Tuesday evening, by which time we're assured temperatures should have risen significantly.

Tuesday 20 December. Northampton v Carlisle United. The Sixfields Stadium. EFL League 2.

As we nursed mild hangovers, following a Monday night out with Jane Hardy and Roger Hardy, Lisa pointed out that Tuesday was going to be a good day, as every member of the family would be doing something they liked and enjoyed: Imogen was meeting up with friends at Xscape for a karaoke session and something to eat; Lisa was lunching and indulging in a bit of retail therapy with the mum of one of Imogen's friends; Ellie was meeting up with a couple of old school friends to go ice-skating and then joining a handful more friends for something to eat; Adam and I were off to Northampton to watch Carlisle. I did point out that while Adam and I were doing something we liked, there was no guarantee that enjoyment would be involved!

So three days later than originally planned Adam, Ben and myself headed down the M1. The journey was pretty straightforward. We drove about five miles to join the M1 at J39, and a similar distance to reach the ground when we left the motorway near the end of our journey.

Sixfields Stadium is an odd little ground. Like several relatively new lower-league grounds (see Doncaster Rovers, Scunthorpe United and others), it's part of a relatively large out-of-town/edge-of town retail park. When I wound down the window close to the ground to ask for directions to car parking the response was along the following lines. "Turn right at Nando's, drive up the hill past Pizza Hut, and if you reach McDonald's, you've gone too far." Once in the ground the neon lights of Cineworld and other entertainment outlets were clearly visible.

The ground itself sits in something of a natural bowl, and looked moderately impressive as we approached it, brightly illuminated by the floodlights, and tidy in design, with an all-seater capacity of just under 8,000.

Only eighteen years old, apparently attempts to increase the capacity have been thwarted by financial constraints and legislation limiting the further development of out-of-town sites if such development might be deemed detrimental to the town or city centre.

Needing to collect our tickets on arrival, we located the ticket office as we walked down the steps to the main stand. From there we were redirected to a small portacabin a few yards away. From there we were redirected around the corner of the main stand to an even smaller portacabin for away tickets. When we finally made it to the turnstile, we were told that none of the free hot drink vouchers, which had been promised as a token of thanks for turning out on a cold Tuesday evening just before Christmas, were available. We were advised to come back a bit later. When a few of us did so at half-time, the stewards claimed they hadn't been given any, and the people running the refreshment franchise claimed similar ignorance. A nice gesture in principle, but rather lacking in execution!

Following the quite positive impressions we'd received as we approached the ground, one of the first comments I made to Adam once we'd finally reached our seats was how utterly lacking in atmosphere the ground was. There was no sense of any build-up to the kick-off, and precious little noise from the home fans. There wasn't a lot from the away fans either, but I think that a turnout of 225 in a crowd of 4,700 for a game rearranged at three days' notice, and that involved a round trip of about nine hours from Carlisle (okay, only half that for the Wakefield Blues!) was quite impressive. A lot of away teams fail to bring that number to Brunton Park for Saturday games at much warmer times of year.

From a very early stage of the game, it became evident that Carlisle would settle for a draw and a point from the game. As a partisan fan, you tend to see your own team as paragons of virtue, while the opposition are purveyors of all manner of cheating and chicanery. The reality is more prosaic. Last night "we" were guilty of all kinds of nefarious practices: kicking the ball away when a free kick had been conceded; taking an inordinate amount of time over goal-kicks and throw-ins. The sort of shenanigans that would have had the Brunton Park faithful incandescent with rage. Probably the "best" moment came when Morgan Feeney shamelessly stole 25-30 yards on a throw-in. The ball went out of play just in front of us, about twenty yards from the Carlisle goal line. He must have been close to the halfway line when he finally released the ball! Cue much hilarity in the away section.

By half-time the Carlisle fans seemed to have bought into the idea that a draw would be a decent result away from home against a team in the automatic promotion places, particularly given how mediocre the quality of play had been in the first half, with little to excite one on a cold December evening.

Expectations were raised early in the second half when left wing-back Jack Armer scored his first goal of the season, despite Northampton claims for offside. A real smash and grab performance suddenly seemed a possibility. Such optimism lasted a mere six minutes, in which time two defensive lapses had gifted Northampton a 2-1 lead.

Numerous substitutions followed as Carlisle were forced to chase the game. The most worrying was that of striker Ryan Edmondson. As he challenged for a long clearance from goalkeeper Tomas Holi, the Northampton right back 'made a back' for him and brought him crashing to the ground, suffering a dislocated shoulder in the process. Edmondson is likely to be out of action for weeks. The Northampton defender didn't even get a yellow card.

Edmondson's replacement, Tobi Sho-Silva, did net in the 87th minute, only for the linesman to flag for offside. Paul Simpson later claimed the linesman's decision was a reaction to the abuse he received earlier from Northampton fans for not giving an offside in the build-up to Carlisle's goal. From our position for both allowed and disallowed goal, I think Simpson had some justification. This was another game (see Orient at home) where the club later received an apology from the EFL for a refereeing error, but again the points had already been lost.

A win would have taken us into fourth position. As it is we sit in seventh. That is way above expectations at the beginning of the season. Automatic promotion is probably beyond us, but a place in the play-offs is now a realistic expectation. And who knows what might be possible when we have a fully fit squad to pick from?

As we travelled home, a part of me wondered why we'd travelled to within seventy miles of London to watch a mediocre League Two game. But that's part of the deal.

The great days, like Oldham away last season, and Salford away this season, are made all the more special by the disappointment one suffers on evenings like this.

To round off a disappointing evening, our journey home was blighted by the curse of late-night motorway travel, the overnight roadworks. Just about every trip to an away midweek game has been victim to late night delays. An indication of broken Britain?

Monday 26 December. Carlisle United v Bradford City. Brunton Park. EFL League 2.

Today saw Ben's induction as a fully-fledged member of the Wakefield Blues, having got a half-season ticket as part of his Christmas present. The corresponding fixture last season, which took place a little later, in January, heralded something of a false dawn during the ill-fated Keith Millen era. A couple of Millen signings in the January transfer window made impressive debuts and two former Bradford players scored the goals to twist the knife in a 2-0 Carlisle win which suggested better things ahead. Unfortunately, Bradford's next few results revealed what a poor team they were at the time, and sadly so did Carlisle's!

The context this season is rather different. Before today's game Carlisle occupied the final play-off position, with Bradford equal on points to us but with an inferior goal-difference. Of the four League matches we have lost this season, all but one has been against the teams in the automatic promotion places. Against other teams in or around the play-offs we've got a pretty decent record, evidenced by comprehensive victories over Doncaster Rovers and Salford City, and a solid draw against Swindon Town. So, this game was a significant one, particularly given a disappointing draw and a defeat in our two previous League games. It was also our first trip to Brunton Park in over three weeks since the lacklustre draw against Sutton United.

What used to seem like an awfully long trek from Crofton to Carlisle now seems to slip by in no time at all. It takes just over an hour to reach Scotch Corner and a break for Greggs' sausage rolls and pasties, before completing the second leg of the journey in about seventy-five minutes. We tend to arrive early enough for me to be tempted by the treasures (or tat!) on offer in the Blues Store! There was a minor panic after we'd got into the ground, and I mislaid my season ticket. Having retraced my steps to no effect, I went back to the turnstiles, where I was directed to the ticket office. This didn't recover my ticket but did enable me to spot Tony Caig, a Carlisle goalkeeping legend to rival Jimmy Glass, in the fanzone. No time for a picture this time unfortunately. Caig's penalty shoot-out saves against Colchester at Wembley were instrumental in Carlisle winning the Auto Windscreens Shield back in 1997.

Having gone back into the ground, I did discover my season ticket in a hitherto undiscovered pocket in my jacket. And that is the cue for a short digression on the topic of football- watching attire!

Gone are the balmy days of August and September when we could watch games in just a replica top and thin jacket. Even the afternoon kick-offs are pretty cold now and have been for about the last month. Mindful of the fact that I was so cold at Harrogate on a freezing Tuesday evening back in January that I was reduced to buying a half-time cup of Bovril, I resolved to upgrade my winter apparel. A quick trip to Sports Direct sorted a set of skins (formerly known as thermal underwear!). A new coat/jacket was a little more problematic. Thickness and warmth were a priority, as was sufficient length to keep my bum warm! A Christmas shopping trip to Trinity Leeds resolved the problem. I saw the perfect jacket in Next, the only problem being that it cost about three times as much as I'd normally spend on such an item. A quick conversation with Lisa and this year's Christmas present was sorted!

Saturday was the new gear's second outing (the first being Northampton last Tuesday), both tests passed with flying colours. I wouldn't say I was warm at either game, but it made a nice change to not be uncomfortably cold.

Once the game started, it was hard to believe the two teams were equal on points. It soon became evident that Carlisle had rediscovered their mojo after a couple of slightly disappointing performances as they dictated the tempo of the game. Bradford spent a lot of time trying to play the ball out from the back, a tactic for which they didn't really have the skill or technique. When I commented on that to Adam at half-time, he said that was exactly what Bradford fans were tweeting. Carlisle's superiority was rewarded in the 34th minute when a Taylor Charter's corner was swung to the far post where Paul Huntington headed home comfortably. It was a goal that was simple and unspectacular, almost anti-climactic. The only concern at half-time was that we should have been at least one more goal ahead, given our dominance.

The difference in performance was down to one player, Jon Mellish. He missed the Northampton game through illness but was back for this one. We tend to play with three centre backs, and he's the only one of the three who is really confident bringing the ball out of defence. He also links up impressively well with left wing-back Jack Armer. He may lack finesse, but his work rate and tireless running are immense. He's also perfectly capable of switching to a midfield role if the situation demands it, with the defence adjusting to a back four.

Such was the case in this game when he moved forward in the second half to counter the increasing midfield influence of Bradford's Richie Smallwood. He embarked on a series of barnstorming forward runs that saw the Bradford defence parting like the Red Sea (cliché time again!). One particular run took him to the by-line before he crossed the ball, not to the advanced striker but to Jordan Gibson arriving near the penalty spot in support. How Gibson managed to blaze his shot over from such a perfect set-up only Gibson knows!

Despite Bradford offering a bit more threat in the second half, Carlisle looked the more likely team to score in the closing stages. When the final whistle went, Bradford left Brunton Park for the second season in succession, and the second time this year, having failed to manage a single shot on target. From Carlisle's point of view, it was definitely one of those games when the result was much more important than the quality of performance.

A word about Bradford's support. They are by far the best supported home team in League Two with average home gates well into five figures. They brought a respectable 1300 travelling fans to this promotion six-pointer, though that is significantly less than the 2,000 Carlisle took to Valley Parade for a dead game at the end of last season. What surprised me was how little noise they made, apart from their booing of Jordan Gibson, who Carlisle have obviously succeeded in making a better player than Bradford did. Admittedly their team didn't give them a lot to shout about, but surely that's where a substantial travelling support come in, making some noise, lifting the atmosphere, and energising their team. The attendance of 8,296 was the highest at Brunton Park since 2010, excluding play-off games or those where there's been some sort of ticket promotion. Let's hope that the performance and result will encourage the extra numbers to keep coming back.

I've never been a great fan of Bradford manager Mark Hughes as either a player or manager. As a player he was undoubtedly talented, but was a dirty, niggly and incessantly whinging forward. He had managed exclusively in the Premier League before taking the Bradford job, but with no success of any note. It was quite satisfying to see him scurry down the tunnel almost as soon as the final whistle went.

Credit where credit is due. The referee for this game was the best we've seen all season. He was keen to play the advantage whenever possible and quick to spot the sort of niggly professional fouls that often go unpunished. The biggest compliment I can pay him is that he was barely noticeable. His control of the game was excellent, with only two yellow cards awarded, both to Bradford players. So, a very Happy New Year to you Adam Herczeg!

Thursday 29 December. Crewe Alexandra v Carlisle United. Gresty Road (definitely not The Mornflake Stadium!). EFL League 2.

Adam owes me big time after this evening. First, he announces about three days ago that his girlfriend Holly is coming round this evening and that therefore he's not up for going to Crewe tonight and ticking another new ground off the list. I didn't fancy the four and a half hours round trip on my own, so he's already deprived me of watching the game in the flesh. To compound his crime, he then disappears upstairs with my laptop this evening so that he and Holly can watch the live stream of the game on I-Follow in his bedroom, thus depriving me of the opportunity to watch it myself, rather than being able to plug the laptop into the television in the lounge where we could all have watched it.

All this wouldn't have managed so much if it hadn't been such a bloody good performance! For the fourth time this season we scored three or more goals away from home. Having moved into fourth place after Monday's win, the top play-off position, this 3-0 win almost halved the gap between Carlisle and Northampton in third place, the final automatic promotion spot.

I think tonight was probably the point at which hope turned into real expectation. To be in fourth place at the half-way point of the season, when we've never had anything resembling a fully fit squad to select from, is remarkable. With the opportunity to strengthen the squad in the January transfer window, anything less than a play-off place at the end of the season will be a real disappointment. I'm optimistic enough to believe that an automatic promotion place is possible. I just hope these words don't come back to haunt me!

What's really encouraging is that not only are we delivering good results against teams close to us in the league table, but we're also despatching teams from lower in the table with the minimum of fuss, this result being a case in point. I've managed to assemble a reasonable picture of the game from video highlights and match reports, so here goes with an attempt at my own match report.

Yet again Carlisle benefited from an early away goal (see also Grimsby, Tranmere and Salford). When there's a good away following that have generated a really good pre-match atmosphere, an early goal makes a significant difference in maintaining and improving that atmosphere. In this case it came in the sixth minute from an Owen Moxon corner that was bundled home by Morgan Feeney. Another key feature of Carlisle's success so far this season has been the number of goals they have scored from set-piece situations, with defenders often playing a key role.

Things got better immediately after half-time when Carlisle doubled their lead in the first minute of the second half. Paul Simpson talks repeatedly about the need to ensure that if the first contact isn't good, then the second contact needs to be. This goal was a classic example of that. An over-hit cross from the right was kept alive on the left by Jack Armer who turned the ball back into the danger area. A deft first touch from Owen Moxon enabled him to turn and side foot the ball home.

The game turned decisively, though not conclusively, in Carlisle's favour ten minutes later when a Crewe defender received a straight red card for a fist in the face of Carlisle striker Jack Stretton in an off-the-ball incident.

The conclusive moment came in the 72nd minute. Following a Crewe corner, Jack Armer hoofed the ball clear from near his own goal-line. His clearance fell to Kristian Dennis, on as a second-half substitute, and still ten yards inside the Carlisle half. Already five yards clear of the last Crewe defender, he raced forward, holding off the chasing players, going half the length of the field before lashing home a rasping left foot shot that gave the goalkeeper no chance.

That meant it was pretty much game over, though there was still time for Jamie Devitt to hit the bar with a fierce dipping and swerving shot from thirty yards that bounced down and unfortunately away from the goal line.

Having watched the Pitchside Blues video of the post-match celebrations, my only regret is that the impressive way following of 820 was not supplemented by two more, to join in the joyous celebrations at the end of what had been another magnificent evening in a momentous year for supporters of Carlisle United.

Friday 30th December.

So, the footballing year of 2022 is over for me. I know that football is measured in seasons rather than years, but this has been a remarkable year in the fortunes of Carlisle United.

The portents on New Year's Day were not good, and they got worse over the next few weeks. And then mid-February saw a turnaround that no-one could have foreseen. Paul Simpson returned as manager and saw the team embark on a series of results that dismissed any fears of relegation. But the real test was to come in the 2022-2023 season, when Simpson had time to assemble his own squad and backroom staff.

Simmo has passed the test with flying colours. There have been so many memorable moments and matches in the last ten months that I'm not going to attempt to pick out specific examples. That may have something to do with the fact that I've been to far more games than I've managed ever before in a calendar year, but it also has a lot to do with the transformation that Paul Simpson has brought about in a team that seemed destined for the National League.

The current rapport between the supporters and players is brilliant, as is the rapport between the fans and the manager. And if you push me for a moment of the year, it's got to be Morgan Feeney's winner in the dying seconds at Oldham in March, which set Carlisle on the road to survival and Oldham on the road to relegation.

Let's hope that expectations for 2023 don't prove to be false ones.

JANUARY 2023

Sunday 1 January 2023. Doncaster Rovers v Carlisle United. The Keepmoat Stadium. EFL League 2.

One or two preliminary issues need sorting out regarding the naming of the ground before we get going in earnest. Google Maps informs me that Doncaster Rovers play at the Eco-Power Stadium but as previously stated, I refuse to bow to the imperative of commercial naming rights. The problem is that when Doncaster moved to their current ground from the abject ruin that was Belle Vue, it was named the Keepmoat Stadium after the construction company that built it, in much the same way that Huddersfield Town's current ground was originally called The McAlpine Stadium. So commercial imperatives are unavoidable in this case.

The Keepmoat Stadium is probably the best of the relatively new grounds we've visited. Like Sixfields it's part of an edge-of-town retail park development, which means that it's easy to reach and has plentiful parking very close to the ground. With a capacity of just over 15,000 it just about merits calling itself a stadium. It's a neat, well-appointed ground, with generously spaced bar areas and excellent sightlines once you take your seat.

Furthermore, I think we probably benefited from a Rovers New Year ticket promotion as mine cost just £15 and Adam and Ben's a mere pound each. Mind you, given the entertainment that followed, it's arguable that we were overcharged! A final bonus is that this was our shortest trip of the season, just beating Bradford. We left home just eighty minutes before kick-off and were home again barely an hour after the final whistle.

The atmosphere once we'd entered the ground was vibrant. The Carlisle drummer and a host of fans were whipping up a brilliant vibe in the bar area and the mood was equally good once we took our seats. Another impressive following of 1,222 had made the journey and were in fine voice. The feeling was very much of a club that was on the up, and it's a scenario that was almost impossible to imagine a year ago.

How misleading. What followed was probably the worst forty-five minutes of football I've seen from Carlisle this season. After just six minutes Joel Senior, making a first appearance in almost a year following a serious injury, made a complete hash of a routine clearance and gifted Doncaster an early lead. At that moment he looked like he wanted the ground to open up and swallow him. For the rest of the half the team showed little sign of getting back into the game. Normally reliable players were noticeably off their game. Paul Huntington was far from his usual reliability, frequently being turned and beaten for pace. Owen Moxon and Callum Guy failed to impose themselves in midfield. Tomas Holi's distribution was woeful. Gibson, very much a confidence player, was having a nightmare. When the injury curse struck yet again after twenty-five minutes as Jack Stretton limped off, the pre-match feelgood factor had well and truly dissipated.

It wasn't that Doncaster were all that good. They got behind our defence too easily but had little to show for it. But nonetheless it was a relief that we were only the one goal down at half-time. In conversation with another supporter in the sausage-roll queue at half-time, he commented justifiably that we looked like a threadbare team that was nursing injuries and were down to the bare bones.

Gibson was replaced with Jayden Harris at half-time, the supporters found their voice again and the performance improved in the second half but not enough to prevent Doncaster scoring a second goal in the 67th minute. Carlisle surged forward in the closing stages and Kris Dennis scored a typical poacher's goal from close range after Tobi Sho-Silva headed the ball into his path in the 87th minute. Dennis nearly scored again a couple of minutes later with a vicious shot that the Doncaster keeper saved at the second attempt, and a late Morgan Feeney header went narrowly wide, but to be honest we never really deserved a point from the game.

The chant goes that "We've got super Paul Simpson, he knows exactly what we need.". Today was possibly an occasion when he didn't. The familiar decision to switch Jon Mellish from central defence to midfield didn't pay sufficient dividends and should perhaps have been reconsidered. It was right to take Jordan Gibson off at half-time, but I'm not sure that Jayden Harris was the right replacement. Harris is a work in progress, having been signed from the National League. I thought a handful of supporters were unduly harsh in their criticisms of him, but it's fair to say that he's yet to win over most fans. I'd much rather have seen Jamie Devitt come on at that point. He can dictate the pace and pattern of a game and can find time and space in a way that few League Two players can. He had relatively little opportunity to do so when he finally came on after eighty minutes.

The officiating was back to the usual appalling standard. Numerous instances of pushing, holding and shirt-pulling went unpunished, and on the odd occasions when advantage was played, none accrued. Most significantly a high boot to Jack Armer's head received only a yellow card when it was clearly a red. The linesman on the left side was just as bad. There were at least three occasions when he and the referee waited at least ten seconds for the other official to make the call on a throw in before one of them took it upon themselves to make the wrong decision.

We remain in fourth place, but today was slightly worrying given another injury, and the current lack of alternatives in a threadbare squad. It's a relief that we now have a fortnight's break with the F.A Cup next weekend. It's to be hoped that a few injuries have time to mend, and that some good business can be done early in the transfer window to enable new players some time to bed into the squad.

No match day. Saturday 7 January 2023.

Our elimination from the F.A. Cup in Round 2 at the hands of Walsall meant that Carlisle had a blank weekend as Round 3 took place, with no option to reschedule any previously postponed game. It was probably a good thing, with the squad ravaged by injuries, and two loan players recalled to their parent club. In one case, striker Jack Stretton was recalled to Derby in order to be sold to another League Two club, Stockport County. Apparently, Carlisle matched the transfer fee Stockport were offering, but couldn't match the wages offered – more of that later.

Carlisle have made two signings so far this transfer window, both half-season loans, and probably intended to provide cover rather than go straight into the starting eleven. We've signed Jack Robinson, a left-sided defender, from Middlesbrough, and midfielder Alfie McCalmont from Leeds United. A Leeds supporting Durkar Devils parent tells me that he's a good player, with a similar style to Adam!

Harking back to the F.A. Cup this was one of the better rounds for upsets in recent years. Honourable mentions go to Sheffield Wednesday, Wrexham, Stevenage and Blackpool. Unfortunately, modern-day giant-killing feats have to be tempered by the fact that the fallen giant has usually made at least eight changes from the team that started their previous league game. Wrexham's 4-3 win at Coventry was impressive but shouldn't be over-egged. With Hollywood money behind them they are regularly able to lure League Two players to drop a division by offering them triple the salary they could earn at most League Two clubs. American money is queering the pitch of the National League in the same way that Middle Eastern money (Manchester City and

Newcastle United) and to a lesser extent American money (Liverpool, Chelsea, Manchester United) is queering the pitch in the Premier League.

Saturday 14 January 2023. Carlisle United v Newport County. Brunton Park. EFL League 2.

A round trip to Birmingham on Friday to take Ellie back to uni meant that I'd clocked up well over five hundred miles in two days by the time we got home from this weekend's football – not that I'm complaining! Good weather on the journey to Carlisle usually heralds a good performance and result, for the superstitious amongst us. The weather was sunny and clear until we were well north of Scotch Corner, though we encountered some blustery wind and rain as we crossed Stainmore and approaching Penrith. A metaphor for what was to follow?

This was Carlisle's first game for almost a fortnight following three games in six days over the holiday period. How would they respond following the disappointing performance and result at Doncaster? Fortunately, given their inactivity, they were still in fourth place before kick-off, despite other teams around them having played league games in the meantime. The club had made another half-season loan signing on Friday, bringing 19-year-old Crystal Palace striker John-Kymani Gordon until the end of the season. Taking players on their first loan deal can be a bit of a gamble – would this be one?

I suggested to Adam on the way to Carlisle that, with Jack Stretton having left the building, Gordon might start the game, providing an element of the unknown, as he certainly wouldn't have featured in Newport's pre-match scouting of Carlisle. And so it proved, with him being the only change from the team that started the Doncaster game. With my acumen, I sometimes think I'm wasted writing blogs! The other loan signings were both on the bench.

The first half was not encouraging. The defence appeared to be half asleep, there was no cohesion or pattern in midfield, and the attack, trying to incorporate a new signing, were left feeding off meagre scraps. Newport didn't have a lot to offer, their main threat coming from former Carlisle striker Offrande Zanzala, though the threat had a lot to do with his physicality and consistent fouling of defenders. But Carlisle didn't appear to be able to take advantage of mediocre opposition. The predictable decision to move Jon Mellish from left centre-back to midfield failed to have the desired effect. I'd already said to Adam that Simmo needed to get them sorted at half-time when the fourth official indicated two minutes of added time.

In the dying seconds of the half, the Newport defence embarked on a prolonged game of head tennis in an attempt to clear the ball from their own area. Watching the highlights, it's fascinating to see how Kristian Dennis watches the ball, trying to anticipate where it will eventually fall, starting to make moves and then holding back. Inevitably he got it right, and when the ball finally hit the deck, he was perfectly positioned to side foot the ball home from about six yards via the far post and notch his fifteenth goal of the campaign. I suspect that he probably said to his new strike partner before kick-off, "The six-yard box is mine!" There was a notable lack of smiles in the goal celebrations. Perhaps the players were like the fans, scarcely able to believe that we were taking a one goal lead into the interval after playing so badly. It had almost been as bad as the first half at Doncaster a fortnight ago.

Nineties Carlisle legend Dean Walling was presented to the crowd at half-time, before a second half that thankfully saw an improvement in Carlisle's performance. They started to take the initiative, playing on the front foot far more than in the first half. A second goal duly came in the 57th minute, and it was in marked contrast to the scrappy nature of the first goal. Kris Dennis did very well to control an awkward ball forward and lay it into the path of John-Kymani Gordon. He still had a lot to do but turned the Newport right-back inside out before coolly slotting the ball home. What an impact on debut! It earned him a standing ovation when he was substituted ten minutes later. He was subsequently named man of the match and was also named in the League Two team of the week. Let's hope he continues to have such an impact.

His departure meant a return to first-team action for Omari Patrick, missing through injury since scoring two goals in the 3-1 win at Hartlepool in early October. Patrick can be frustrating at times, but he was certainly up for it on Saturday. His pace and trickery, along with his ability to cut in from the flanks and finish clinically, offer Paul Simpson another option in attack, whether he starts a game or comes off the bench.

At 2-0 it was really game over, as Carlisle have become increasingly proficient at closing games like this down. In fact, the final margin could have been even greater, particularly when Jordan Gibson, who can be as frustrating as Omari Patrick, cut in from the left and curled a beautiful shot towards the Warwick Road End goal, only for it to rebound from the far post.

To be honest, this was not a great performance. But what is really encouraging is that Carlisle still managed a comfortable 2-0 victory, which could have been better, while being well below their best. The ability to grind out results when not at your best is the stuff of which promotion campaigns are made. I fervently hope these next few sentences don't come back to haunt me, but I feel that we can now seriously begin to consider and contemplate promotion. Northampton lost on Saturday, which means that if Carlisle win their game in hand they will be within one point of the automatic promotion places. From their current position I'll be incredibly disappointed if the team don't at least make the play-offs. A top half finish would represent good progress from last season, but Simpson's impact has raised expectations.

An interesting by-line. Our on-loan right wing-back Fin Back is currently back at his parent club, Nottingham Forest, undergoing rehabilitation following a serious injury at Salford a couple of months ago. Not only have Forest said they will pay his wages while he works his way back to fitness, they will also send him back to Carlisle as soon as they think he is ready. I take this as an encouraging sign that the Premier League isn't always about money. It's also a possible dividend from Paul Simpson's time at the F.A. as manager of one of the age-group teams, when one of his colleagues was Steve Cooper, currently the manager of Forest.

Saturday 21 January 2023. Bradford City v Carlisle United. Valley Parade. EFL League 2.

This was another game that wasn't. We were suitably hyped up for what is our second shortest road trip of the season, only for the game to be postponed following a midday pitch inspection. Frozen areas of the pitch, and the failure of the sun to break through freezing fog and help the thaw were given as the reasons. Not particularly helpful for the 1,000 away supporters who would be well into their journey from Carlisle.

The one event of note during the week was the signing of thirty-four-year-old striker Joe Garner from Fleetwood Town. The transfer had been heavily rumoured for some days, the only surprise being that he's signed an eighteen-month contract rather than just until the end of the current season. Garner played for Carlisle very early in his career and was a notable success, moving on to Nottingham Forest for a club record transfer fee of £1.14 million. In a well-travelled career, he's also played for the likes of Preston North End, Ipswich Town and Glasgow Rangers. Fellow Carlisle striker Ryan Edmondson (currently injured) spent time on loan at Fleetwood Town. He says he was assigned to spend a whole day working solely with Garner, during which he was given a comprehensive lesson in the dark arts of forward play. Hopefully Garner will prove to be the grit in the oyster that helps produce the pearl of promotion.

So, we have to wait another three days for our first sighting of late-career Joe Garner at Tuesday evening's home fixture against Hartlepool, the first midweek League match of the current campaign. I just hope that the temperature is a bit warmer and the driving conditions are more favourable than they have been today!

Tuesday 24 January 2023. Carlisle United v Hartlepool United. Brunton Park. EFL League 2.

I have to admit that there were times as Tuesday measured its steady progress that I wondered just why I was making a 270-mile round trip to the north-west outpost of England to watch a League Two football fixture on a cold January evening. Fortunately, the football on display put paid to any such heresy!

I've written recently on the tendency of the weather as we travel north to be a precursor of the performance that we're going to see. The portents weren't promising. It was fully dark by the time we reached Scotch Corner and we were enveloped in thick fog as we crossed the Pennines over Stainmore. However, the fog cleared as we lost altitude and when we parked and disembarked in Carlisle, the temperature was a good three or four degrees warmer than what we'd left in Wakefield. It was still a cold January night, but not the bitter kind that drives you to buy hot Bovril to counter potential hypothermia.

My score prediction was for Carlisle to win either 4-0 or 5-0. This was based on the fact that we beat Hartlepool 3-1 away at the Victoria Ground earlier this season, along with the fact that Hartlepool remain embroiled in a relegation battle while Carlisle have improved enough to be on the verge of the automatic promotion places.

Fortunately, Carlisle started on the front foot, imposing their game on the opponents from the kick-off, which had not been the case in the previous two games. They were rewarded as early as the sixth minute when the Hartlepool defence failed woefully to deal with a corner from the Carlisle left and captain Morgan Feeney was left with a simple tap-in.

Carlisle continued to surge forward with slick passing and strong running. Wing-back Jack Armer and centre back Jon Mellish were particularly impressive overlapping down the left. It was little surprise that the lead was doubled after twenty-six minutes and little surprise that the threat came from the left flank. A barnstorming run by Mellish took him almost to the by-line, and again the Hartlepool defence proved unable to deal with a low cross from the left, leaving Kris Dennis plenty of time to pick his spot and sidefoot the ball home. My score prediction was looking eminently achievable.

Unfortunately, Carlisle offered Hartlepool a way back into the game almost immediately. Following a long clearance from the Hartlepool goalkeeper, midfielder Owen Moxon ("he's one of our own") hesitated before playing a woefully under hit back-pass towards goalkeeper Tomas Holy. A Hartlepool striker was quick to seize on the error and slot the ball home to halve the deficit.

Except Hartlepool weren't really back in the game. Carlisle had at least two gold-plated chances in the remaining twenty minutes of the first half, hitting the post on one occasion. The only surprise at half-time was that the margin remained at just one goal. Both teams were demonstrating why they are in their respective positions.

It continued in a similar vein in the second half. A piledriving, dipping twenty-five yard shot from Callum Guy almost put an end to the goal of the season debate, or the goal of any season to be honest, only for the Hartlepool keeper to partly redeem earlier failures by tipping the ball over the bar. In the 66th minute Kris Dennis was played in by Owen Moxon but instead of going for goal he chose to return the ball to Moxon. He then scampered into the goalmouth and was perfectly positioned to head home a pinpoint cross from Moxon.

Having failed to convert a good chance to complete his hat-trick, Dennis was substituted a few minutes later, replaced by Omari Patrick who is still returning to full match fitness after a lengthy injury absence. He appeared determined to repeat his feat from the away fixture by scoring twice against Hartlepool in the second half. He didn't, but with ten minutes left Simpson also brought on Leeds loanee Alfie McCalmont and returning fans' favourite Joe Garner, an indication of the increasing options and riches at his disposal. It's no longer a case of "If you're fit, you're in the match-day squad.". No further goals ensued, but in the closing stages songs and chants were emanating from all three sides of the ground occupied by Carlisle fans as we celebrated a job well done, dispatching a struggling team with minimum fuss. Statistics can be misleading, but the shot count is telling. Hartlepool had eight shots of which only three were on target. Carlisle had fourteen shots, eleven of which were on target. The scoreline could easily have been doubled, exceedingly even my optimistic prediction.

Carlisle's situation is beginning to look very, very promising. This win means they are only one point behind Northampton in the third automatic promotion place. With twenty league games to go, the tally of forty-two goals already exceeds the pitiful thirty-nine scored in the whole of last season. We are League Two's highest scoring team and possess the division's joint highest goalscorer in Kris Dennis. According to statistical analysis rookie midfielder Owen Moxon is the best player in League Two to date. And our next game is against bottom-of-the-table Rochdale. What is there not to be happy about?!

Saturday 28 January 2023. Rochdale v Carlisle United. Spotland (not the Crown Oil Arena!). EFL League 2.

This was one of our shorter trips – not as convenient as Doncaster, Bradford or Harrogate but a pleasant change from the long slog to Brunton Park on Tuesday evening. It was just an hour's trip over the M62, with Ben and John Clark supplementing the numbers of the Wakefield Blues.

John has agreed to write an alternative account of today's game for this post. We were sat next to each other watching the same game and supporting the same team, so it will be interesting to see how our match reports differ. I suspect that John's account might be a bit more objective, considered and dispassionate! I've promised not to edit his account in any way, and not to alter my account in the light of his.

There is no parking at Spotland but we were able to find street parking next to a municipal cemetery less than ten minutes' walk from the ground, and were in our seats on the half-way line a good forty-five minutes before kick-off. The atmosphere gradually built as more and more Carlisle fans took their seats during the build-up – more about the travelling support later.

As on Tuesday night Carlisle started the game on the front foot, snapping into tackles and pressing defenders when they attempted to play the ball out from the back. This game was another object lesson in not trying to play out from the back when you don't have players with the necessary technique. In the eighth minute a hoofed clearance was beautifully controlled by Kris Dennis, poacher turned provider, who played a superb through ball to set John-Kymani Gordon clear. He had some distance to go to goal, but there never appeared to be any doubt that he would do what was required, and he calmly slotted the ball home. Once again, the impressive travelling support had been rewarded by an early goal. It initially appeared that it might be the catalyst for further goals against the bottom side in the division. It was therefore slightly disappointing to still be only one goal ahead at half-time, but not a great cause for concern.

But Rochdale were made of sterner stuff than Hartlepool and a couple of substitutions early in the second half changed their pattern of play and enabled them to gain a foothold in the game. There were a couple of anxious moments when the ball pinged about the Carlisle area before eventually being cleared, and Carlisle players seemed to be too ready to stand off the Rochdale players and give them room to build attacks. Nonetheless, Carlisle seemed to be demonstrating their recently acquired habit of closing a game down and seeing out a result.

Until the 89th minute. A Rochdale free kick from the right was floated into the Carlisle area, headed on and then headed home. The Rochdale players wheeled away in celebration, and a shocked hush descended on the away stand. Then Paul Huntington could be seen in animated discussion with the linesman. That discussion was eventually joined by the referee, and after what seemed like an eternity the linesman raised his flag to indicate offside. We celebrated like we'd scored a second goal! That moment apart, the officiating was predictably poor. Shortly after the final whistle went to confirm our fifth win in the last six games, and to keep us in fourth place, one point from an automatic promotion place, but six points ahead of the fifth placed team.

It's worth taking a couple of minutes to consider the impact that John-Kymani Gordon (already popularly known as JK) has had on the team since his arrival on loan from Crystal Palace three games ago. He's started all three games before being substituted somewhere between sixty and seventy minutes, each time to a standing ovation. He's scored two goals, each of them showing great coolness and composure after being superbly played in by Kris Dennis. It looks like we've got a good 'un!

It's always a bit of a gamble taking a player from a Premier League club on their first loan. There's no way of knowing how they'll cope with life away from their parent club, and how they deal with life away from the training ground in an unfamiliar environment. They're of a similar age to undergraduates experiencing their first extended period away from home, and as parents with children of a certain age will know, it's a nervous wait to see how they will settle. It's also impossible to predict how they'll cope with the rigours of first-team football, up against seasoned old pros who know every trick in the book. According to Paul Simpson, JK, who is sharing a club house with Alfie McCalmont (on loan from Leeds) is settling in well and already developing his culinary skills. On the pitch he demonstrates a knowledge of the dark arts of attacking worthy of a player ten years his senior.

Carlisle had similar good fortune with the signing of Dynel Simeu, a Southampton centre back, for the second half of last season. After looking worryingly raw in his first couple of appearances, once he tuned in to his teammates he produced an impressive series of defensive performances, using his impressive physicality to good effect. His exuberant, chest-thumping celebration of goals and victories quickly made him a fans' favourite.

Similarly, JK was spotted kissing the badge following his goal on Saturday!

I referred earlier to the travelling support. The attendance at Spotland was 4,042, of which 1,634 were Carlisle fans. In other words, the away fans constituted well over a third of the total gate. And that number represented about a third of the crowd who attended last Tuesday's game against Hartlepool, despite a round trip from Carlisle of 255 miles. I can't imagine any club in League Two has better travelling support, particularly given Carlisle's geographical remoteness. I'm sure there's a statistician out there who could come up with a formula based on average home crowd, set against average travelling support as a proportion of home attendances. And throw in distance travelled as a key variable!

In an interesting sideline, the Cask and Feather, a pub close to Rochdale's ground is running a league table of away fans, based on the number of Jagermeister shots ordered in a single round. Carlisle fans absolutely smashed the record for a single round, beating previous table-toppers Newport County's paltry 120 with an impressive 340! They also exceeded Hartlepool's overall record of 520, raising the bar to 526. Not that I'm encouraging or condoning pre-match drinking of course!

What follows is John Clark's alternative view of the game, seen from the adjacent seat to mine. And I was right- it is more objective and considered than mine!

Rochdale 0 Carlisle United 1.

Saturday 28th January, 2023.

There are some fixtures which resonate throughout the football world, fixtures which denote a fierce rivalry built up over local, industrial, religious or regional differences. Think El Classico, think Liverpool versus Manchester United, the Old Firm derby or any other number of derbies for that matter; encounters where pride, passion and tribal identities are brought to the fore. But Rochdale versus Carlisle United? Maybe not so much, although to side with that view is to ally yourself to the big club, premiership, size-matters arrogant attitude which currently dominates football discussion and administration.

No, this game on Saturday did matter and, as the words of the song go, if you know your history, Rochdale v Carlisle does have considerable significance. Carlisle fans of a certain age will tell you that Rochdale's Spotland ground on February, 1995 was the scene of a 2-1 victory for Rochdale which was wildly cheered by Carlisle fans as it marked the very first occasion when Carlisle reached a Wembley final in what was then called the Auto Windscreen Shield. Carlisle had won the Northern Final by virtue of a 4-1 victory achieved during a downpour in the first leg at Brunton Park.

Eleven years later, on May 2nd, 2006 Carlisle were back again at Spotland under the management of a certain Paul Simpson to wrap up a 2-0 victory, and with it, the League 2 Championship. Football history, eh? It's enough to make your heart go whoa, hoa, hoa, hoa!

Hearts were beating again on Saturday. A little over a year earlier, Carlisle seemed to be preparing notices of imminent decease after a comprehensive defeat against Swindon at Brunton Park and even the most optimistic supporters were left looking into rapidly draining glasses, but now the club was back in the game and the Blue Army was mobilising. After the return of Paul Simpson as manager, Carlisle were proving to be a formidable force in League 2, steadily gaining points to sit in a play-off place, three points behind third placed Northampton. The team had been galvanised and the club appeared to be running on a more efficient basis. Recruitment had been impressive as additions were made to the squad with a view to increasing selection options rather than just fill gaps. What's more, that Blue Army mobilisation was evidenced by rising home gates and an astonishing away following and no one is in any doubt that the catalyst had been the appointment of Paul Simpson.

But it was also time to issue a warning note. As Saturday's game approached, Rochdale were in twenty-fourth position. As the old joke goes, they had a strong team, strong enough to hold up the rest of the league. But to make jokes, even corny ones like that is to tempt fate, to ignore the fact that teams in Rochdale's position need points just as much, more desperately even, than teams lying in fourth place. Many a team with aspirations for higher things has come unstuck against a relegation threatened side and a first look at the Spotland pitch suggested that it wasn't so much a scrap for points that was in store but a battle. You can insert your own favourite cliché here.

Still, after posting figures for tremendous away support at the likes of Salford and Doncaster, Carlisle fans numbered a total of 1,653 for their "close to home" fixture involving a 248-mile round trip. Blue Army! Blue Army!

The support is acknowledged by both players and management and it features in motivational preparation. In return, the supporters relish the local identity of the team with Owen Moxon regularly lauded as "one of our own," playing alongside Paul Huntington. Denton Holme and Trinity School, take a bow. Paul Simpson and his first-team coach, Gavin Skelton also have impeccable Cumbrian credentials. Does this matter when tribal identities are being asserted? Of course it does.

Despite expectations though, the fourth placed team against the bottom of the league game on a patchy looking pitch did not provide a great game. Flowing football was sporadic and the players who distinguished themselves did so through effort and application and then a bit more graft; tracking runs, blocking shots and throwing themselves into tackles. Jordan Gibson deserves special mention at this point, a player who must surely regard himself as a flair player, one who might prise open opposition defences, but on Saturday he demonstrated that he understood the job specification. His match stats tell one story: no goals, no assists and no shots on target, on the pitch for seventy-nine minutes. But the other story is the constant closing down and harrying, nipping at opposition players in possession and generally being a thorough nuisance to play against. His midfield mate, Callum Guy can be included in the same tribute. You have to earn the right to sit in fourth place. There will be other occasions when you can strut your stuff.

Let's also look at Kristian Dennis. As the league's joint top scorer, he resisted the temptation to rest on his current reputation. He is constantly on the move, a nightmare to mark in the six-yard box, and also capable of some very impressive first touches outside the box. But he won his biggest round of applause on Saturday for running twenty yards to close down a defender attempting to make a clearance and conceding a throw in in the opposition's third. The fans loved it and you can imagine what his team mates thought as their goal-scoring colleague was putting in as big a shift as anyone else at the top end of the pitch. But back to that first touch and Dennis's first meaningful contribution to the game when he was first to react to a bouncing ball just inside the Carlisle half. His beautifully weighted first-time ball was a gift for John-Kymani Gordon to lock on to. That he would beat the Rochdale centre-half for pace was never in doubt and his finish past the keeper was equally certain. Eight minutes played and Carlisle were one up. Cue mayhem in the visiting supporters' stand.

But, beware of the early goal. Beware of complacency and of expectations of an easy victory. Be wary of any team who have just conceded. It was time to dig in and not make any mistakes for the remainder of the first half. This is what Carlisle did. Rochdale huffed and puffed, they had two dangerous looking forwards in Rodney and Dodgon but they lacked guile in getting the ball to them. The Carlisle central pairing of Huntington and Morgan Feeney were able to deal with the lofted ball straight down the pitch. Jon Mellish, in a disciplined performance, was on hand to offer his considerable support, while Keeper, Thomas Holy, commanded his box and competently gathered anything that came his way. Another goal for Carlisle would have been useful but nobody would turn down the clean sheet they held at half-time.

More patchiness in the second half. Gordon menaced a visibly nervous defence and took a battering for his pains, but boy, was he up for it. A loanee from Crystal Palace, he's bought into something at Brunton Park and he is certain to become a crowd favourite. Despite his efforts though, Rochdale were still only a goal down and still in the game, only a deflection or an unpredictable bounce away from a precious point. They changed personnel, they upped their huff and puff and started to look for angles from which to launch their high balls into the box and all credit to them for not folding after conceding an early goal.

Carlisle made their first substitution, replacing the potent Gordon with Omari Patrick in a surprise to some observers. Surely the Rochdale defenders would be relieved to see the back of Gordon. Stating the obvious, substitutions are a crucial part of football and a manager's reputation can be won or lost in his ability to read the game and make changes accordingly. A like for like swap must be made in the hope of a positive difference. This is what Patrick actually achieved, offering a different kind of threat; equally pacy but with good close control skills, he triggered an improvement in Carlisle's performance. Moxon chose this moment to illuminate the whole match with a Zidane type drag back and turn which he followed with a lofted ball to Gibson who killed it instantly with a perfect first touch and Carlisle mounted a period of pressure which included a series of corners. This was proof positive of telling use of substitutes and as the Carlisle fans well know, in their dug out they've got Super Paul Simpson.

In the end, Rochdale showed their own depths of resilience, Carlisle were unable to get a second goal and that almost cost them dearly. A cheap free kick conceded, another lofted ball into the box which Huntington for once could not clear and a Rochdale player pounced on the resultant second ball to plant his own header past Holy. A late goal conceded, we've been there before and it hurts, but the referee was persuaded to go and consult his assistant who had been dilatory with the use of his flag. With sixteen hundred Carlisle fans behind him offering their opinion, the assistant decided that yes, the Rochdale player was indeed off-side. The decision was greeted like a winning goal, but it was close folks, it was close. Have a check on YouTube.

Tough on Rochdale, but as a resigning Prime Minister once said, "Them's the breaks." The players had dug deep, the Carlisle fans had done really well, including when graciously applauding the girls football team as they paraded their piece of silverware on their half-time lap of honour. Class from team and fans alike, but now it was time to go home.

The Cumbrian diaspora means that not everyone was heading back over Shap. Our party crossed the Pennines back towards Yorkshire navigating the light fog and drizzle on the M62, with the thought of another three points in the bag and each of us, I suspect, accompanied by the earworm, "He knows exactly what we need."

John Clarke

Tuesday 31 January 2023. Carlisle United v Barrow. Brunton Park. EFL League 2.

After Carlisle's season-defining win at Oldham in early March last year, I wrote the following words. "This was the kind of day that makes the years of defeats, disappointment and disillusionment seem worthwhile." Tuesday night at Brunton Park was another of those occasions.

There wasn't quite the degree of jeopardy that was involved in the Oldham game but there was still plenty at stake. With Barrow the opponents, this counted as a 'local' derby, even though the two teams are from opposite poles of the county. That's what counts for local in an area as remote as Cumbria! Pre-match ticket sales suggested that the game was likely to be played in front of Brunton Park's highest attendance of the season. Most importantly, a win would take us into one of the three automatic promotion places. I admitted to Adam that I had a worrying hunch about this game. I've been to similar games before where there's been high anticipation and a big crowd, and Carlisle have tended to freeze and fail to deliver.

The first sign that things were going to be different from the previous week's Tuesday game against Hartlepool was when we had to queue on the slip road as we left the M6. We crawled along Warwick Road for about ten minutes before arriving at our usual car park to find it almost full. When we arrived at about the same time last week it was barely a quarter full! I sent Adam and Ben ahead to secure a crush barrier place in the Paddock while I parked up. Warwick Road was heaving with supporters as I walked to the ground, and there was a sense of excitement I hadn't experienced in a long time.

Paul Simpson sprang some surprises in his team selection. The two strikers who had scored five of Carlisle's previous six goals were both on the substitutes' bench. Neither Kris Dennis, joint leading scorer in League Two, nor JK Gordon, scorer of two superb goals since arrival on loan, got a start, though they were both to play a part in due course. They were replaced by Joe Garner and Omari Patrick who had both come on as substitutes in the previous two games. Ben Barclay, who had not played in the first team since August due to a long-term injury replaced Joel Senior at right wing-back. In our wisdom, we Wakefield Blues decided that this was a shrewd ploy to outflank Barrow's tactical preparation for the game, rather than ill-advised meddling with a winning combination! If Simmo thought this was the best thing to do, then we trusted his judgement. Barrow's starting eleven featured three former Blues: competent defender Patrick Brough; Richie Bennett who Carlisle originally signed from Barrow when they were still in the National League, a tall but slightly lumbering and clumsy striker; and goalkeeper Paul Farman, he of the strange match-ball-rubbing pre-match ritual and purveyor of intermittent howlers.

It was indeed the highest home attendance of the season, 9,351. Barrow brought almost a thousand supporters, but that still meant that there was an increase of more than 3,000 in the number of Carlisle fans who turned up, compared with last week's midweek game.

For the first forty-four minutes, in unpleasantly wet and windy conditions, Carlisle seemed to be confirming my pre-match fears that they would bottle the big occasion. Barrow dominated possession, were quicker to claim loose balls, and were stronger in the tackle. As half-time approached I reflected that Barrow had 'won' the first half on points, that we were lucky to reach half-time on level terms, and that Simpson would have to make some tweaks at the interval. He'd already made one adjustment, moving Jon Mellish from left centre back to midfield, in an attempt to counter Barrow's dominance of possession, though apparently to little effect.

In the final minute of the half, Mellish received the ball on the edge of the area in what the highlights suggest was a suspiciously offside position. He took one touch to control the ball and then prod it past the advancing Farman. It was a lead Carlisle barely deserved, but there were no offside protests from the Barrow defence. It re-enforced the cliché that when you're doing well fortune tends to favour you. Even so, Adam admitted later that he thought that having gained an unmerited lead, the second half would be a case of careful game management, seeing things out to clinch the points.

How wrong he was! The second half was an entirely different affair and was the best forty-five minutes of football I've seen Carlisle play this season, indeed for a number of seasons. God knows what the final score would have been if they could have maintained this standard for a full ninety minutes.

The second half was just five minutes old when Owen Moxon won a robust challenge in the Carlisle half and played a defence-splitting long pass into the path of Joe Garner, some ten yards outside the penalty box. He carried the ball forward before cutting inside and drilling a low shot home. His delight at scoring his first goal for Carlisle in ten years was clear for all to see. To describe his celebrations as energetic would be an understatement!

It was effectively game over in the 67th minute when Jordan Gibson slipped the ball through to Mellish just inside the Barrow penalty area, and he took a moment to steady himself before confidently slotting the ball past Farman.

But Carlisle weren't finished. Five minutes later, Moxon who had produced a "Zidane-like turn" (copyright John Clarke) against Rochdale on Saturday, produced a similar moment of magic, but this time inside the opposition penalty area. He would have been perfectly justified in having a shot at goal himself, but instead he laid the ball back on a plate to the oncoming Omari Patrick who calmly side footed home.

Two minutes later Simpson decided that his strikers had done their business for the night and substituted them both. What a luxury – your team is 4-0 up, and you can bring on the joint leading scorer in the division as a substitute! That's why I'm so optimistic about the rest of the season. Rather than having a bare-bones squad who produce the goods against the odds, we now have quality options in all areas of the pitch.

The euphoria was slightly dampened in the 84th minute when Barrow pulled a goal back, denying Carlisle another clean sheet. Even then they had to rely on Carlisle to score the goal for them! A cross into the Carlisle box was bound for the head of a Barrow striker only for Ben Barclay to intervene and head into his own net.

I turned to Adam and said to him that there was still time for Kris Dennis to add to his tally. He duly obliged. In the 88th minute yet another superb pass put Gordon in the clear, but with plenty still to do. As he rounded the keeper for what looked like his third excellent finish in four games, Farman maintained his reputation for periodic howlers to bring him crashing to the ground. Dennis calmly dispatched the ensuing penalty.

Adam is still struggling to come to terms with what we witnessed. He's only ever seen Carlisle score more than three goals once, and that was in our 4-1 win at Salford a few weeks ago. In fact, I can only remember a couple of such occasions myself and they were both back in the Seventies! I can remember a 6-1 Boxing Day win against Preston before promotion to the First Division, and a 5-0 victory over Swindon Town following relegation back to Division Two.

This result means that we have scored six more goals than any other team in League Two, and our positive goal difference of twenty-one is matched only by Stevenage. Kris Dennis is now out on his own as League Two's leading goal scorer having scored seventeen goals (plus one in the Carabao Cup). Carlisle are currently the form team in League Two with six wins in their last seven games, the only blip being the New Year's Day defeat at Doncaster Rovers. Most importantly we now occupy the third automatic promotion place.

It's remarkable how expectations have gradually been ratcheted up as the season progresses. After Paul Simpson's stunning rescue act in the final third of last season, I'd have happily settled for mid-table this season, threatening neither the relegation or the play-off places. As a solid start to the season developed, I began to think that the play-offs might be a possibility and was delighted when we actually made it into the top seven. As the good form continued, I began to wonder if we might challenge for the automatic promotion places, though Orient, Stevenage and Northampton were well clear of the chasing pack. Well, we overhauled Northampton with this result, and are just six points behind leaders Orient, who have won only once in their last six games. A few weeks ago, Orient and Stevenage seemed to be disappearing over the hill and out of sight. Now they appear eminently catchable.

I fervently hope that the extra 3,000 Carlisle fans who turned out on Tuesday evening are motivated by this magnificent performance to come back to Brunton Park on Saturday, when the visitors are Harrogate Town.

FEBRUARY 2023

Saturday 4 February 2023. Carlisle United v Harrogate Town. Brunton Park. EFL League 2.

I hate Harrogate Town! Tim Pocock voiced vary similar sentiments back in November when we bumped into each other on the way out of the ground, after a last-minute equaliser from Owen Moxon had salvaged a 3-3 draw in the reverse fixture at Wetherby Road. Harrogate are undoubtedly Carlisle's bogey team. In seven fixtures since Harrogate gained promotion to the Football League we've failed to beat them once, in either League or cup competition, losing more games than we've drawn.

Nonetheless, we travelled with the perfectly reasonable expectation that this would be the day on which this particular bogey would be laid to rest. Surely a team that had won six out of their last seven games, the most recent being a 5-1 thrashing of a promotion rival, would see off a team that had not won in their last five games, amassing just two points along the way.

Paul Simpson rang the changes again, replacing Tuesday night starters and scorers Joe Garner and Omari Patrick with the scorers in the three previous wins, Kristian Dennis and JK Gordon.

I didn't expect a repeat of Tuesday night's champagne performance against Barrow, but I certainly didn't expect the comedown to be quite so brutal. Carlisle started the game in the same way they finished Tuesday's game, slicing through the Harrogate defence with ease, and creating two chances in the first minute of the game. Six corners to Carlisle and none to Harrogate in the first half tells its own story. Carlisle were so dominant that surely it was only a matter of time before a goal came? Even though it didn't, I comforted myself that the first goal in Tuesday night's 5-1 win (have I mentioned that before?) didn't come until the 45th minute.

As the second half progressed and the breakthrough still failed to materialise, frustration grew both on the pitch and on the terraces. Rain sweeping across the ground further dampened the spirits of the supporters. The situation wasn't helped by some appalling officiating by both referee and his assistants. This was best summed up when Kris Dennis screamed in frustration at the linesman on our side of the pitch, "Just try using your fucking eyes!"

But surely the statistics should speak for themselves. Carlisle had nineteen shots, eight of which were on target. Harrogate had three shots, none of which were close to being on target. Carlisle had ten corners to Harrogate's two. So how the hell did Harrogate manage to win when they didn't have a single shot on target? It looked like we were simply going to be frustrated by our failure to take more than a point from a game we should have won easily.

The answer came in the eighty second minute. Harrogate harmlessly booted the ball upfield from a Carlisle attack. All that was required was a simple cushion header from Mr Reliable central defender Paul Huntington to goalkeeper Tomas Holy. I don't know whether there was a breakdown in communication, but Huntington inexplicably let the ball bounce before side-footing it past the advancing Holy. It was the worst kind of own goal, gifting three points to a team who had shown a total inability to score themselves.

Garner and Patrick, already on as substitutes, generated more chances, none of which were converted. The nearest Carlisle came to an equaliser was a swerving and dipping free kick from another substitute, Jamie Devitt, which was heading just under the bar before the keeper tipped it over.

There were always going to be days like this. Having made it into the top three, it would be naïve to think that the rest of the season would progress serenely, winning six out of every seven games. Nonetheless this was a pretty harsh reality check. It's important that this is only a blip, rather than the beginning of the type of bad run which we've yet to experience.

There was a minor Brunton Bonus for Adam on the way home. As usual we broke our journey home at Scotch Corner services. Adam and Aden went into Burger King to get some fries and who should be sitting there waiting for his order but midfielder Alfie McCalmont, currently on loan from Leeds United. Apparently, Paul Simpson had given the squad a couple of days off, with no midweek fixture, and Alfie was on his way home to West Yorkshire. It must have been a pretty short after-match debrief for him to have got to Scotch Corner before we did! Anyway, Adam had a brief chat with him, both agreeing that the afternoon's fare had been pretty dismal!

The attendance was 6,422, almost 3,000 down on Tuesday night. However, Barrow had brought almost a thousand fans while Harrogate could only just manage a hundred! So the underlying home attendance was up by over a thousand, though it would have been nice to retain more of Tuesday's supporters.

After three trips to Carlisle in twelve days, with further trips to Birmingham and Rochdale thrown in, I'm quite relieved that the next home fixture isn't until a week on Tuesday. Saturday's away game at Wimbledon is out of range. Nearly four hours in each direction is too far to drive and the train fare to London is prohibitive.

Saturday 11 February 2023. AFC Wimbledon v Carlisle United. Plough Lane (not the Cherry Red Records Stadium!). EFL League 2.

I'm glad we didn't travel to this one! As I stated in my last post, I didn't fancy the drive, and a £200 return train fare for Adam and myself was out of the question, probably due to not checking prices until about a week before we might have travelled. Not that such factors prevented more than a thousand Carlisle fans making the journey to Plough Lane, more than six times the number of Wimbledon fans who made the reverse journey back in September last year. Interestingly, if I was to book train tickets now for our away game at Orient on 1 April, it would cost less than half the price.

I've also looked at prices to London for the last game of the season, on the Monday Bank Holiday following the king's coronation. Kick-off is at 12.30, which is ridiculous given the distance Carlisle fans will have to travel, for what might be a season-defining game, determining whether we secure automatic promotion or qualify for the play-offs. If things are at stake we want to be there. But if it's a dead game, for whatever reason, do we want to be booking train tickets now (still at considerable expense) for what might be a meaningless game? Maybe I should check the train operators' cancellation policies. Ah, the delights of public transport in the 2020s.

Before I embark on the details of today's game, I want to pay tribute to everyone associated with AFC Wimbledon over the decades. I'm old enough to remember when non-league Wimbledon took the then mighty Leeds United to a hard-fought F.A. Cup reply in 1975, largely thanks to the heroics of their goalkeeper. How many of my readers remember Dicky Guy? Remarkably, just over thirteen years later, Wimbledon defeated Liverpool to win the F.A. Cup, having achieved a dizzying ascent to the topflight of English football.

However, following a number of changes of ownership, Wimbledon became the first victim of franchise football in England, with the club relocating to Milton Keynes and being renamed MK Dons. All credit to the supporters and officials who proceeded to establish AFC Wimbledon and fight their way through the non-league pyramid to regain league status.

Not that any of that counted for anything today. We needed to bounce back quickly after last Saturday's misfortune against Harrogate Town. After certain technical difficulties, which it transpired were a result of a power cut at Plough Lane, we finally managed to get the live feed of the game. We hadn't missed anything. The first half was poor, the ball spending far too much time in the air and neither team really fashioning meaningful chances.

In the final quarter of the game Carlisle were very much on the front foot, putting the Wimbledon defence under frequent pressure, though The Dons did have their chances on the break.

League Two's leading scorers have suddenly become toothless, failing to score in their last two games and only picking up one point. Simmo needs to decide what is the best attacking selection, given the potential embarrassment of riches at his disposal. I have my own view, but I'll keep that to myself for the moment. We're still in third place and two games without a win hardly constitutes a crisis, but we need to get back to winning ways when we travel up to Carlisle on Tuesday evening for the home game against Mansfield.

Tuesday 14 February 2023. Carlisle United v Mansfield Town. Brunton Park. EFL League 2.

That'll teach me to go to Brunton Park on a Tuesday evening rather than stay at home for a Valentine's Day meal with Lisa!

This was an utterly dreadful evening. Just a fortnight ago, after the 5-1 thrashing of Barrow, I was writing about that being one of those special nights that make all the agonies of being a committed supporter worthwhile. Just a fortnight later I find myself at the other end of the spectrum. This game was a nightmare, the like of which you fervently hope never to witness again. Ironically it came almost a year to the day after last season's low point, the 3-0 home defeat to Swindon Town, which I described as one the worst days in my long career as a Carlisle supporter. That was the game that prompted the return of Paul Simpson as manager. One can only hope that last night's debacle prompts the same kind of winning run that followed the humiliation against Swindon.

I should have read the signs. Adam, Ben and I left Crofton under blue skies in bright, late afternoon sunshine. As we approached the A1M/A64 junction near Aberford, it appeared that someone had suddenly dimmed the lights. The sky clouded over, and we were already driving through early evening gloom. By the time we were heading north of Wetherby things had worsened, with fog rolling in. It didn't slow us down unduly, but it made driving a bit more stressful – no chance of flicking on cruise-control! The fog persisted until we were about 5-10 miles beyond Scotch Corner, when the grey gloom finally dispersed. As we were heading west, the last vestiges of daylight were still visible in the sky for some time.

On arrival, the car park was significantly emptier than on recent visits, and the walk along Warwick Road to the ground was noticeably less busy. I popped into the

Blues Store to see if I could pick up a back copy of the programme for the Wimbledon game in September, the only one missing from our collection for this season. It transpired that the programmes for that game had sold out in no time, as apparently everyone wanted a programme for the first home game after the death of the Queen. That's why we didn't have one in the first place – might have to resort to Facebook or Twitter!

The pre-match playlist was selected by captain Morgan Feeney. It consisted largely of songs from the Seventies and Eighties, which was music to this supporter's ears!

And then the game started. The initial signs were promising. Carlisle appeared to be on the front foot, winning tackles, and showing quick movement and slick passing. Then, after fourteen minutes, Mansfield crossed from the left and a player rose to head home unchallenged. A setback maybe, but there was plenty of time to get things back on track.

Ten minutes later Tomas Holy tipped over a speculative ball into the box which appeared to be dipping just below the crossbar. The ensuing corner, again from the left, was again headed home unchallenged. Only four minutes later Morgan Feeney was penalised (perhaps harshly?) for a challenge in the area, and the ensuing penalty made it 3-0 and started to take us into the realms of the scarcely believable.

But there was still time for it to get worse before half-time. On thirty-nine minutes the Carlisle defence was again sliced open with alarming ease, and Mansfield were 4-0 ahead, all the goals scored within a twenty-five-minute period.

By this point I was casting my mind back to see if I could recall any worse performances by Carlisle at Brunton Park. I recalled a dismal day in the Seventies when we lost 6-0 at home to Southampton in what used to be the Second Division. The next paragraph will be meaningful only to readers of a certain vintage, but I'll go ahead anyway!

Research reveals that the said game took place on 22 January, in front of 9,617 fans, of which I was one, having hitch-hiked home for the weekend from Durham University, mainly to watch this game. What is remarkable is the Southampton line-up that day. It included, amongst others, Alan Ball, Peter Osgood, Ted MacDougall and Mick Channon. Some of that team might have been in the twilight of their career, but it was a team that had been good enough to beat Manchester United to win the previous season's F.A. Cup, as a Second Division team.

Back to Tuesday night. Simmo went for bust after half-time. Two defenders were taken off, and two strikers were brought on, meaning all four of Carlisle's fit strikers were on the pitch together. Carlisle duly poured forward in the second half, creating a number of chances, but they were up against a Mansfield team who knew that they only had to protect the massive lead they'd already established. The support from the stands and terraces remained remarkably positive, perhaps a reflection that the attendance of 4,645, merely half of the crowd for the Barrow triumph, probably represented the hard core of support, who stick with the team through thick and thin.

Despite the second-half endeavours, there were too many cases of missed challenges, misplaced passes and passes that went straight into touch. How can a team that had won five out of six games, and become the division's leading goalscorers suddenly only gain one point from a possible nine and fail to score a single goal in three games, if you discount Ben Barclay's own goal against Barrow? Remarkably, we've still clung on to third place, but the cushion we'd established over chasing teams four games ago has all but vanished, and we desperately need a win over Colchester on Saturday, which will be the first home league game we've been unable to attend this season.

It was a long drive home!

Saturday 18 February 2023. Carlisle United v Colchester United. Brunton Park. EFL League 2.

That was more like it!

It was slightly odd missing a home league game for the first time this season, but I can't say I missed the drive to Carlisle and back. The journey is usually pretty straightforward, but it's a long time at the wheel, particularly when games are coming close together. I like to think it's a case of driver fatigue rather than loyalty fatigue!

As Carlisle looked to get back on track after failing to score in three games and only gaining one point in those games, Colchester United weren't the ideal opponents. Having struggled at the wrong end of the table for the first half of the season, they spent big in the January transfer window, and it appeared to have paid dividends. They came into this game having lost just once in eleven matches, and a win in this fixture would set a club record for successive away wins. They were very much the form team in League 2.

Paul Simpson made four changes to the line-up that started Tuesday night's debacle against Mansfield. Jack Ellis returned at right wing back following injury, and the strikers were rotated again, with Joe Garner and Omari Patrick starting in place of Kris Dennis and JK Gordon. The biggest surprise was the selection of Leeds United loanee Alfie McCalmont as an attacking midfielder in place of Jordan Gibson. Previously McCalmont had only made a couple of late appearances off the bench. It proved to be an inspired choice. With barely four minutes gone, McCalmont seized on a weak headed pass to his goalkeeper by a Colchester defender and calmly side footed the ball home. It was just the start Carlisle needed.

We were watching the live stream of the game, and as the first half progressed, it was difficult to see why Colchester were on such a successful run. To be fair to Carlisle, that was probably because the home team gave them little chance to establish a foothold in the game.

1-0 at half-time turned into 1-0 at full-time. Both sides had chances during the second half, but Colchester failed to manage a single attempt on target in the whole game. This was another game where the result was much more important than the performance. Not that the performance was bad, but this was a day when it was essential that Carlisle ground out a result, and that's exactly what they did.

This result means that Carlisle have re-established a three-point margin over Northampton Town in fourth place, who lost their game. It also means they are seven points away from dropping out of the play-off places. Furthermore, the attendance of 5,550 was a distinct improvement on Tuesday evening, as Colchester brought only 150 supporters. Hopefully things are back on track.

Thursday 23 February 2023.

This is not a match report (when have EFL clubs played games on a Thursday evening?!) but it would be remiss of me to let the first anniversary of Paul Simpson's return to the managerial hot seat at Brunton Park pass without comment.

Exactly a year ago Carlisle United were in 23rd place in League Two, occupying one of the two relegation places. As I write, they are in third place, occupying one of the automatic promotion places. That in itself is remarkable. What is equally remarkable is that this transformation has been achieved with a team largely composed of the same players who struggled through last season. On a weekly basis the starting line-up only has three or four players who have joined the club since the end of last season.

I'm not going to imitate Jon Colman, in the Carlisle News and Star, who assembles an impressive array of statistics to demonstrate the transformation Paul Simpson has brought about. Instead, I'm going to focus on raw passion and emotion. The home defeat to Swindon Town, just over a year ago, that precipitated Simpson's return, was one of the most depressing and discouraging afternoons I have ever spent at Brunton Park. It bore all the hallmarks of a club in terminal decline. The run of fifteen games at the end of last season that saw Carlisle climb to comfortable safety was one of my best experiences as a supporter of more than fifty years vintage.

Nonetheless, I think there was a widespread feeling that "The Great Escape" was a one-off, and that we would have to settle for a more prosaic reality this season. How wrong we were! This season may have lacked the jeopardy that hung over the end of last season, but it has been full of memorable performances and moments to match last year's survival.

But the transformation that Paul Simpson has brought about is not just about performances on the pitch. The whole mood surrounding the club is entirely different. Home attendances are significantly improved, and the away support is absolutely magnificent, particularly given the geographical remoteness of the club. There are very few negative words on the terraces and in the stands, even on the occasional bad days. There is a sense that the supporters have an underlying belief in the work that Paul Simpson is doing and are happy to tolerate the occasional blips because they believe in the bigger picture of progress.

Simpson has also assembled an impressive backroom team, particularly in bringing back former manager Greg Abbott as Head of Recruitment. As a result, we are now attracting loanees from Premier League clubs rather than last season's Championship recruits, who largely failed to impress.

I should also pay tribute to our former Director of Football, David Houldsworth. His departure coincided with Simpson's arrival at the club (no prizes for deducing that the two events were connected!). His absence from the club has facilitated many of the changes that Simpson has introduced, that would not have happened under his stewardship. Thank god he went.

On a final, personal and egotistical note, it looks like I've found a publisher for this and last season's journal, which will hopefully be in print by the end of the year.

Saturday 25 February 2023. Crawley Town v Carlisle United. Broadfield 'Stadium'. EFL League 2.

There was never a realistic possibility that we would make the lengthy trek to Crawley, Carlisle's longest away trip of the season. Massive respect, therefore, for the 504 hardy souls who did make the journey, most of whom had a considerably longer trip than we would have had from Wakefield. And boy, were they richly rewarded for their loyalty!

I'd gone into Wakefield to shop for some new clothes (a fruitless mission!) so Adam and Ben had decided to watch the first-half round at Ben's house. That meant

I had no access to the game when I got home at about ten past three. I was reduced to checking my phone for score updates – and it seemed that every time I did so, another goal had gone in! To be 4-0 up, away from home, after less than forty minutes was behind anyone's wildest expectations. Even better, all the first-half goals were scored at the away end, in front of the delirious travelling fans. By half-time, it felt as if the horror show eleven days ago against Mansfield, when we were on the receiving end of a similar blitz, had been fully exorcised.

Without wishing to sound complacent, it was reasonable to assume that it was game over by quarter to four. I've seen the first-half goals since, and there are some real crackers. A superb run down the left flank by Jon Mellish was followed by an excellent cross. It was met by right-wing back Jordan Senior racing into the area to score with a powerful diving header. A few minutes later an excellent through ball was calmly slotted home by Omari Patrick. No assist was needed for the third goal, Owen Moxon embarking on a mazy run through the Crawley defence before calmly planting the ball in the net.

Adam and Ben were back here by four o'clock, which meant I was able to enjoy the second half, courtesy of Ben's firestick. It was all a bit anti-climactic to be honest! Crawley pulled back a goal early in the second half, but it didn't take long for Carlisle to restore their four-goal advantage when Jon Mellish bundled home one of numerous Carlisle second-half corners.

On sixty-five minutes, with his team 5-1 ahead away from home, it appeared that Paul Simpson was adding insult to injury by bringing on Kris Dennis, League Two's joint leading scorer, as a substitute. Crawley did score a second goal shortly before the end of the game, but it was pretty academic by then.

I'm going to indulge in a few statistics to extend this post. by winning today, Carlisle didn't just consolidate their third place in League Two, they moved above Stevenage into second place. After Carlisle beat Crawley 1-0 on the opening day of the season at Brunton Park, the two clubs have followed diametrically opposed trajectories. While Carlisle sit second from the top, Crawley are second from bottom, occupying a relegation place, just a year after Carlisle occupied a similar situation. The bright future that their new crypto-currency owners were meant to bring has failed to materialise, as they are currently on their third manager of the current season.

Last season Carlisle failed to score more than two goals in a game during the entire season. This season they have managed to score three goals or more five times in away games alone. When you add to that the fact that they have achieved the same feat in four home games, that means that they have scored at least three goals in more than a quarter of their league games this season.

It's a long time since supporting Carlisle has been as good as this, and for such an extended period. I'm increasingly optimistic about end-of-season outcomes.

MARCH 2023

Saturday 4 March 2023. Carlisle United v Grimsby Town. Brunton Park. EFL League 2.

It felt like an age since we'd last attended a game in person, and indeed it was by this season's standards. It was a whole eighteen days since we witnessed the shambles against Mansfield. I wasn't particularly looking forward to the long drive to Carlisle and back, but the journey in both directions proved to be surprisingly quick and trouble-free.

It was difficult to know how to view this game in advance. Grimsby arrived at Brunton Park fresh from their F.A. Cup triumph over Premier League Southampton just three days earlier, a win that made them the first team from the fourth tier of The Football League to reach the last eight of the competition in God knows how many years. At the same time, they occupied a very modest sixteenth place in League Two, and we had beaten them on their own patch back in October. There were some supporters who feared that we were coming up against a team who were flying high, while others, me included, felt that their players would be preoccupied with the cup run, and would be desperate to avoid injury before the quarter final.

The team selection by Paul Hirst, the Grimsby manager, suggested that he felt their League status was relatively safe, and that he was prioritising the cup. There were seven changes to the starting line-up that had humiliated Southampton. In contrast, the only change to the Carlisle team was the recall of Jordan Gibson to play at right wing back in place of Joel Senior, who had been suffering from illness in the latter part of the week, though he was well enough to take a place among the substitutes.

Early signs were encouraging. Carlisle pressed Grimsby hard and were quick into the tackle. However, in possession things weren't quite clicking. Too many well-intentioned passes either failed to find their target or went straight out of play. If anything, Grimsby fashioned a couple of the best chances in the first third of the game, and Tomas Holy had to make an excellent one-handed save to keep his goal intact.

However, Carlisle continued to press the Grimsby defence, and in the 36th minute pressure from the front three paid dividends. The ball fell to Alfie McCalmont who calmly curled the ball home for his second goal in three starts. It was probably a slightly undeserved lead.

In the 45th minute Joe Garner found Owen Moxon in space, and he in turn played in Jordan Gibson down the right. He beat his marker convincingly before finishing decisively with a cross shot. A 2-0 halftime scoreline was probably slightly flattering to Carlisle, but the secret to success is sometimes still scoring goals even when not playing particularly well. For any stats freaks out there, this was the ninth time in thirty-four games this season that Carlisle have scored in the last couple of minutes of the first half, and on the last six occasions it has led to a victory.

The second half was much more fluent, though ironically with no more goals to show for it. I'm not a great fan of stats, but I'm happy to use them when they're in my favour! Grimsby had 56% of possession overall, and managed three shots, only one of which was on target. From their smaller share of possession Carlisle managed thirteen shots, five of which were on goal. I think that an early goal in the second half might have opened the floodgates, and calmer finishing in front of the Warwick Road end would certainly have ensured a wider margin.

Nonetheless, this was a business-like win, the third in a row. We're into the final quarter of the season, and we still haven't experienced a significant blip. Our mood was further improved by the news that Stevenage had suffered an unexpected defeat at Rochdale, the bottom club in the division, meaning that we leapfrogged them back into second place. Automatic promotion is now a very real possibility, with a place in the play-offs the minimum expectation. But there remains the nagging worry that it could all fall apart in the last twelve games. I don't think it will but, without wanting to wish my life away, I'd rather we were a bit closer to the final denouement!

Saturday 11 March 2023. Swindon Town v Carlisle United. The County Ground. EFL League 2.

This game saw the beginning of a challenging run-in to the end of the season. Of the twelve remaining games, nine are against teams in the top half of the league table as it currently stands, and they still have to play every team in the automatic and play-off places. It's a double-edged sword really – every game is a demanding fixture, but every win is worth more as it extends the gap between Carlisle and their rivals. This really is the "business end" of the season.

At this point last season, the club were embarking on the remarkable run that took Carlisle well clear of the threat of relegation. On the corresponding weekend last year, a Jordan Gibson penalty in the final minute of time added on earned a win over promotion hopefuls Northampton Town. This weekend we sat in second place in the division, with the focus being on retaining that place.

We didn't travel for this game, Swindon being a bit beyond our range, but Adam, Ben and I did settle down to watch the live stream of the game. All credit to the 558 fans who did make the trip from even further afield.

The first half was largely unremarkable. Swindon had the lion's share of possession, but Carlisle probably fashioned the best chances. The only remarkable thing was the incompetence of the Swindon commentator and summarizer. They spent the first thirty minutes, mistaking Omari Patrick for Crystal Palace loanee JK Gordon, who was sat on the bench throughout the first half. I suppose it's an easy mistake to make – they're both black and both sport dreadlocks! I really thought that kind of howler was a thing of the past.

Things fortunately livened up in the second half. In the 51st minute an Owen Moxon corner was curled towards the near post. Swindon's Charlie Austin headed against the angle of post and crossbar. As the ball rebounded it was scuffed clear, but only into the path of Carlisle left-wing back Jack Armer, who lashed home a superb right-foot volley into the top corner of the goal. Armer is putting together a very strong case for being player of the season.

There were a couple of further half-chances, but as time ticked on Carlisle seemed to have settled for containment and game management. We grew increasingly uneasy as Swindon were allowed to come at Carlisle, and our worst fears were confirmed when Swindon scored an eightieth minute equaliser. Carlisle suddenly had to reset from defending what they'd got to getting back on the front foot in search of the win.

By this stage Carlisle's strike force had completely changed. Ryan Edmondson, returning after an almost three-month injury lay-off, had replaced Joe Garner in the 68th minute, and immediately after the Swindon equalizer John Kymani Gordon replaced Omari Patrick, no doubt causing further confusion to the Swindon commentary team. Leading scorer Kristian Dennis appeared to have been relegated to fifth-choice striker! I shouldn't have doubted Paul Simpson's judgement.

As Carlisle went in search of a late winner, I'd already settled for a draw, and was hoping for an early final whistle. When a surprising five added minutes were announced I was concerned rather than pleased, as it allowed more time for Swindon to snatch an undeserved winner. A clash of heads meant that yet more time was added. It did, however, allow Carlisle to win a couple of further corners. The first was wasted as Owen Moxon merely floated the ball onto the roof of the Swindon net. The second was won when the pressing of Gordon forced a defensive error in the dying seconds. This time Moxon's delivery was perfect. The ball swung in towards the far post where Edmondson headed home from about three yards. Cue bedlam as most of the substitutes and coaching staff raced along the touchline to join the celebrations. When the game restarted the referee played just twenty further seconds before blowing the final whistle.

Exactly a year on, we had again won with a goal in the dying seconds. Paul Simpson's attacking substitutions proved to be spot on, with one striker winning the decisive corner, and the other putting it away. The win keeps us in second place and means there's currently a nine-point margin before we'd drop out of the play-off places. Euphoria was mingled with disbelief at the end of the game!

Next up are Stevenage at Brunton Park, who are just a point behind us, with a game in hand. A win would be massive and it's probably the biggest game of the season to date. Unfortunately, I won't be there, as parental duties summon me south, to watch eldest daughter Ellie in a dance production at Birmingham University. Adam and Ben are desperately trying to find an alternative way of getting to Brunton Park on the 18th of March, not helped by the fact that that date sees further strike disruption to the rail network. Normal service will be resumed when we head to Valley Parade the following Tuesday.

Saturday 18 March 2023. Carlisle United v Stevenage. Brunton Park. EFL League 2.

Adam and Ben's travel problems were quickly resolved. My good friend, John Clarke, who had originally contacted me in the hope of a lift to the game, decided he was going to go anyway under his own steam, and generously offered to take the lads with him. And given my commitments elsewhere, I'm indebted to John for much of the content of this post.

The much-vaunted "biggest game of the season" turned out to be something of an anti-climax. Firstly, because I wasn't there myself; secondly because John and the lads had a massive traffic delay at Penrith that meant that they missed the first few minutes of the game; thirdly because the result was a largely unimpressive 0-0 draw (see below for John's match analysis).

About 250 miles south in Birmingham, I feel I was very self-disciplined during Ellie's dance production. I only checked for score updates every two dances. Given that there were over thirty numbers in the show, I think that's an impressive act of self-denial!

The draw means that we've dropped out of the automatic promotion places, with Northampton leapfrogging us, but a win against Bradford on Tuesday will return us to second place. Paul Simpson admitted that the team weren't at their best, but also felt that the referee was found wanting on two occasions. The first was when Paul Huntington had his shirt ripped off at a Carlisle corner and the second when substitute Ryan Edmondson was hacked down when through on goal. The rules dictate a red card, but only a yellow was shown.

The crowd was an impressive 8,029, the second-best attendance of the season, and all the more pleasing because it consisted almost entirely of Carlisle supporters. Stevenage, sitting in second place, brought a measly 141 supporters to the game. Four times as many Carlisle supporters travelled an almost identical distance to Swindon a week before.

It's over to John for the majority of the rest of this post.

"Two heavyweight fighters were stepping into the ring at Brunton Park on Saturday, second versus third in the league in what could have been described as a "must win" game in order to make a decisive promotion statement. I was reminded of December 27th, 1994 when Carlisle and Bury were the two teams battling it out for promotion from what was then the third division although it was the fourth tier of English football. Anticipation levels were high as over twelve thousand fans piled into Brunton Park to witness a handsome 3-0 victory for Carlisle.

A large crowd of eight thousand fans on Saturday weren't going to witness anything remotely handsome. In truth, the match could have been better described as a "mustn't lose" fixture as these two contenders measured each other up, dodged and feinted but failed to land any serious blows or get anywhere near delivering a knock out.

Despite my opening analogy though, this is football. Not every game is going to be a rip-roaring thriller and sometimes the spectator has to content him or herself with a tactical battle; negate your opponent's strengths and maximise your own threat. Sadly, on Saturday the match never got beyond the former. Very few chances created and no serious save made by either keeper with both back fours dominant throughout. If the battering ram isn't working then find another way, like introduce some craft and guile. In other words, get the ball down and play some football, get behind the defence and get the ball in the box. It's a truism that competent big defenders will gobble up long diagonal balls into the box, whereas turning and facing their own goal gives them indigestion. But the Stevenage defenders were never offered that problem. In the few opportunities Carlisle had to play down the wing, on each occasion the attempted cross was blocked or else it was delivered way beyond any attacking players.

It wasn't the fare which the large crowd expected. The were offered too few chances to burst into vocal support, although when Steve Evans, the Stevenage manager emerged huffing and puffing from the dug out he was soon reminded of his corpulent state and alleged illegitimacy of birth. Otherwise, the crowd watched two dominant defences and midfield play which consisted of closing down, harrying and hacking. Measured balls were few, most were lofted into a tricky wind for further bouts of scrapping when it reached ground level again. Be physically dominant and press, wait for your opponent to make a mistake, it's the pragmatic form of fourth tier football I'm told, and this is all well and good except that if your game plan is to hold on to the point you started with, it soon leads beyond football artistry towards what is euphemistically called game management. Chuckle if you will at the so-called "dark arts" but time wasting, blatant pushing, shirt-pulling and being all too ready for a bout of macho posturing, flaring-up, disrupts the flow of the game and it shortchanges the spectator.

It would be naive of anyone to expect professional footballers to act solely with regard for the beautiful game, they will do whatever they have to do and whatever they can get away with. Consequently, Saturday's game was marred, as was the home fixture with Sutton and there are no doubt other matches you might wish to add. So, what to do about this? Ideally, the home team should score early and ensure that a contest takes place, but that is not always possible of course. So, here's another idea: why doesn't the person charged with running the game actually fulfil his obligations? Too many referees turn up looking like early career teachers wanting to be friends with a class of kids who are all too ready to bend the rules as far as they will go. Letting the game flow is a laudable aim, but all too often it doesn't flow, it degenerates into a miasma of niggle. Shirt-pulling is an offence, a bookable offence, so act upon it. A player running with the ball directly towards goal with only the keeper to beat has a goal scoring opportunity. Bringing that player down is also an offence – a sending off offence – so act upon it. Until they do discharge their responsibilities efficiently, match officials will be conniving in the dark arts to the detriment of the game.

Rant over with just enough time to deal with some specifics. Callum Guy was awarded Man of the Match and this was fair enough when there was no outstanding candidate on either side. Guy was committed throughout, nicking the ball to win possession, often taking a good kicking himself for his pains, and then spraying some delightful cross field passes which were as lovely as shafts of sunlight on a gloomy day. Alfie McCalmont also looked good, crafty at close quarters and showing awareness of the pattern of play (such as it was.) He will find better showcases for his talent than Saturday's drab affair.

And a good word for Matt who took part in the half-time crossbar challenge. After a first miserable effort, he preceded his second attempt with an attempt to gee up the Warwick Road end faithful by clapping his hands above his head in the manner of an Olympic high jumper gathering rhythm and momentum. Having built up expectation he then turned to the ball and grubbed another miserable effort along the ground, lucky to reach the goal line let alone the crossbar. Undeterred, Matt then gestured for further approbation from the Warwick. Full marks for chutzpah, young man. It was another shaft of sunlight.

As was the appearance of Trinity School girls under fourteen football team parading a trophy and doing a half pitch lap of honour to suitable applause. As they passed before our section of the Paddock, I turned to my young companion and told him that Trinity, before the introduction of comprehensives, was my alma mater. I then added that in my day, they didn't have girls there. As an afterthought I added that they didn't have football either.

So concludes Methuselah who still mourns the days of Chris Balderstone applying his craft and vision on the Brunton Park turf, and opposition teams who turned up and then were consigned to their fate as lesser mortals. A thought to toy with on trailing out of the ground.

And, in the manner of Colombo, one more thing: why do scoreless draws and score draws have parity in terms of points earned?"

Tuesday 21 March 2023. Bradford City v Carlisle United. Valley Parade. EFL League 2.

It was good to be on the road again, a whole seventeen days since I last attended a Carlisle game in the flesh. And fortunately, we chose the right road to the game. This was our shortest trip of the season, though not the quickest. We wisely didn't stay on the M62 longer than necessary, unlike Bradford supporter Tim Brookes, who spent three hours stuck on said motorway, and was reduced to listening to the audio commentary on Radio Leeds. A pity, because Tim was going to provide an opposition perspective on the match!

Bradford's Valley Parade ground towers above much of the surrounding cityscape. It is, by some distance, the most impressive stadium in League Two, and fully merits being called a stadium. The impression is slightly undermined when you enter the ground, with a rather pokey little stand at one end of the ground, and the corner from which the players emerge looks more like the changing rooms for some municipal pitches, than those of a former Premier League ground.

But there was minor drama before we even got into the ground. On being frisked as we queued for the turnstile, the steward asked me what was in one of my pockets. I explained that it was an epipen, which I always take to matches as Adam has a peanut allergy. The steward explained that it could be regarded as an offensive weapon because of the needle it contains. I don't know whether he thought I might run onto the pitch and plunge the epipen into the thigh of a Bradford player, giving him an unwanted adrenalin surge! After consultation with his superior the steward allowed me to proceed – I was just trying to be a responsible and caring parent!

The impressive stadium was matched with an equally impressive crowd. Over seventeen and a half thousand turned out for a League Two fixture, including well over twelve hundred Carlisle supporters. Even more impressive is that this was a midweek evening fixture, making it more difficult for people to get to the game.

But this wasn't just a run-of-the-mill League Two game. Carlisle started the game in fourth place with Bradford just two places behind. Both teams came into the game on the back of five-game unbeaten runs. Perhaps that explained the ensuing stalemate! The first twenty minutes were scrappy, with both teams seeking to impose themselves on the game without any real success and without any fluent football. As the half progressed, Carlisle began to dominate and had a period in the fifteen minutes before half-time that really should have been rewarded with a goal.

It was a different story in the second half. Bradford were very much in the ascendance, with the Carlisle defence straining every sinew to keep them at bay, epitomised by skipper Morgan Feeney deflecting a goal-bound shot onto the woodwork. Even so, the game almost had a dramatic denouement in the final minute of time added on, when substitute Jordan Gibson's shot hit the inside of the Bradford post before rebounding to safety. Perhaps two 96th minute winners in three games were a little too much to expect!

This game was one of those rare events, a goalless draw that was vibrant and entertaining. On the way back to the car I asked John Clarke how it compared to last Saturday's goalless draw against Stevenage. He replied that he was still trying to decide whether it was five or six hundred times better! Whatever the case, the point gained was sufficient to restore us to the third automatic promotion place.

Unfortunately, we won't be at another game for over a fortnight. The next two Saturdays see us travel to Gillingham and Orient, both very long hauls. So, we'll have to wait until the Good Friday game against Tranmere, for which the club are doing a ticket promotion, in the hope of attracting a 10,000 plus crowd.

And from that point we'll be at every game until the end of the season, assuming our status as season ticket holders will enable us to get tickets for poxy little grounds like Barrow's and Sutton United's. We've already bought train tickets to Sutton for the last game of the season, in the hope that it will be an occasion for wild celebrations!

Saturday 25 March 2023. Gillingham v Carlisle United. Priestfield Stadium. EFL League 2.

Oh dear!

This was a game that we watched live, but from afar. The long slog to Gillingham was just a bit too far, with a busy end to the season approaching. A significant number of Carlisle fans obviously felt the same way. The travelling support of 475 was significantly down from the 1250 who made the trip to Bradford on Tuesday night, though it represented a similar proportion of the overall attendance.

Thank God we didn't spend significant amounts of time and money on this game! Paul Simpson was pretty unambiguous in his verdict that this was the worst performance of the season to date. I agree, and that means that there's relatively little for me to comment on in this post. Substitute Kris Dennis hit the post fairly late in the game, but that was about it. Perhaps our leading scorer might have been more accurate if he'd had more game time recently?

That apart, there were far too many misplaced final passes, too many runs into blind alleys, and too many aimless clearances that immediately concede possession back to Gillingham. Despite that, it looked as if we were going to hold out for our third goalless draw in succession, but it was little surprise when we were hit by a sucker punch, Gillingham scoring the winner in the 94th minute.

Northampton's win means that we drop to fourth, out of the automatic promotion places, and only two points and no goals in our last three games are causes for concern. However, last time we suffered a similar mini blip we responded with four wins on the bounce. That's exactly what's needed right now.

We'll be passing on another long trip next weekend, to Leyton Orient. But after a short break in Bruges in the first week of the Easter holiday, we're aiming to be at every one of the last seven games of the season, in the hope that one of them will be the scene of celebration, of either qualification for the play-offs, or even better automatic promotion. Train tickets to Sutton, for the final game of the season, have already been bought!

APRIL 2023

Saturday 1 April 2023. Leyton Orient v Carlisle United. Brisbane Road. EFL League 2.

This likely to be a fairly short post: not because I'm disaffected after yesterday's result, but because of pressures of time. We have an early start in the morning, as we head off as a family for a short break in Bruges. But fear not, we will be back in time for the Good Friday game against Tranmere Rovers!

This was the last game of the season for which we were *in absentia*. On our return from Bruges, Adam and I will embark on an itinerary that will, ticket availability allowing, see us attend every one of the last seven games of what has been a remarkable season.

Despite Adam and Ben live-streaming the game, I didn't actually get to watch much of it. This was first against fourth in the division, and there was a sense that there were some scores to be settled, as a couple of major refereeing errors had allowed Orient to ease to a barely deserved 3-2 victory at Brunton Park earlier in the season. The impression I got from the snatches of the game I watched, was of two teams below their best. There was some good midfield and approach play from both sides, but relatively little incisive play in the final quarter of the pitch from either team.

The winning goal, which I didn't see, was an own goal, apparently twice deflected. Despite a second successive defeat, we remain in fourth place, just a couple of points away from an automatic promotion place. I would settle for a place in the play-offs, but expectations have been raised so far that failure to achieve automatic promotion will feel like a bit of a disappointment. What's most worrying at the moment is that Carlisle have only taken two points from the last twelve and, having been the division's leading scorers, have failed to score a goal in four games. If I had any criticism to make of Paul Simpson's management it would be that, following the signing of Joe Garner, leading scorer Kris Dennis has no longer been an automatic starter. Consequently, when he does start a game, he tends to lack the sharpness that saw him race to eighteen goals. But the bigger picture is that I still have confidence in Simpson to see the club through to a successful conclusion to the season.

Friday 7 April 2023. Carlisle United v Tranmere Rovers. Brunton Park. EFL League 2.

This was a highly significant game for at least two reasons. Firstly, the club had decided to go for a ticket promotion, with prices slashed to £10 a ticket for adults (no bonus for us season-ticket holders) and other ticket offers available, in the hope of attracting a five-figure attendance. That target was exceeded spectacularly, with 12,694 home fans in a total gate of 13,410. It was the biggest crowd I'd seen at Brunton Park in many a year, and the first time Adam had ever seen the Waterworks End open to supporters. Whichever way the team were kicking today, there were home supporters behind the goal. Secondly, the game came after a poor run of form, with a good result needed to get the promotion campaign back on track.

Given the expected attendance, we set off half an hour earlier than usual, in order to claim our usual crush-barrier position in The Paddock and enjoy the pre-match atmosphere generated by a bumper crowd. It's a good job we did! Our progress was slowed significantly by congestion as the A1M and M1 merged just south of Aberford which extended as far north as Wetherby. Having then raced up to Scotch Corner we hit further congestion on the A66. A combination of satnav diversions and local knowledge to avoid delays at Penrith meant that we hit Warwick Road just before 2.40, having foregone our usual break at Scotch Corner. I made a snap decision to abandon our usual car park. Adam jumped out and headed down Warwick Road in the hope of securing us a reasonable place in The Paddock, while I parked up nearly a mile from the ground and hobbled along Warwick Road as quickly as my arthritic knee would allow. I finally made it into the ground just as the teams were emerging from the tunnel.

It was great to see all sides of the ground almost full, and I fought my way through a packed and sold-out paddock, failing dismally to find Adam. I decided to enjoy the moment and find Adam later. It proved to be a wise decision as, in the third minute, a defensive mistake allowed Omari Patrick to take control and set up

Kris Dennis, who side footed home from close range. It was the perfect start in front of a bumper crowd. The team's first goal in five games settled nerves both on and off the pitch, pre-empting any premature moans from the more impatient among the crowd.

Shortly after the goal I spotted Adam a few yards to my right and squeezed my way along the packed Paddock to join him, only for him to be verbally abused by a vertically challenged spectator who seemed to question his commitment to the cause. Adam pointed out that we'd travelled from Wakefield (as always) to attend the game and could have added that we'd flown home from Bruges the day before to ensure our attendance!

Carlisle proceeded to dominate the rest of the first half. Tranmere were another League Two team determined to play the ball out from the back, despite not having the requisite skill or composure to do so. An effective high press by Carlisle's strikers tended to result in Tranmere's defenders eventually having to hoof the ball forward indiscriminately, usually conceding possession in the process. They dominated possession in the game as a whole (63% to 37%) but managed only eight shots, just one of which was on target. From their relatively meagre share of possession Carlisle fashioned fifteen shots, eight of them on target. Tranmere indulged in much neat passing, but much of it was sideways and in non-threatening areas.

Carlisle duly extended their lead in the 39th minute. An excellent cross from the right by Owen Moxon was met at the far post by Jack Armer who headed across the face of goal for Kris Dennis to slam the ball into the roof of the net. That meant that Dennis had scored five of the team's six goals against Tranmere this season. It also made him Carlisle's first twenty-goals-in-a-season striker since Karl Hawley in 2006. Paul Simpson was also in charge at that time, and the campaign ended in promotion!

Omari Patrick had a gilt-edged chance to make it 3-0 just before half-time but was foiled by an excellent save. There was a sense that another goal at that point might have opened the floodgates in the second half. As it was, the second half followed a similar pattern, with Carlisle comfortably in control of the game. They had the luxury of being able to bring on two strikers of the quality of Joe Garner and Ryan Edmonson for the final quarter of the game. Ben Barclay deservedly won the man-of-the-match accolade for a superb performance in central defence, and it was good to see Jamie Devitt get a decent run-out after replacing Callum Guy at half-time.

So, mission accomplished. The winless run is over, and the result takes us back into the third automatic promotion place. Most importantly, perhaps, the team didn't mess up on the big occasion, in front of so many fans. Only six games to go, and the tension gets ever higher!

Monday 10 April 2023. Walsall v Carlisle United. The Bescot Stadium. EFL League 2.

Well, that was a long way to travel for a frustrating goalless draw!

It wasn't quite as far as Good Friday's trek to Carlisle, and this time we weren't bedevilled by Bank Holiday traffic delays, though we did drive in and out of some pretty gruesome weather on our way to Walsall. It was pretty much the same journey that I made less than a fortnight ago to collect Ellie from uni, apart from the last few miles. We arrived just after two o'clock and were able to park right next to the ground, though for a fairly hefty premium of £7. We were luckier than those who had travelled the longer distance from Carlisle, who had to contend with no fewer than three accidents on the M6 as they made their way to the game. Despite travel issues, the Blues travelling support again impressively topped 1,000.

Carlisle went into the game with an unchanged starting eleven and substitutes' bench. They made some early inroads without having the quality to finish some promising build-ups. There was also some concern that Walsall, with only one win since New Year's Day, were cutting through our defence rather too easily. A setback occurred in the 22nd minute when right wing back Jack Ellis fell victim to the injury curse that seems to have bedevilled that particular position this season. He was replaced by Jordan Gibson. While Gibbo might be very effective in the "wing" part of that job description, I don't think anyone would describe him as a natural defender!

As half-time approached, there was a sense that neither team had done enough to deserve a lead, despite the Carlisle fans putting Walsall's support to shame with their constant chants and encouragement. However, events took a dramatic turn on the hour when Walsall captain and former Carlisle player Hayden White made a crunching challenge on Jack Armer that earned him a straight red card. Surely, with thirty minutes left against ten men, Carlisle could make their numerical advantage count to clinch three invaluable points.

Alas, it wasn't to be. Carlisle poured forward in numbers in the final third of the game, but there was more sweat and graft than quality about their endeavours and ten-man Walsall had their share of opportunities at the far end. Despite six minutes of added time, the final touch was still missing.

One of Walsall's second half substitutes was midfielder Joe Riley, a Carlisle player only a year ago. Although his appearance was greeted with predictable boos and chants of "Carlisle reject" there was also a fair smattering of appreciative applause for services rendered. I wonder if he was contemplating, at the end of the game, whether he might have been wiser to accept the offer of a new contract at Carlisle last summer?

A couple of footnotes to a frustrating afternoon. Firstly, Walsall's gamesmanship was appalling. I lost count of the number of times a player went down with an apparent injury, and the referee bought it every time, summoning on the physio and destroying the flow of the game. Which leads conveniently on to my second footnote. The standard of officiating was appalling. I've banged on about this before, and as a father of an U17 player I fully back the efforts to deal with the abuse of grassroots officials. However, when it comes to the professional game, when significant numbers of supporters have travelled significant distances, at significant expense, we have a right to expect better from match officials. The nadir was reached when Jamie Devitt was flagged offside when he received the ball in his own half! I didn't have the presence of mind to take a picture of the free kick that ensued, but I can assure you that it took place within the Carlisle half! It's such a rudimentary mistake it beggars belief. Before anyone dismisses this as the frustrated ramblings of a biased supporter, let me quote from Paul Simpson's post-match interview.

"I thought we showed a real desire to get the winner but I think Walsall played the game for the whole game. I was really disappointed with the number of times they were diving and unfortunately, look, you know me, I don't like having a go at referees, but I think that's one of the poorest performances from a pair of officials I've seen for a while."

"The referee and the assistant on the near side, I thought they were absolutely shocking over the whole of the game. Listen, that's not the reason we haven't got the full three points, but saying that, I think it's a penalty in the first half for a pull on Jack Armer. I've seen it back, the referee says there's no contact, I think there was. Who knows, we might have got something more out of it if that had been given, but too many things were allowed to happen."

"There was too much timewasting, too much delaying of the game, slowing down restarts, and it just became a really bitty game because of that against a team that are really struggling to get results at the moment."

"I thought we showed real character and determination to try to win it and, like I say, we might be looking at it as a really important point."

"I don't understand it, I really don't. I don't know what the ref is seeing. We can talk about so many poor decisions he's made, but what I find really frustrating is that they talk about this Respect campaign, and he's shown no respect to our players at all, or to their players for that matter as well."

"I don't like criticising referees, because I think they have a really tough job to do, but that standard from him was very poor. I'm told that when the players tried to talk to him he just laughed at them. I don't think that's acceptable."

"In the first half, I asked the fourth official something and he told me I needed to calm down otherwise I'm going to get myself into trouble. Their bench were effing and blinding at him, and he just accepted it. At no point did I swear at him, wag my finger at him or anything like that. I tried to treat him with respect, and he chucked it straight back at me, so that's really disappointing."

"Those things are something I need to take up with the referees group the PGMOL, and it isn't the reason we didn't get three points, but it certainly has an effect on making a game of football flow better."

The result drops us out of the automatic promotion places, though only on goal difference. The next two games, both at home, are absolutely crucial. They're against Northampton Town and Stockport County, both close rivals for the automatic and play-off promotion places. Two positive results would put us in a very strong position. Let's stay positive, however squeaky the bums may be becoming!

Saturday 15 April 2023. Carlisle United v Northampton Town. Brunton Park. EFL League 2.

This was not an easy watch!

I've waited a couple of days before committing my thoughts to print, because I struggled to get my thoughts into perspective in the immediate aftermath of Saturday. We are really at the sharp end of the season now. Before this game, there were just five fixtures remaining. Wins in the next two home games, against Northampton Town and Stockport County, the two teams immediately above Carlisle in the League Two table, would put us in a very strong position to win automatic promotion.

Ben was back with us for this trip, having missed the last couple of games. John Clarke was also in the picture, though the agreement was that we would meet him in The Paddock. The circumstances behind this arrangement are far too complex to bear recounting here! We arrived in good time, with none of the delays we encountered on Good Friday, and by the time I'd parked up and popped into the Blues Store John and the lads had already met up. It only took another ten minutes for John, a native of Carlisle, to encounter two former school contemporaries, dating back some five decades!

The crowd was over 8,200, a good turnout considering there was no ticket promotion, and the long haul from Northampton meant The Cobblers only brought about 540 fans. The stakes and the expectations were high. I confessed to John beforehand that I was a bag of nerves and didn't expect to gain a lot of enjoyment from the afternoon!

Carlisle started the game positively with some fluent attacking moves, but relatively little in the way of chances. At times Northampton cut through Carlisle's midfield a little too easily for comfort, but similarly had little to show in terms of attempts on goal. It wasn't a bad first half, but the final bit of quality was lacking from both sides, which probably accounted for the crowd being a little quiet after a noisy start.

Disappointingly the second half continued in a similar vein with relatively few clear-cut attempts on goal from either side. Some attacking substitutions failed to make a significant difference, and when the crowd raised the volume again in the final quarter it was probably more in hope than expectation. I was reduced to praying for a repeat of last season's fixture at Brunton Park when a 95th minute penalty from Jordan Gibson gave us all three points. Alas it wasn't to be.

My first comment to Adam after the final whistle was that just one win in seven games, and only two goals scored in those seven games, is in no way promotion form. Our defence is rock solid, conceding only two goals in the same run of games, but each of those goals cost us three valuable points. It's hard to pin down exactly what the problem is, other than the blatantly obvious lack of goals. The effort and work rate are still there, but without the fluency and finishing that made us the leading scorers in the division. Simmo continues to ring the changes up front but is struggling to find a winning combination.

This result felt more like two points dropped rather than a point gained. Northampton will be happier with the result as it consolidates their automatic promotion place, while Carlisle drop a place to fifth. We're still well positioned to make the play-offs, but if that is to be our fate it would be nice to take some semblance of form into that end of season lottery.

Tuesday 18 April 2023. Carlisle United v Stockport County. Brunton Park. EFL League 2.

Wow, what a game!

I'm writing this in the immediate aftermath of the game, only about forty minutes after the final whistle. That should be enough to tell you that I wasn't actually at Brunton Park tonight (of which more later), but the live stream came pretty close to making me feel as if I was there. I'm going to record my immediate reactions, though I'll probably wait until I've heard the views of those who were there before I post this report.

This seemed to be an evening on which Carlisle rediscovered their attacking mojo but lost a little bit of discipline in defence. Whether that is due to the absence of Morgan Feeney (injury) and Ben Barclay (on loan from Stockport so not eligible for tonight's game) is not for me to decide.

As usual Carlisle made a pretty positive start. As usual they were on the front foot, the difference being that tonight they were creating some real chances. They had two opportunities to take the lead in the first half-hour. Firstly, a glorious Jack Armer volley was just tipped over by the Stockport keeper as it arrowed towards the top left corner of the goal. If it had gone in it would have been goal of the decade. Secondly, an excellent Kris Dennis shot was only parried by the keeper, and Jordan Gibson should have done better than put the rebound wide of the right-hand post.

It was perhaps little surprise that Stockport took the lead shortly after the second Carlisle chance. They were given too much space in the final third, and curled home a shot that gave Tomas Holy little chance. As the half-time whistle went, I felt that Stockport's lead was slightly undeserved.

Before I embark on the second half, a word about the referee. This was the same man who had refereed our home defeat against Orient fairly early in the season. His performance was bad enough for the EFL to issue an apology to Carlisle for two serious mistakes, one of which resulted in a Carlisle player being sent off, and the other of which led to an Orient goal. It defies belief that someone at the EFL deemed it appropriate to appoint him to such a vital promotion game at the sharp end of the season when he had such negative recent history with one of the teams involved. His performance was predictably dire, but he did maintain his average of five yellow cards a game, which suggests an official who struggles to manage the players in front of him.

Fortunately, Carlisle struck back early in the second half. An Owen Moxon corner was bundled home off his shin by Jon Mellish. Mellish's muted celebration suggested that his goal was fortunate rather than deliberate, but he had the intuition to be in the right place at the right time.

Despite a couple of attacking substitutions and some impressively vocal support, it took until the 83rd minute to reap any dividends. Ryan Edmondson won possession and drove forward before squaring the ball to Owen Moxon, whose curling shot gave Carlisle the lead. It proved to be short lived as defensive laxity allowed Stockport to score an equalizer just three minutes later. Despite a series of late corners and free kicks, a winner was not forthcoming.

The crowd tonight was about 7,100, with about 1,000 from Stockport. The Radio Cumbria commentator on the live stream was quick to praise Stockport's travelling support, but failed to mention that Carlisle took more than 1,200 to Stockport in November for a game that had rather less significance.

The result means that a place in the play-offs is much more likely than automatic promotion. With three games to go, we just need to hold it together and pick up a couple of wins from our remaining games.

It was my full intention to be at Brunton Park tonight. However. Imogen, my daughter was suffering from an upset stomach, and as Lisa had a parents' evening at school, things were put on hold. I left things until the last minute, but Imogen's health hadn't improved, so at quarter to four I messaged Adam to say that we wouldn't be going, then phoned John Clarke with the same message.

About five minutes later, John phoned me back to say something along the lines of "Damn it, I really want to go to this game, would Adam and Aden like to go with me?" I rapidly accepted his very generous offer and drove them over to John's house. As I type, they're probably on the A1M somewhere south of Scotch Corner! As the final whistle went, I have to admit to a certain relief that for once I wasn't faced by the long drive back to Wakefield!

A day on, it's time to report the views of those who were actually there. John Clarke's view was that "Carlisle may not have deserved all three points but they very nearly got them. Agonizingly close. My nerves were shredded." Adam says that it was one of the best games he's seen at Brunton Park (he doesn't have the rich heritage that John and I can draw on!). His friend Aden isn't as invested in football as the likes of John, Adam and myself, but Adam tells me that he thought the second half was brilliant.

It's looking increasingly likely that Carlisle's season is going to be extended by the play-offs. I love the idea of Carlisle's season ending with a successful trip to Wembley, but I'd much rather promotion was put to bed without that stress.

Saturday 22 April 2023. Barrow AFC v Carlisle United. Holker Street (not the So Legal Stadium!). EFL League 2.

The drama surrounding this fixture began almost three weeks ago. Due to the limited capacity of Barrow's ground (a paltry 5,400), away tickets were limited to 650. That meant that there had to be a priority system for ticket sales, with season ticket holders having first bite at the cherry. Tickets went on sale to them at 10.00 a.m on Monday 3 April. So far so good, as we belonged to that privileged group. The only problem was that as a family we were due to fly from Manchester Airport to South Charleroi Airport in Belgium for a short break in Bruges at 12.45!

As we approached Manchester Airport and the clock ticked to ten o'clock, Adam was immediately on the phone, but to no avail. The ticket office was deluged with calls, and he couldn't even get placed in a queue. This continued as we checked in and made our way through security and passport control. Meanwhile, back in Crofton, Ben was also busy on the phone, with the same end in mind. Glory be, as we moved to the departure lounge, the news came through that he'd been successful, and we had our golden tickets!

Before I move on to the game itself, a few comments about ground capacities. In recent months, Carlisle have frequently taken more than 1,000 supporters to away games, even at distant locations like Leyton Orient and Gillingham. Barrow was the shortest journey of the season for supporters from Carlisle, so one could have expected an away support of 1500 plus at a ground of a decent capacity. What was particularly galling was that Barrow failed to sell out the home tickets. The official attendance of 4,515 was almost nine hundred short of the ground's capacity. Almost a thousand more Carlisle supporters could have attended the game.

While it might have been the shortest trip of the season for Carlisle based fans, it was ironically the longest journey of the season so far for the Wakefield Blues, though that may be exceeded in a couple of weeks' time by our trip to Sutton United for the final game of the season. We were a man down, because John Clarke doesn't have a season ticket and therefore had no chance of being there. Another way of putting it is that he's got far too much common sense to commit to driving from Wakefield more than twenty times in a nine-month period! An early start meant that we arrived around two o'clock. Despite growing up in Cumbria, I'd never previously travelled this far south in the county. I'd done my pre-match research and identified a car park just 100 metres from the ground, albeit with limited capacity. We were early enough to get a place, but experienced a problem when I had nothing less than a £10 note to pay the very reasonable £2 parking fee, and the car park attendant didn't have enough change. I delved into my pocket for loose change and managed to produce £1.50. I was more than impressed when the attendant shrugged and said, "That's fine, that'll do."!

Holker Street is a horrible little ground. It must rival Harrogate Town's Wetherby Road ground as the worst in League Two, though I believe Forest Green's ground may run them close when they make an ignominious return to League Two next season. There were only two turnstiles for away fans, which meant that a sizeable queue had assembled even an hour before kick-off. Once inside the ground, there was limited space, and a complete lack of crush barriers in the corner in which we chose to take our position. Sight lines down the touchline were limited as well. There was no spectator accommodation at the far end of the ground. I don't mean that it wasn't open, as is usually the case with the Waterworks End at Brunton Park. There are just no seats or terracing there. The predictable chorus of "Barrow's a shithole, I wanna go home" was fully justified, at least as far as the ground is concerned.

John waxed critical to me a week ago about the lack of humour and imagination in some of the Carlisle songs and chants. I'm pleased to report that they/we redeemed themselves/ourselves on this afternoon. The stadium announcer handed us a gift shortly before kick-off by playing The Dave Clark Five's "Glad All Over". The original lyrics were almost immediately drowned out by the raucous chants of "We've got – Joey Garner, we've got – Joey Garner". There was also a new (to me at least) song. "We are Carlisle, the mighty Carlisle, we always win away. We are Carlisle, the mighty Carlisle, we always win away. We win away, we win away, we win away." to the tune of "The Lion Sleeps Tonight".

Of course, this was our 'local derby', and while Barrow didn't really have a great deal to play for at this stage of the season, the memory of our 5-1 thrashing of them at Brunton Park in February was still fresh in the minds of both teams' supporters. Carlisle, of course, had everything to play for, with automatic promotion still a realistic possibility. Paul Simpson went for a change of formation, moving Jon Mellish from central defence into midfield, changing shape from 5-3-2 to 4-3-3.

The game was predictably tense, nervy and scrappy, but to be honest the result was all that mattered. Our nerves were settled in the sixteenth minute when an Owen Moxon corner from the right was headed on at the near post by Kris Dennis. In the ensuing goalmouth scramble Ben Barclay had a couple of efforts blocked before finally backheeling the ball over the line.

There weren't many standout moments. Although Barrow had more possession, Carlisle defended manfully, and when they did get attempts on target Tomas Holy was in impressive form in goal. As Barrow piled on the pressure towards the end, hope that some good counterattacks might result in a second goal that put the result to bed alternated with fear that we would concede a late equaliser. I derived absolutely no pleasure or enjoyment from the last quarter of the game! Finally, after five minutes of time added on, the final whistle blew, and enjoyment returned as we celebrated a vital win.

The 20th clean sheet of the season equalled a club record, set during Simmo's first spell in charge of the club, and broke the club record for the number of clean sheets by a single goalkeeper. Two more will have a massive influence on the final outcome of the season.

Saturday 29 April 2023. Carlisle United v Salford City. Brunton Park. EFL League 2.

A full complement of the Wakefield Blues headed north, knowing that a win could, depending on results elsewhere, keep alive hopes of an automatic promotion place. Although it was never mentioned, it's possible that we were all buoyed by the memory of Carlisle's coruscating 4-1 away victory over Salford at the Peninsula 'Stadium' earlier in the season, a game that we all witnessed.

Carlisle fans turned out in their thousands. The attendance was 10,927, with only 450 Salford fans making the trip. That represented the second-best crowd of the season, without a cheap ticket promotion to swell the numbers. It meant that there was a buoyant atmosphere prior to kick-off, with the Waterworks End again open to provide support on all four sides of the ground.

Unfortunately, for the first time this season, Carlisle failed to produce the goods in front of a bumper home crowd. After an encouraging opening ten minutes the midfield and defence were scythed through far too easily for Salford to score their first goal after twenty-three minutes. Just five minutes later a fairly routine shot was badly fumbled by Tomas Holy, doubling Salford's lead. The Carlisle thousands were pretty much silenced. The rest of the first half was pretty dire, as passes went astray, and Carlisle showed little sign of getting back into the game.

Half-time saw striker Ryan Edmondson replaced by midfielder Alfie McAlmont, but the half began in much the same style as the first half ended. In an attempt to improve affairs, Paul Simpson brought on Jordan Gibson and loanee Jack Robinson in the 64th minute. That meant that we witnessed the rare event of Jack Armer failing to complete a game. He's only been substituted twice previously this season, both times in the dying minutes as a time-wasting tactic. Joe Garner also joined the fray just a minute later. In the seventy-fifth minute Garner appeared to have got Carlisle back into the game, heading home a Jack Robinson cross, before a dubious offside flag cut short the celebrations. Adam thought he was offside; I was full of righteous indignation at an incompetent linesman. There again, I'm just a passionate committed retiree, while he's a calm, rational and objective teenager.

It mattered not. Just two minutes later Garner repeated the trick, superbly heading home an Owen Moxon free kick to get Carlisle back into the game. Only five minutes later we were right back in contention when the referee awarded a penalty for a foul on Garner. At that point all hell was let loose, as Salford tried to do everything within their power to delay and disrupt the taking of the penalty. Most significantly, Salford's Elliot Watt (a former Carlisle loanee) pushed Jon Mellish in the chest. Mellish responded in exactly the same manner, at which point Watt fell dramatically to the ground, clutching his face. A red card for Mellish immediately followed. Fortunately, Kris Dennis kept his head amongst all the carnage, and eventually dispatched the penalty to draw us level, and restore the voices of 10,500 home fans.

Having watched the incident back I will be very surprised if the red card is not rescinded, and the club receives yet another apology from the EFL. That counts for nothing as the red card fundamentally affected the outcome of the game. Mellish was missing from his left-sided central defence position five minutes later when Salford cut in from their right to score their winning goal. I can identify at least three games this season where confirmed refereeing mistakes have cost us points, points that would otherwise have seen us in an automatic promotion place.

The nine minutes of added time at the end of the second half were a testimony to Salford's time-wasting, disruptive approach. It should have probably been closer to fifteen minutes. I lost track of the number of times a Salford player fell to the ground when Carlisle were in possession and mounting an attack. And the referee bought it every time. The feigning of injury to disrupt the opposition's momentum is a blight on the game and needs to be eradicated as soon as possible, based on my extensive experience of League 2 this season.

As time added on began, Carlisle were reduced to nine men, when Jamie Devitt suffered a season ending injury. It may even mark the end of his Carlisle career, with his contract up for renewal.

The upshot of all this is that automatic promotion is no longer a possibility. However, a play-off place is almost, but not entirely, assured. To miss out, we would need to lose our final game while Mansfield win theirs, overturning an inferior goal difference of eight in the process. Hopefully our final game at Sutton United will be about determining exactly who we face in the play-offs.

All credit to Sutton. Despite a ground capacity of just over 5,000, they initially allocated 1,050 tickets to Carlisle, nearly double Barrow's meagre allocation. They have since released another 430 tickets to Carlisle, raising the possibility that away fans may outnumber home fans, despite the significant travelling distance involved and a ridiculous lunchtime kick-off.

MAY 2023

Monday 8 May 2023. Sutton United v Carlisle United. Gander Green Lane. EFL League 2.

And so the season finally reaches its end – except it doesn't!

The equation was simple. A draw would give Carlisle the one point they needed to guarantee qualification for the promotion play-offs, irrespective of results elsewhere. Those other results would then determine who Carlisle faced in the play-off semi-final.

Ironically, given that it was the last game of the regular league season, the day saw two significant firsts. It was our first visit to Sutton United's ground, and the first time we had travelled to a match by train. I'll do my best to avoid cliched railway metaphors about the promotion campaign being "on track", defenders "steaming" forwards, or substituted players having "hit the buffers"! The prospect of driving to South London and back on a Bank Holiday Monday didn't appeal, so at 7.30 a.m. Adam, Ben and I boarded the LNER service departing Wakefield Westgate. Just two hours later we pulled into Kings Cross, made the short walk to St Pancras and continued our journey. The trip from North to South

London took at least half as long as the journey from Wakefield to London! The absurdity of a 12.30 p.m. kick-off time meant that the transport arrangements were even more ridiculous for those travelling all the way from Carlisle.

A short walk of two hundred yards took us to the Gander Green Lane ground, though we had to walk at least twice as far to reach the away fans' turnstiles (all two of them!). at this point it's appropriate to give a nod to an excellent website that has guided our travels this season. www.awaygames.co.uk is a veritable compendium of information for travelling fans. For every ground it has details about public transport links, car parking close to the ground, pubs that welcome away supporters and much more. It's been an essential companion for our away trips.

The ground itself reeks non-league. It's got a bigger capacity than Harrogate's Wetherby Road, and is in a better state of repair then Barrow's Holker Street, but that's probably as much as can be said for it. There's covered terracing or seating on each side of the ground, with open terracing in each corner, but nowhere does it extend back more than about ten rows or steps. There's a growing tendency for clubs to earn promotion from the National League by getting it right on the pitch, without really having the infrastructure to support membership of the EFL.

Official figures say that 1,366 Carlisle fans made the long journey to Sutton, which was almost 30% of the overall attendance. I suspect that many of the Carlisle supporters had, like us, made early travel arrangements to minimize the cost of train fares, in the hope that this might be a day on which we celebrated automatic promotion, and we all wanted to be there. That was no longer a possibility, but we were still determined to end the season on a high note, and the packed away end was in impressive voice as kick-off approached.

With Jon Mellish absent through his suspension for a totally ridiculous red card (see previous game) Jack Armer moved to left-sided centre back, with Jack Robinson, on loan from Middlesbrough, making the first start of his loan spell at left wing-back. In familiar fashion Carlisle started the game well, on the front foot for the first ten minutes of the game. However, a tendency for defenders to stand off attackers allowed Sutton to take a rather too easy lead in the sixteenth minute. The rest of the first half was pretty woeful, with a lack of fluency and cohesion. The only redeeming feature was a Kris Dennis shot that rattled the Sutton crossbar following a short free kick. The ball spent far too much time in the air, playing into the hands of Sutton's large and physical side. There were some boos to be heard as the teams trudged off at half-time.

Things picked up in the second half. Carlisle attacked with more intent and aggression, provoking much more noise from the travelling support, but chances continued to go begging. In the end it took a slightly comical own goal, following a long throw-in from Ben Barclay, to restore parity. The nature of the goal mattered not. It meant that our play-off place was guaranteed, and that we could spend the last few minutes of the season in celebratory mood. The chants of "We're the famous Carlisle United and we're going to Wemberley" might have been a touch premature, but we were entitled to dream of a potentially glorious end to our extended season.

As we walked back to West Sutton station, we were engaged in conversation by a friendly Sutton fan who asked us how long our journey home would take. Having confessed that our journey would be shorter than that of most Carlisle fans, having only travelled from Wakefield, he wished us well in the play-offs, admitting that the trip up to Carlisle for the return fixture had been a bit too far for him. It was a nice moment at the end of a game that held out the prospect of our first success in many years and meant that I travelled home with a largely positive impression of Sutton United.

The draw meant that we retained fifth place and therefore face Bradford City in the play-offs, our higher position meaning that we enjoy home advantage in the second leg of the semi-final. I anticipate a packed and hostile Valley Parade for the first leg, with a similar atmosphere at Brunton Park six days later. It can't be said that we go into the play-offs on a good run of form, but I don't think that matters. None of the teams in the play-off positions won their final game. I think that the play-offs bear little relation to the season that has preceded them. It's all about the team that manages those three one-off games better than the rest.

I'd have been delighted at the start of the season if someone had told me this is where we'd finish, given what happened last season. But now it will be bitterly disappointing if our season doesn't end with a day of glory at Wembley!

Sunday 14 May 2023. Bradford City v Carlisle United. Valley Parade. EFL League 2 play-off semi-final, first leg.

The dream lives on! We may have lost 1-0 yesterday evening, but the tie is only at the halfway stage, and the performance, particularly in the second half, gives massive reason for encouragement. Hopefully the job will be almost completed at a vibrant Brunton Park on Saturday afternoon.

Unsurprisingly a full complement of the Wakefield Blues made the short trip to Bradford, with John Clarke joining Adam, Ben and myself for the first seven o'clock kick-off on a Sunday evening that I can recall. The vagaries of live TV scheduling! Having entered a car park postcode into the satnav, we arrived at our destination to find the shutters firmly closed. A quick consultation led to Adam and Ben setting off for the ground while John and I sought out alternative parking. Having done so there remained the further issue of picking up John's ticket. On arrival at the away turnstiles, we were directed to the main ticket office, which entailed walking around two sides of the ground and fighting our way through massed crowds of Bradford fans. Having finally made it, John was promptly redirected to the away turnstiles, where apparently there was a man with a white box for ticket collections. As we retraced our steps, we were beginning to cast anxious glances at our watches and beginning to wonder if we'd be able to either get into the ground before kick-off or locate Adam and Ben. We finally got in with about fifteen minutes to spare. Just as I was about to text Adam about their whereabouts, I spotted him and remarkably, given that the away allocation of tickets was sold out, they'd managed to save two seats for us. When I say seats, the only time we actually sat on our seats was during the half-time interval!

Valley Parade was a fitting venue for such an important game. Almost two sides of the ground are surrounded by two highly impressive and large two-tier stands. On a third side a pretty decent stand housed the away fans, but the remaining third of the ground does rather give the impression that the money ran out before the redevelopment was complete. The attendance was an impressive 20,575, with 2,415 away fans. To put that into League Two perspective, the away following was half the total attendance at the other semi-final the previous day, and the overall attendance was more than four times the total gate at Salford City's ground the day before.

It took only a few moments inside the ground to realise why it was so important to be there. This was Carlisle's biggest game for six years, since they faced Exeter City at the same stage of the season in 2017. There was a little lump in the throat as the teams walked out into a vibrant atmosphere. Both sets of supporters were in full voice as kick-off loomed. Carlisle had made two changes from the previous game, Garner replacing Dennis in attack, and Joel Senior taking the place of Jack Robinson by playing at right wing back, meaning that Ben Barclay moved into central defence and Jack Armer returned to his usual left win back role, though without his usual partner in crime (the unjustifiably suspended Jon Mellish).

The opening minutes were fairly even, with both teams probing for openings. In about the 10th minute Carlisle were denied a blatant penalty when Alfie McAlmont was unceremoniously dragged to the ground by a Bradford defender. A few minutes later a superb, swerving, instinctive volley from Joe Garner on the right rattled the Bradford crossbar, though it wouldn't have counted because the referee had given a free kick for a handball in the build-up, an offence that only he in the entire stadium seemed to have noticed. Predictably, Bradford immediately went up the other end and scored. That subdued the Carlisle fans for the next few minutes, engendering nagging fears that an early goal in front of a sizeable home support might open the floodgates. Fortunately, we didn't go the way of Sheffield Wednesday at Peterborough a couple of evenings earlier and reached half-time just the one goal behind.

Omari Patrick was clearly struggling up front, bereft of confidence, and it was little surprise when he was replaced by Ryan Edmondson on fifty-seven minutes, with Kris Dennis also replacing Joe Garner. From that point onward Carlisle were very much on the front foot. Jack Armer was back to his usual reliable and enterprising self at left wing back after a slightly uncomfortable afternoon at Sutton in central defence, and Owen Moxon was constantly initiating attacks from a deep-lying midfield position. Numerous chances were created and all that was missing was the final finishing touch. Taylor Charters also impressed from the bench and if Callum Guy fails to recover from injury, there is a more than able deputy lined up.

We may have lost 1-0, but I think the general feeling among fans was that we bossed the second half and have nothing to fear from Bradford in the second leg. They were the team hanging on at the end, and it was noticeable that they had left the pitch well before the Carlisle players and staff had finished saluting their supporters. I am confident that Carlisle can complete the job at a bouncing Brunton Park on Saturday afternoon and secure an overdue return to Wembley.

What follows is a "behind enemy lines" account of the game from Bradford supporter Tim Brooke. Tim and I go back a long way. When I started teaching at Boston Spa Comprehensive School over forty years ago, Tim was a Year 10 student. About three years later we both performed in a staff-student production of "Hamlet". I was also a colleague of Tim's dad, John, in Wetherby Labour Party in the Eighties. In the intervening years our paths have crossed numerous times, at gigs, comedy shows, our children's primary school, and school parents' evenings. Having attended the same game as me on Sunday evening Tim will be co-hosting a live poetry event in Wakefield tomorrow evening with Lisa! The world moves in mysterious ways!

Paul Simpson and the width of a post.

These days, whenever we play Carlisle United, I am immediately reminded of Sunday 9th May 1999, Paul Simpson being the unmistakable cause of my reminiscence. Overall, 1998/99 had been a strange season: starting badly, not gaining a win until the end of August and stuttering during the first half of the season until the axis of Lee Mills and Robbie Blake began to truly fire.

So where does the mercurial Paul Simpson fit into it all of this I hear you say. Well, any Bantams fan of a certain age will understand immediately. On the 9th of May I travelled in hope rather than expectation to Molineux. We needed a win to beat Ipswich to the last automatic promotion spot which would herald a return to England's topflight after an absence of 77 years. Like many a fan I believed that we had already squandered the opportunity the week before when we drew 0-0 at home against relegation candidates Oxford United, with Stuart McCall missing a golden chance with a misplaced header. Yes, it was certain that we would be facing the horrors of the playoff lottery. Still, I had my ticket for the last game, what the hell, I would go even though I knew that Wolves who were pushing for a playoff spot themselves would win. The game didn't get off to the best of starts with City conceding to Flo in the 12th minute, however three goals from Beagrie, Mills and Blake and we looked comfortable, we also look liked like we could afford to miss a Peter Beagrie penalty. Paul Simpson however, had other ideas. Simpson had been bothersome to City's defence most of the game and in the 81st minute he slotted home to rank up the nerves in the last few minutes. Those nerves reached stratospheric proportions when Simpson crafted a free kick that had Gary Walsh beaten all ends up and which cannoned off the inside of the post and by a miracle didn't go in. Such is football, an inch further to the right and that would I'm sure been the end of our Premiership dream. That is why Paul Simpson is indelibly marked on my memory.

So, to the game. A lot has happened to me since that day at Molineux, I'm retired from teaching, I still follow City, who are now a million miles away from the Premiership and I have a nineteen-year-old son. Joe unlike me was born in Yorkshire not too far away from Elland Road. All his friends apart from one support Leeds United. Joe doesn't, he supports Bradford City. However, he supports them with a zeal that my forty plus years of support doesn't come close. There are many things I love and respect about my son, his random acts of kindness, his encyclopaedic knowledge of European football, his love of the Stone Roses, The Jam and the Undertones but also his commitment to hopeless causes. As usual we picked up his friend Reilly, (his only Bradford City supporting friend) and drove along the M62 in virtual silence. The car is usually alive with football or music talk but not today, we had something else on our minds. Parked up at the end of Manningham Lane we normally turn left down North Parade either to have a pint in the Sparrow or to walk down to the City Vaults. Not tonight, we were going to observe our usual end of season ritual and walk to Lumb Lane for a pre match curry at the excellent Sweet Centre. Although the tension was still apparent, we shared some thoughts about our current Gameweek37 Fantasy performance, Pochettino's decision to drink from the poisoned Chelsea chalice and the potential outcome of tonight's game.

Curry consumed we walked to the ground, and I climbed the steps to the Upper Kop where I have spent a considerable part of my adult life. Like me when I was his age Joe is still struggling to shake off an air of Danny

Dyer and he and Reilly go to stand at the top of the Kop with the last remnants of the 'Ointment' Bradford's hooligan fraternity most of which I taught at some point although I'm not sure what I taught them.

Before the game started there was a minute's applause in memory of Mark Matthews City's Academy Coach who recently died of cancer at the age of 56, the same age as me.

The game started brightly for City, we are usually slow starters, needing to be provided with the incentive of going a goal behind before being encouraged to start playing. Not tonight-our early movement was purposeful and energetic; passing was determined if not always accurate. However, Carlisle's Joe Garner, gave an early indication of his potential to worry City when he let fly from distance to rattle the bar as the City faithful bayed for a handball, which was granted by the once foul mouthed referee Ross Joyce. In the 18th minute Jamie Walker collected the ball from Scott Banks to slide the ball home from inside the box and both City players and City fans entered a state of delirium. City continued to build throughout the half, but so did Carlisle, the goal appearing to spark them to become increasingly direct with their play. The game was very even with both sides coming close; Jamie Walker dragged another shot wide on the half hour mark. City's defence was tested by Carlisle's excellent set pieces through the work of Moxon and Whelan. Scott Banks continued to trouble Carlisle's defence and a surge into the box as half-time approached saw Holy have to deal with a rasping shot.

The second half started in the same vein with arguably Carlisle edging it. Harry Lewis was kept busy by Alfie McCalmont and Joe Garner, but Bradford still managed to hold onto the lead. During the 69th minute Ryan Edmondson dispossessed Romoney Chrichlow in the Bradford box, he fired across the face off goal at a tight angle only for Jack Armer's shot to find the side netting. Bradford then enjoyed a rare period of second half pressure as Andy Cook who had been well marshalled throughout the game managed a couple of chances. However, as the game ended the momentum seemed to be Carlisle. Bradford continued to defend their slender lead and after a tense five minutes of injury time managed to do so. Though in reality it's only Half-Time, Bradford will head to Cumbria on Saturday with a one goal advantage to preserve with another ninety minutes plus stoppages to play. Oh, the joy of the Play-Offs!

Up the Chickens!

Saturday 20 May 2023. Carlisle United v Bradford City. Valley Parade. EFL League 2 play-off semi-final, second leg.

In a break with normal practice, I'm composing the first part of this post the day before the game, though there's good reason for that.

Tomorrow afternoon's match is probably the biggest game at Brunton Park in eighteen years, since the second leg of the Football Conference (as it then was) semi-final against Aldershot, when Matty Glennon's heroics in the penalty shoot-out helped Carlisle return to the

Football League at the first attempt. There have been League One playoffs since, but the context is different. There have been trips to Wembley. But the big moments over the last eighteen years have taken place away from Brunton Park.

The anticipation is verging on unbearable already! It's probably been heightened by watching the unbelievable game at Hillsborough last night when Sheffield Wednesday overcame a four-goal deficit against Peterborough to reach Wembley via a penalty shoot-out.

I've been at vital games at Brunton Park before, most notably the legendary Jimmy Glass game, but I've never been so invested in the team as I will be tomorrow. I may have seen the club play in the former First Division, but I've never remotely approached the approximately 75% of games I've seen this season.

The game will also see the biggest crowd at Brunton Park for many a year. Earlier today over 12,000 home tickets had been sold, and when the away allocation is added, we can anticipate a crowd of around 14,000 to 15,000. The allocation of away tickets has been exactly the same proportion of ground capacity for both ties, so that can be discounted from what I'm about to say. Let's put to rest one or two myths about Bradford's 'amazing support for a team in League Two'. A crowd of 20,500 at Valley Parade last Sunday represented just under 4% of Bradford's population. If the attendance tomorrow reaches 15,000, that will represent 13.6% of the population of Carlisle. So which team is really the better supported?

I fervently hope that this won't prove to be the final post of a remarkable season!

It isn't! Our season is still alive!

Where do I start to recount an epic afternoon in the life of Carlisle United Football club? Perhaps with an expression of sympathy for Ben, who, due to an athletics competition, had to miss out on the biggest game of his time as a Carlisle supporter. The rest of the Wakefield Blues made an earlier start than usual, in the hope of securing our usual parking place and position in The Paddock. We travelled in glorious sunshine, and as we reached Junction 43 on the M6 we joined a queue that stretched all the way back to the beginning of the exit slip-road. Despite it only being 1.30 p.m., we were one of the last cars to secure a place in our usual haunt, the Riverside car park. There's normally plenty of space left at 2.15! Adam went ahead to secure a crush barrier place, with the "old gits" following at a more sedate pace once we'd parked up.

We paused on our journey to buy a matchday programme, as this was the last time the club would be selling a print version. That was reason enough to make it a collector's item. It now has added cachet as the programme for the game that saw the club reach Wembley! How fitting that the programme contains a crowd shot from this season's League game at Valley Parade in which both Adam and John are clearly visible.

We were in position just after two o'clock, able to fully savour the build-up to kick-off as the ground gradually filled up and the players went through their pre-match routines. The official attendance was 15,401, with just under 2,000 Bradford fans present, creating a brilliant atmosphere. Interestingly, the gate receipts from the play-off semi-finals are split equally between the EFL and the four clubs involved. Given that the attendance at Brunton Park yesterday was greater than the aggregate attendance at both Stockport v Salford ties, that might appear a little unfair, particularly when last Sunday's attendance at Valley Parade was over 20,000.

Carlisle began the game in the way they finished Sunday's first leg, creating chances and pinning Bradford back. Bradford enjoyed the majority of possession, but it was largely confined to unthreatening areas of the pitch and tended to consist of lots of cross-field passing with little penetration.

John-Kymani Gordon, available again after a three-match suspension, had replaced Omari Patrick in attack in the one change from the first leg starting line-up. He was superb in the first half, controlling awkward balls out of defence, running at Bradford with real intent and aggression, and constantly closing down Bradford defenders when out of possession. He had already had a shot tipped onto the post before Carlisle took the lead in the 21st minute. Joel Senior cut in incisively from the right flank before a deft interchange of passes with Owen Moxon. A subtle backheel from Senior set up a shot from Moxon that was parried by the Bradford keeper but fell to Gordon. His goal bound shot was helped into the net by a lunging Bradford defender. Most of the ground erupted, and the tie was all square.

Carlisle suffered a major scare just moments later when a Bradford header hit the post, and Tomas Holy pulled off an excellent point-blank save from the follow-up. That apart, it was slightly disappointing that Carlisle were only a goal ahead at the interval.

As the second half progressed, the atmosphere remained vibrant. The Bradford fans were predictably vocal, but whenever they burst into song, they were invariably quickly drowned out by the response from 13,000 plus fans on all sides of the ground. On seventy minutes Simmo made predictable but pro-active changes in attack to find the winning goal. Despite some good chances it wasn't to be, and we faced the prospect of extra time.

Only six minutes of extra time had elapsed when an Owen Moxon corner was cleared as far as the right corner of the Bradford penalty area, where it fell to Callum Guy. He adjusted and hit a superb low volley which bounced once before arrowing into the far corner of the net. Cue bedlam, as Wembley beckoned. But it was never going to be that simple. Just two minutes into the second period of extra time Bradford equalised. They possessed League Two's leading scorer in Andy Cooke. He had failed to score in our three previous games against Bradford this season and captain Paul Huntington had comprehensively beaten him in the air on this afternoon – so much so that John questioned whether he was on a contract bonus for the number of aerial challenges he won! However, he was less impressive on the ground, and was comprehensively beaten for pace before the ball was squared for Bradford to draw level on aggregate.

I think that at this point most of the crowd were readying themselves for the unbearable tension of a penalty shoot-out. But there was one more twist to come. In the 112th minute Owen Moxon curled a tantalising ball into the Bradford area, where it was met by the deftest of glancing headers by Ben Barclay to restore Carlisle's aggregate lead. For the remaining minutes it was a case of game management, keeping the ball as far away from the Carlisle goal as possible.

There was a moment of jeopardy in the dying seconds as Carlisle fans in the Warwick Road End started to spill onto the perimeter of the pitch in anticipation of a pitch invasion at the final whistle. The referee had to halt the game briefly while the fans were pushed back. A few seconds later the final whistle blew, and we were through to the play-off final at Wembley as fans poured onto the pitch. The "old git" in me thinks it would have been nice if the fans had stayed off the pitch and allowed all the supporters in the ground to acknowledge all the players in the accustomed manner, but the old romantic in me fully understands the desire of younger fans to celebrate our biggest moment in over a decade in an emotional and visceral way. Pitch invasions seem to have become de rigeur when the home team qualifies for a play-off final.

Adam eventually joined the throng on the pitch while John and I attempted to salvage a shred of dignity by maintaining our place on The Paddock terrace. Finally, the pitch cleared, and we reluctantly departed the scene of Carlisle's greatest moment since the EFL Trophy Final in 2011. Once you've left the ground, the marvellous immediacy of the moment is over.

Tragically (and I use the term advisedly as a former English teacher), Ben Barclay, having scored the goal that took Carlisle to Wembley, will be ineligible for the final, as he is on loan from Stockport County who we will face at Wembley in a week's time. He is out of contract at Stockport at the end of this season and has surely done enough to earn a contract offer from Carlisle United.

Given extra-time and the post-match celebrations, by the time we finally departed the Riverside car park we would normally have been breaking our journey home at Scotch Corner! It mattered not. We're on our way to Wembley and can revel in the moment.

A brief footnote. Despite Ben Barclay's ineligibility, Jon Mellish will be available for the play-off final. If you cast your mind back a couple of posts, Mellish received a red card in the penultimate game of the League season for pushing Nathan Watt of Salford City in the chest. This was in response to Watt doing exactly the same to him. The difference was that Watt collapsed dramatically to the ground clutching his face. All credit to Mellish's mum who posted on Twitter, following Salford's defeat to Stockport, "Aargh, Watt a shame."

I'm invested in this year's end of season play-offs to an extent I never have been before. Quite apart from Carlisle's involvement, I have friends who support three of the other five teams involved – Liz Currie and Barnsley, Mark Shaw and Sheffield Wednesday and Paul Fisher and Luton Town. We can't all be happy, but it would be great if three of us could!

Sunday 28 May 2023. Carlisle United v Stockport County. Wembley Stadium. EFL League 2 play-off final.

THE BUILD UP

The big build-up starts here! The euphoria from Saturday's brilliant semi-final triumph over Bradford lingers on but will count for nothing unless the team can finish the job on the grandest of football stages. It's eleven years since Carlisle last appeared at Wembley. On that occasion they defeated Brentford (yes, the same Brentford who are now an established Premier League club close to qualifying for European competition) 1-0 to win the EFL Trophy, then known as The Johnstone's Paint Trophy.

The tickets are bought, though not yet delivered, and car parking is booked. It only remains for four more days to tick past, and we'll be on our way. Unfortunately, only three of the Wakefield Blues will be at Wembley. John Clarke, an increasingly frequent companion at recent games, has a prior engagement. In a scenario slightly reminiscent of Ben Barclay's situation (scoring the goal that takes Carlisle to Wembley but ineligible for the final) John has watched the two games that took Carlisle to Wembley but won't be there on Sunday. As organiser of Wakefield's Red Shed Poetry Competition, he will be hosting the awards ceremony on Sunday afternoon. So, he won't even be able to watch it live on the telly! Ironically, one of the shortlisted poets for the Wakefield Postcode Prize is one Lisa Falshaw! Tim Brooke, who recently provided a Bradford perspective on the first leg of the semi-final is also shortlisted. I suspect the poetry awards may be punctuated by a number of messages from Wembley!

I'm determined not to overthink the final. As stated previously, every time Paul Simpson has started a season as Carlisle manager, they've won promotion. Let's just leave it at that!

Only four days to go now! The most important aspect of today's build-up was the arrival of the all-important tickets. Our few days in the sporting spotlight saw Kris Dennis interviewed on Sky Sports News at lunchtime, and this afternoon came the news that regular captain Morgan Feeney is fully fit and available for Sunday's game. With Jon Mellish also returning from suspension, that gives Paul Simpson an interesting but welcome selection headache in central defence, despite Ben Barclay's ineligibility.

Debate in the Falshaw household today has centred around which shirt I should wear on Sunday. Adam favours the 1997 deckchair shirt in Eddie Stobart colours (now worth a cool £300!) but I'm inclined to go for a more original and unique choice. Not a mere replica shirt, but a genuine Carlisle United Number Nine shirt, as worn by the legendary Chris Balderstone, probably in the late sixties. Chris originally gave it to my dad as a thank you for selling lots of copies of his testimonial brochure. It's now working its way down the Falshaw generations.

It's now Friday evening and the team and staff are already in London. In fact, as I write, they're conducting a preliminary visit to Wembley Stadium. It's about thirty-four hours until we start our own journey to the national stadium.

I still can't quite believe that a season that started with moderate expectations and a mildly encouraging 1-0 home win against Crawley is concluding on the grandest stage of all. Nor can I quite comprehend that by this time on Sunday the League Two football season will be over, and our fate will be determined. We might even have arrived home!

Yesterday saw a meeting of the Wembley dads for afternoon drinks. Paul hasn't managed to get Luton Town tickets for tomorrow's Championship Final, but as we head back from Wembley on Sunday Mark will be travelling in the opposite direction to support Sheffield Wednesday in Monday's League One Final. We're all confident that we'll be reconvening shortly to celebrate three promotions!

Whichever team wins on Sunday it will be quite a story. If Stockport prevail, it will be their second successive promotion, having only gained promotion from the National League a year ago. If Carlisle triumph it will represent a remarkable turnaround from fifteen months ago, when Paul Simpson took charge with the club in the League Two relegation zone. Not quite as spectacular as the promotion of Luton or Coventry to the Premier League tomorrow, but pretty impressive nonetheless.

Saturday has unapologetically been spent willing the hours away and wishing it were Sunday! I did take time out from wishing my life away to watch Luton Town's dramatic penalty shoot-out win in the Championship play-off final, which means that the first leg of the Wembley dads' treble has been successfully completed.

THE MATCH

OH MY GOD! WE'VE ONLY GONE AND BLOODY DONE IT!

In the words of the immortal Paul Simon, "These are the days of miracle and wonder."

About fifteen months ago I stated the following, after a season-defining win at Oldham Athletic. "This was just magnificent. This was the stuff of which dreams are made. This was the kind of day that makes the years of defeats, disappointment and disillusionment seem worthwhile." Take that statement and multiply it by a factor of at least ten to describe the events of 28 May 2023.

Over thirty hours on I'm still on Cloud Nine and in no fit state to provide an objective and dispassionate account of yesterday's events (as if that was ever the intention). So, you'll have to settle for a ridiculously subjective and utterly passionate account instead!

I think I'll start with a narrative of the day's events, before going on to the ramifications of the day's events, their significance, and all the emotional stuff.

A 1.30 kick-off meant that we set off at 7.30 for our longest trip of the season. It wasn't particularly fan-friendly scheduling for two teams from the north of England, the far north in Carlisle's case. The losing semi-finalists would also have had a similar journey to Stockport, from Bradford and Salford. But the money the club receives from Sky Sports probably makes it worth it. At least it was only Wakefield to Wembley for us, rather than Carlisle to Wembley.

Our first service station break saw us comprehensively outnumbered by Stockport fans, but at our second break the numbers were more equal, as the routes from Carlisle and Stockport converged. We arrived at Wembley at about 11.30. The car parking fee may have been exorbitant, but was probably worth it, as we were less than five minutes' walk from the stadium. That gave us plenty of time to soak up the pre-match atmosphere, and revel in the fact that Carlisle United were actually at Wembley. Adam and Ben headed for the Carlisle fan zone, while I stood and watched the Carlisle fans pouring up Wembley Way. Just about every Carlisle shirt from the past thirty years was on display, including some that I'd completely forgotten. I'd finally opted for the Eddie Stobart deckchair shirt, not wanting to embarrass Adam with other possibilities!

We entered the stadium at about 12.30, though for a while the best atmosphere was to be found in the concourse, where Carlisle fans were in full voice in the bar area. Eventually the seats began to fill as the atmosphere built towards kick-off. There were no real surprises in the Carlisle line-up, Paul Simpson opting for the same line-up that started the semi-final second leg against Bradford, apart from Jon Mellish replacing the ineligible Ben Barclay in defence.

When the teams finally emerged at about 1.20, there was inevitably a lump in the throat watching my own team walk out onto one of the greatest stages in football. The pre-match formalities were quickly concluded, and it was time for the serious business of the day, the small matter of a game of football.

The opening half-hour was reasonably even, with neither side fashioning many clear-cut chances. Carlisle's best opportunity was a powerful header from Joe Garner. Disaster struck in the 34th minute when Jon Mellish attempted to block a Stockport shot, only for the ball to loop up off his boot and drop agonisingly over the head of goalkeeper Tomas Holy. Nonetheless we reached half-time perfectly confident that Carlisle were capable of getting back on even terms.

In the second half, Carlisle were attacking the end populated with their own supporters. As is usually the case, Paul Simpson started to ring the changes around the hour mark. And as usual, the changes were to the strike force, with Ryan Edmondson and Omari Patrick replacing Joe Garner and John-Kymani Gordon. Stockport were now faced with two very different kinds of striker running at them.

As the equaliser still failed to materialise, Simpson made further changes, bringing on Jordan Gibson to bolster the attack, and Taylor Charters to bolster the midfield. In the 80th minute the final substitution was made, with leading scorer Kris Dennis replacing left wing back Jack Armer, Charters switching to left back and Jon Mellish moving from central defence into midfield as the formation was switched from 5-3-2 to 4-3-3. With ten minutes to go, and the possibility of extra-time, Carlisle had played all their substitution cards.

With the game in its final stages, for the first time the fear surfaced that this might just not be Carlisle's day, a feeling reinforced in the 82nd minute, when a goal bound shot from Jon Mellish struck a Stockport defender, on the goal-line, on the arm, only for the referee to wave away fervent appeals for a penalty. It mattered not. In the 84th minute Jordan Gibson cut in from the right before Joel Senior helped the ball into the penalty area. A scuffed shot from Ryan Edmondson was half-cleared to the edge of the area, from where Omari Patrick drilled a low and accurate shot just inside the left-hand post. I've rarely experienced crowd celebrations quite like the ones that took place in the next few moments!

In the remaining few minutes Carlisle were dominant in search of a winner, Stockport happy to just cling on and take the game to extra time. There was a certain inevitability about the whistle that brought normal time to an end and heralded a further thirty minutes. Both teams had a golden opportunity to win the game in extra time. Tomas Holy superbly tipped over a shot from Jack Stretton (on loan at Carlisle in the first half of the season) and Kris Dennis had a glancing header equally well saved by the Stockport keeper.

As time ticked by, it became clear that the final game of the season was going to go to the point of last resort, a penalty shoot-out, and so it proved. Stockport won the toin-coss to determine at which end the penalties took place, and unsurprisingly chose the goal in front of their own fans, which meant we had to look on from a distance.

The shoot-out, once it began, was over remarkably quickly and with surprisingly few nerves on my part. I think a sense of destiny had taken over by that point! Carlisle's first four penalties were dispatched clinically, none of them offering the goalkeeper a glimmer of a chance. Tomas Holy gave Carlisle the upper hand by guessing correctly and diving to his right to save Stockport's second penalty. As young Taylor Charters strode forward to take the final penalty, he knew that the result of the game, and so much more, was in his hands. Seconds later he'd calmly driven the ball home and Carlisle were once again a League One team. Cue pandemonium!

But enough of calm and rational analysis – time for some passion!

As Taylor Charters wheeled away in triumph following his promotion-winning penalty, I let rip a primal roar of celebration while Adam slumped to the ground in floods of tears. I don't think Ben was in a much more composed state. Despite our underlying belief in the team, I don't think any of us could fully comprehend that the moment of fulfilment had really arrived. Seventeen years since our last promotion and nine years since we dropped into League Two Carlisle are on the up again!

The post-penalties scenes are unforgettable. There were wild celebrations on the pitch by players and staff in the immediate aftermath, matched by the mayhem in the stands. The stadium DJ kept the atmosphere fully pumped up as everyone awaited the post-match formalities. Then came the long walk up to the Royal Box where captain on the day Paul Huntington and club captain Morgan Feeney finally hoisted the trophy aloft, to the acclaim of the rapturous acclaim of the supporters. As the trophy was passed along the line, predictably the loudest cheer was reserved for when it finally reached the hands of Paul Simpson. Then it was back onto the pitch for the tickertape and champagne celebrations, followed by further parading of the trophy in front of the fans.

It strikes me that there's something inherently unfair in the play-off system, though I'm delighted we were the beneficiaries of that unfairness. The teams that end up in second and third place in the division get no trophy, just the satisfaction of promotion. As League Two Champions Orient get a trophy but no grand finale. Carlisle have effectively finished the season in fourth place yet get both a trophy and a glorious day at Wembley! It was cruel on Stockport too, who didn't even get losers' medals for the play-off final.

Paul Simpson's achievement in fifteen months at Carlisle United is truly remarkable. The club he inherited in February 2022 was broken. Performances on the pitch were dire, coaching was sadly inadequate, and the management of the club behind the scenes was woeful. I can't believe that anyone who trudged disconsolately along Warwick Road, following the home defeat to Swindon that prompted Simpson's arrival, truly believed that we would be celebrating promotion just over a season later. We'd just sunk into the League Two relegation zone and the fans were chanting "Hello to the National League".

Six wins in his first seven games saw the spectre of relegation banished and persuaded Simpson to sign on for a further three years. Even so, I'm sure most supporters would have settled for mid-table mediocrity this season, comfortably safe from either relegation or promotion dogfights. It wasn't to be. A solid start established the team in that comfortable mid-table position before a series of impressive away performances saw Carlisle climb into the play-off places. A run of six wins in seven games led to the heady heights of an automatic promotion place. That couldn't quite be sustained, but Simpson had made excellent signings, transformed average performers into good ones, engendered a superb team spirit and ethic, and got the supporters vociferously behind the team again, in significantly greater numbers. As we headed into the lottery of the play-offs I had little doubt that Simpson had the nous and ability to see us through. There were few moments during either the semi-finals or the final when I doubted the team's ability to succeed.

Of course, this success sustains the remarkable record of Carlisle gaining promotion in every season that Simpson has started as Carlisle manager. When I cited that fact just over a year ago, after Simpson had committed to the long haul, it was a flippant aside, stated far more in hope than expectation. I'll end this song of praise to Paul Simpson with a couple of quotes from supporters. Within minutes of the end of the final Adam said to me "Start building the Simmo statue now", and last October, following an exhilarating away win at Hartlepool, Eric Hornsby simply declared "He's a god!".

As we travelled to the first game of the 2021-22 season, we were delayed on the A66 by a horse drawn traveller caravan, to such an extent that we almost missed the kick-off. In a remarkable moment of symmetry (or irony?), as we drove home from the final event of the 2022-23 season, we were again delayed, this time on Wakefield Eastern Relief Road, by a pony and trap.

And so, I come to the end of the final post of an amazing season. In fact, they've been two remarkable seasons that I've chronicled. It's been a wonderful journey. I cringe at the use of the word "journey" by talent show contestants to describe their experience but given the miles we've covered in the last two seasons I think I'm perfectly justified in using the word both literally and metaphorically. The Wakefield Blues have covered a total of 12,544 miles following Carlisle United over the last two seasons. While we're talking numbers, the overall attendance at the fifteen EFL play-off games was 437,358, a new record. That is an average attendance of 29, 157. Since eight of the teams involved have a ground capacity lower than that it is a remarkable statistic.

When the vague possibility of these self-indulgent ramblings being turned into a book became a reality, I had a ridiculous dream of the book concluding with the perfect ending of promotion. The play-offs can be nerve-shredding, but if you emerge victorious then there's no better way to win promotion. I'm still coming to terms with the fact that my flight of fancy has become a glorious reality.